Books of Merit

Prototype

PROT⊕TYPE

How Canadian Innovation
Is Shaping the Future

William Illsey Atkinson

Thomas Allen Publishers
Toronto

National Library of Canada Cataloguing in Publication Data

Atkinson, William Illsey, 1946–
Prototype : how Canadian innovation is shaping the future

ISBN 0-919028-47-0

1. High technology industries—Canada.
2. High technology industries—Social aspects—Canada.
I. Title.

HC120.H53A85   2001   338.7'62'000971   C2001-901410-4

Short portions of this book, in slightly different forms, have previously
appeared in *The Globe and Mail* and in *Biotechnology* magazine.

Jacket and text design: Gordon Robertson
Editor: Michael Holmes
Cover image of car interior: David Laurence
Author photograph: Bayne Stanley

Published by Thomas Allen Publishers,
a division of Thomas Allen & Son Limited,
145 Front Street East, Suite 107,
Toronto, Ontario M5A 1E3 Canada

Printed and bound in Canada

For TSHN

You disap-
    pear at parties
                       but

I still cut in

ACKNOWLEDGEMENTS

Critics admit that a film is a group activity, but the myth persists that a book is produced solely by its author. Not so. *Prototype* would never have seen light without the intense and protracted involvement of many skilled and committed professionals. They include my many interviewees without whose incredible dreams and achievements I would have had nothing to report; my publisher Patrick Crean, who believed in this project from first glimmer; Michael Holmes, my substantive editor, who chivvied and cajoled a loose first draft into something tighter and more readable; Alison Reid, who as copyeditor did what I had thought impossible and taught me things about English grammar; Robert Mackwood, the world's best agent; Jim Allen, the CEO of Thomas Allen Publishers and my first fan; and Katja Pantzar, who as senior editor at TAP pulled it all together. "For all, our thanks."

CONTENTS

Due to the unconventional nature of this book, this is an unconventional table of contents. The symbol ≼ indicates the general spot on the page where the cited topic begins.

AUTHOR'S NOTE

———

To unite many personalities and technologies into a coherent narrative, I have adopted the framework of a single continuous voyage. In adapting my material to this framework I have altered minor facts: for example, the Banff nanotechnology workshop occurred in January, not late spring; I golfed with the elk as described, but on another occasion. Further, to protect interviewee confidentiality I have altered certain names and blurred identifying data. Other than this, all people, places, quotations, and technologies are as I found them.

William Illsey Atkinson
North Vancouver
August 2001

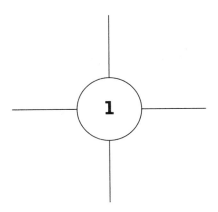

KNOWLEDGE

AND RESOURCES

Dawn. The sky above my head is littered with stars; in the enormous Pacific night my front-door light seems an intrusion. Eastward the dark eases slightly above a sawtoothed line of mountains. From far away comes the harsh rasp of a raven. I lock the front door on a sleeping family and carry my last case to the waiting car.

Today I begin an exploratory journey to discover the basis of Canada's changing economy. I will not merely wander: I have some concrete aims in mind. I want to discover the reality behind the stock-market instability and the dot-com hype: to sense, if possible, where this nation's work is heading. But I will sample rather than try to create a definitive compendium. And like the medieval palmer, I will not overplan my journey. I will go where head, heart, and chance dictate. I will make time for digressions and random meetings. Sometimes my side trips will be physical; sometimes I will explore the ideas that occur to anyone travelling this immense land.

Essentially my journey is one of the imagination. Some of what I find will come from the men and women whose work I explore;

some will come from my own thought—deducing where my interviewees are coming from and where they are so rapidly and confidently going. I go not just to learn, but to associate; both to see and understand. Above all, I want to connect things that have not been connected.

My quarry on this multi-month journey is the knowledge economy. It marks a new way of earning, spending, and investing. It construes the world in a radical new way. It finds wealth not in soil, like traditional farming; nor in rock, like traditional mining; nor on the shop floor, like traditional manufacturing; nor in windowless offices, like traditional finance. The knowledge economy's core premise is that all wealth—jobs, wages, salaries, capital accumulation, everything—rests on data: that is, on useful information. Knowledge is freedom, success, and pleasure; it is sufficiency and power. Knowledge supports all.

What distinguishes today's high-tech firm? How have its common and individual traits created the juggernaut called the knowledge economy? More important, what *human* good can I extract from this undisciplined flood? Can I discover or imagine the ideal high-tech firm? A novel corporate prototype that enriches investors, fulfils employees, and protects the environment all at once? This is the little-known country that I seek. At journey's end, I will have identified and profiled organizations—corporations, government departments, and hybrids of the two—that are in some way crucial to Canada's knowledge economy. Their contribution may be in new technology or in novel approaches to existing technologies: in subject matter or in method. But individually, each will illuminate the Canada of tomorrow. And in aggregate, they will steer us to some broad conclusions about the vast economic and imaginative revolution that has just begun.

Although I won't neglect areas such as marketing and finance, business won't be my first consideration. I am after bigger game: to sketch a whole new way of working.

My journey will be both internal and external. As Saul Bellow (himself born a Canadian) said: "All travel is mental travel." Crossing the country lets me do more than encounter the knowledge economy directly, in all its variety. Just as important, it gives me time to consider what I've seen and heard, to put it into context.

With all I have packed, clothes and computers and reference works, my car is full. I have much to discover and a very long road ahead.

But even a journey of eight thousand kilometres must begin with a first step; so I get in my car, buckle up, check my instruments, shift into gear, and drive away. The journey has begun.

I have come to my present voyage by a long and circuitous route. When I joined the National Research Council of Canada in 1979 as a science writer based in Ottawa, the NRC had just begun an intensive campaign to lobby on behalf of what it had defined as the TIIS, technology-intensive industrial sector. At the time, the NRC was almost alone in its wish that Canada consider a high-technology approach to work and the economy. A parade of governments paid lip service to the TIIS—I know this because I myself wrote many of their speeches and briefing notes—but stopped short of concrete action. Only a handful of firms, such as Bell-Northern Research (later Nortel Networks) and Ballard Power Systems, walked the walk. The rest of Canadian industry hardly bothered to yawn at the NRC's mantra. The country was doing just fine, thank you. The Canadian dollar bracketed US90 cents and employment was high. The world had an endless appetite for Canada's unprocessed resources—metals, potash, lumber—which earned our export revenue. At home, massive government spending cushioned the poor and unemployed.

As for R&D, it hardly mattered that Canada's spending as a percentage of GDP was the lowest in the industrial world, lower than that of Ireland. Let the eggheads sound their warnings: they only wanted more tax money. When times were good, who needed research? When times were bad, who could afford it? Business would weather its boom-bust cycles, laying off and then scrambling to rehire, and life would go on as it had.

We all know what has happened since. Those massive government programs ran on borrowed money and thus on borrowed time. Bit by bit, tax revenues were devoured by the gargantuan debt we had accumulated, until half were lost at the instant of collection. The prosperity of much Canadian business turned out to be fully as illusory. Big, fat companies had operated on assumptions from the mid-fifties, when industry outside North America was in ruins and no effective competition existed. Through various means, including tax deferments and outright tax forgiveness, business itself was on the dole as much as any dirt-poor fishing outport.

But as the German proverb puts it, God repays a lot of little sins at once. Canada's comeuppance in the eighties was bitter. Manufacturing across the country took it on the chin; primary industry such as mining, forestry, and steel production laid off tens of thousands; the dollar plunged. Ontario, where I grew up, became a rust belt. And slowly, haltingly, Canada began to admit that the concept of TIIS might be worth a look. The NRC, nag though she was, had got it right.

Canada is deep into its technological turnaround now, and won't look back. We made a face, took our medicine, and got on with life, just as we did in wartime. In retrospect, we needn't have worried: we Canucks are made of tough stuff. As Churchill said in Ottawa in 1941, "We have not journeyed all this way across the centuries, across the oceans, across the mountains, across the prairies, because we are made of sugar candy." And yet we wouldn't act on warnings or take good advice. We needed the stuffing scared out of us; and fortunately, life did just that.

My present journey will uncover some of the ways that Canadians met and overcame their economic challenge. My examples will come from many sectors of the economy, but all will share one trait: they will harness the most renewable and widely available of all our resources—fresh thought.

There, for example: those offices, a mere six hundred metres from my starting point. They belong to a young company I'll call DeepDive. Manufacturer? Consultant? Engineering firm? All of these, and none. The best description of DeepDive is a *knowledge company*.

Fifteen years ago Roy McKee, a young Canadian marine designer, grew uneasy at the demands being placed on commercial divers. Increasingly aggressive undersea operations, including military activity and exploration for oil and minerals, had literally driven divers to ridiculous depths. Some teams were being asked to operate for hours at a time, two hundred metres below the surface, in water three degrees Celsius above freezing, in inky blackness, wearing scuba gear.

Scuba is an acronym for self-contained underwater breathing apparatus. It's an old technology, developed more than fifty years ago. A scuba diver wears foot-fins for propulsion and steering. Portable tanks of compressed air carried on the back feed through a pressure regulator, delivering each breath at a pressure that counterbalances the surrounding water pressure. So fortified, the diver's chest does not cave in.

Scuba was a breakthrough. In shallow water, down to fifty metres or so, it works well. First in warm water, then in cold, it rapidly replaced its predecessor, the clumsy hard-helmet diving suit whose air came from surface pumps on a boat floating overhead. But as scuba was used more widely, it ran into problems.

No: that's too abstract a way of putting it. What happened is that divers the world over began to suffer horrifying deaths. At extreme depths, breathing pressurized air makes its inert molecular nitrogen dissolve into human blood. The result can be nitrogen narcosis, the "rapture of the deep" that makes divers behave as if drunk. This condition is dangerous enough, but it pales next to another effect of blood-soluble nitrogen: the bends. Too rapid an ascent from deep working levels may cause dissolved nitrogen to boil out of the blood and return to its original gaseous state. The diver experiences an agony so intense and prolonged that it has few equivalents.

People could go deeper than scuba divers, more safely, in rigid unpressurized submersibles. But once there, except for the odd crude grapple, they could do little work. Assembling marine components on site required the dexterous and vulnerable hands of a scuba diver.

Enter Roy McKee. Roy imagined a rigid one-person diving suit: a tiny, tough-hulled submersible that was nearly as small as the diver who operated it. To achieve his aim, Roy made many big and little inventions. One of the most revolutionary was a jam-proof joint that worked when its inner side was at a pressure of one atmosphere and its outer side was feeling twenty tonnes of force, six hundred metres beneath the sea.

The resultant hard-shelled suit, now in its ninth generation and as sophisticated as any marine contrivance in the world, stands two metres tall and weighs half a metric ton. At least, that's its weight in air: underwater it's lighter than a feather, though as stable as stone. It's now far safer for divers to work for up to a *day* on the abyssal floor. Like submersibles, DeepDive suits let their operators work in conditions under which humanity evolved: that is, air at a pressure of one atmosphere. The death agony of the bends, the rapture of nitrogen narcosis—all the results of breathing pressurized gases are things of the past.

This story is fascinating, but how I learned about it is even more so. One day my young son came home from his daycare with detailed spec sheets on a DeepDive hardsuit. The sheets were complete with fold-out whiteprints and engineering parameters. This technical miracle had been handed to my son as scrap paper for him to scribble on.

I stood gaping as I scanned the sheets, then raced for the phone. The drawings were worthless, it turned out, because they were a few months old. In that time, new technology had superseded them. Rev 1.2, the daycare sheet, had reached 1.3 and was still climbing.

Some key characteristics of the new economy, including its omnipresence and its rate of change, snapped into focus for me at this chance discovery. First, Canada's knowledge economy may crop up anywhere. In DeepDive I found a world-class firm nestled between sea and mountains in my own backyard. No noise, no pollution, no PR fanfare: just world-beating ideas—the best small manned submersibles on the face of the Earth, or beneath its oceans. As for economic impact, DeepDive generates millions of U.S. dollars in yearly export revenue for Canada. (In fact the company bills in U.S. dollars.)

My second realization was that the *knowledge* behind the knowledge economy is changing, adapting, and growing with incredible speed. It's here; it's happening; it's with us to stay. Old ways of making money are already obsolete. The motto of the knowledge economy is *No thought, no profit.*

————

It wasn't always like that. In the distant past wealth meant ancestors' accomplishments. To that folk concept ancient empires added the notion of wealth as land and slaves. Much later the capitalist revolution that predated the industrial revolution redefined wealth as money.

But over the past three decades the concept has taken root that wealth is not what you own but what you know. By itself money is just a heap of counters. Resources are no more fecund: even gold is worthless if left in the ground. Knowledge is the only wealth creator. It can turn sand to silicon chips. It can create pollution-free energy from methane by stripping its carbon and running the remaining hydrogen through a fuel cell. It's so obvious: knowledge, and only knowledge, is power and wealth. Yet it took us centuries to see.

One of the most prescient writers on the knowledge economy was an American economist, J. A. Shumpeter, who came to the U.S. from Austria and did most of his key work at Harvard University. Knowledge, Shumpeter wrote half a century ago, is the key to unending prosperity. The most successful products and services are, by definition, those that incorporate features based on new knowledge. Without this wealth-creating information, nothing but price differentiates a product from all competitors—and price is quickly driven down by market forces till the item in question is commonplace, interchangeable, and of low unit value—in other words a commodity. In time, the only people making money on an item are those who run Third World sweatshops and pay workers next to nothing. If an industry does stay in a developed country, it automates production until its human workforce is cut to the bone.

Not only things we think of as typical commodities—potash, sugar, wood—go down this route: since 1980 it's happened to something as complex as the personal computer. Today a PC's parts are sourced less from North America than they are from China, Singapore, and Pakistan. That radio phone you're using may have come from Mexico or Indonesia. If its technology is not at the cutting edge, its status has sunk to that of a commodity. The wave of the knowledge economy has rushed over it and gone on to newer things. Only knowledge underpins success.

There are only two things a nation can do in the face of so pervasive a revolution: embrace it or be killed by it. Canada came so close to the second outcome that it was frightened into the first. Now our knowledge economy is on a roll.

That suits me fine. While I'm not a front-line worker in the knowledge revolution, I've been its acolyte and observer for forty years. To me the knowledge economy is inexorably transforming the world, whatever daily jigs the stock markets dance.

Seen in this context, DeepDive is one more in a long line of miracles that the knowledge economy has an unlimited supply of. Two thousand years ago, the Roman poet Virgil wrote that people are happy when they find the causes of things. For a writer like me, today's knowledge explosion is intrinsically fascinating, a source of constant delight. It's a roller-coaster ride that never ends.

All these thoughts are in passing: I am not yet ready to examine how the knowledge economy has transformed Canadian manufacturing. My first act will be to consider the resources that support the abstractions called Nation and Economy. I will visit the land.

Land as an example of the knowledge economy? Absolutely. One of the CEOs I interviewed in preparing for my trip said with a shake of his head that subscribers to *Fortune* magazine must think the knowledge economy is limited to dot-coms. Nothing could be further from the truth. Technology is percolating into the most basic activities: hewers of wood and drawers of water are becoming as much a part of the knowledge economy as advanced information technology, or IT. Having never read *Fortune*, the knowledge economy does not limit itself to IT with a dash of biotechnology here and there. It flourishes in unlikely business sectors and in out-of-the-way geographies.

In the great tradition of Canadian indirectness, I begin my west-to-east journey by going north. I turn onto the Trans-Canada Highway, toward the great coastal rain forests of the Pacific.

North of Vancouver, Highway 1 becomes what is aptly called the Sea-to-Sky Route. The sun's up now, but no sunlight reaches me: kilometre-high mountains screen it, and I drive totally in their shade. *Rugged* doesn't start to describe this coast. To an urban Canadian, this landscape borders on brutal. The road twists and turns across creeks raging with snowmelt from the mountain summits. I see hard evidence that the force of these debris torrents can roll down boulders, wash out bridges, pulverize trees. It's easy, in this lonely land, to believe a civilized person is only three meals away from savagery. That is, in fact, precisely why technical knowledge is so important: in the old time, it made us predators instead of prey. Technology isn't a recent discovery. It's built into our very genes.

"What did early man feel like?" asks Calvin in Bill Watterson's wonderful comic strip, *Calvin and Hobbes*. "Tiger food!" his friend replies. The answer is exact. Dr. Robert Brain, a paleoanthropologist who has for thirty-five years excavated sites in southern Africa, thinks that at the close of the last interglacial our forebears— our great-grandparents with sixty thousand *greats*—were the main prey of *Dinofelis*, an immense cat species that ruled Africa's plains a million years ago.

Then technology intervened. The proto-hominids, says Brain, learned the management of fire. They kept warm in caves, ate what would have otherwise been inedible, and—most important— defended themselves against the cats that were their predators.

With the taming of fire came a second technology: weapons. At some point merely keeping the carnivores at bay, or out-competing them for food, may have given way to actively killing them. If so, our species was born in that archetypal battle a million years ago, when the tables turned. Now there was no overlord but Man, no dominant creature, no reason for subservience.

Knowledge does a similar thing today. It sweeps away our excuses. It forces us to attempt the impossible, to risk being great. As we leave home for the stars, we may encounter other tigers. But whatever is out there had better start preparing: *H. Tigersbane* is on the way.

Of course, we'll be frightened out of our wits. So much the better. Fright is our ignition switch. Terror is the mother of invention and drives us to devise new tools. That's why knowledge industries don't fear market turmoil, why pundits' gloomy pronouncements about the Death of Technology are absurd. Knowledge, like life itself, defeats all challengers. A stock-market crash is no big deal to a species that got its start by killing tigers.

My thoughts return to the present as the road descends a long grade from sky down to sea. Horseshoe Bay is a U-shaped cove off Howe Sound. The inlets hereabouts are fjords, drowned valleys; water depths abruptly plummet from ten to one hundred metres. This makes the bay a perfect dock site for the big ships that move traffic between the mainland and Vancouver Island. It feels good to park the car, stretch, and climb the stairs to the ferry's observation deck. The whistle roars; the boat gets under way; my destination slides smoothly toward me over the water, forty minutes away.

Only fifty kilometres separate Vancouver from Gibsons, but in many ways what's called the Sunshine Coast is an age, a dimension, and an attitude removed from Vancouver's latte bars. I see how thin a veneer our cities are, how vast and various our geography. Sometimes Canada seems nothing more than thirty city-states strewn across a wild and empty park.

In the cold spring wind that streams across the ferry's bow, I consider again what line of thought has brought me here. Like DeepDive, my destination today shows the pervasiveness of the knowledge economy. But unlike DeepDive, it has none of the popular trappings of high tech—no arcane instruments and flashing lights. Today I go to interview a watershed.

The knowledge economy applies thought to create things that did not previously exist. This process may be evident in giant telephone companies, with their person-centuries of effort and worldwide scope—or, just as likely, in an old-growth forest managed in common-sense ways.

Beyond the beauty of its central idea, that nature may be sweet-talked into doing our will, a manifestation of the knowledge economy need not be complicated: quite the contrary. The simpler an idea, the more useful and long-lasting is its technology. Excrescences such as Victorian apple peelers or some of our own era's clumsy computer operating systems are usually as evanescent as moonrise, though they may make money in the few years they're around. The *high* in high technology means quality, not quantity.

Its goal is whatever works best. And to be economically effective, knowledge need be neither complex nor new. It can just as easily be old wisdom, rescued from undeserved neglect and reapplied. It is to see an example of this that I am travelling today.

➤   Brian Carson meets me at the Sunshine Coast ferry dock. He pumps hands, shoos me into his ancient 4x4 truck, and roars off on a guided tour. Brian is a bearded, energetic man who manages municipal watersheds for the Sunshine Coast. He has the rare knack of tailoring his explanations to his visitor, whether fellow geoscientist, politician, bureaucrat, or—this bright March day—a writer. Whatever the profession, the visitor views a masterpiece: two watersheds that Brian's team has brought to vigorous life after years of systematic pillage.

In 1989 the Sunshine Coast Regional District approached the B.C. Ministry of Forests and asked for a moratorium on logging in its two largest watersheds, those of Chapman and Gray Creeks. The district was concerned about water quality and wanted a breather from ongoing forestry operations to assess the situation.

Not for nothing, however, have watershed restoration engineers in private industry nicknamed the B.C. Ministry of Forests *MoFo*, hip slang for "motherfucker." The district made its request because it had suffered under a MoFo euphemism called Sympathetic Management.

Bluntly put, Sympathetic Management was no management. To preserve jobs and votes in the area, MoFo turned a blind eye to every kind of horror story in watershed logging. One forest company worker said he felt like weeping at what his employer was allowed to get away with—gouging out ill-drained roads with bulldozers, or leaving vast amounts of felled timber to rot in place. These cowboy practices compromised the local water supply, adversely affected fish habitat, and wasted thousands of dollars in pristine first-growth timber. MoFo didn't care.

Finally the district had had enough. While their letter to the ministry was phrased as a request, it was more a cease-and-desist order than a petition. District Council was set to go to court to back up its demand, and had an ace in the hole—copies of MoFo's own paperwork, which documented and protested the violation of the watersheds in confidential memos. MoFo was caught red-handed, and finessed. The province then set up an integrated watershed management plan overseen by members of the district, forest industry, First Nations, and government agencies responsible for fish, trees, wildlife, water, mines, and health.

Over a decade later, two rejuvenated watersheds are the result. As senior watershed manager, Brian Carson is on the brink of committing his land to yield predetermined amounts of clear water and sound timber every year, forever. This achievement—gaining logging's benefits, while avoiding its common consequences of cloudy water and compromised biohabitat—goes beyond local import. It marks a world milestone in resource development.

A third-generation B.C. native with two graduate degrees, Brian Carson spent fifteen years supervising hydrology projects in the Third World. Then he came home from Nepal to find his life work in his own homeland.

These days, Brian's science takes place largely in his truck. It's a thing of beauty, filigreed with corrosion, full of ancient coffee cups and old dead batteries. Its springs are hard to the point of inflexibility, and a ride down a logging road evokes a ride in an English stagecoach c.1675. But when the subject of your expertise is a pair of Coast Range watersheds sprawling over a hundred square kilometres, you can't expect to use a Cadillac. Brian's transportation is perfectly suited to its site.

Chapman Creek rises from snowmelt at the thousand-metre level and brawls westward down forested slopes to meet the sea in Georgia Strait. Even two kilometres upstream of its alluvial fan, it moves fast. Brian points out automobile-sized boulders that the creek has pushed downstream.

As Herodotus says, You can't swim twice in the same river, referring to the water. But as Carson sees it, more than a river's water can change. To his practised eye, every aspect of every stream is in continuous flux—banks, bottom, vegetation, slopes. Here is an oxbow on the brink of short-circuiting, leaving behind it an alluvial plain that alder trees will fill. Here is a valley, dry now, through which the river sluiced during a flood. Here is an enormous Western red cedar, three or four centuries old. The lumbermen left it because it was filled with compression wood, unsuitable for sawing; now it secures an overhanging bank.

Brian explains what he's doing with Chapman Creek, the largest river in the two adjacent watersheds. He's *listening* to it. Brian lets the river tell him what it wants. This requires a familiarity so intimate that it is almost mystic.

Brian's goal, a stable waterway that threatens neither surrounding forest lands nor housing, requires repairing the distortions caused earlier by hasty logging, gravel mining, and other ill-considered consequences of human settlement. A single glance shows Brian the error in earlier attempts at river engineering. Through every ill-considered change of past years, he sees the natural course of Chapman Creek and deduces how to restore it.

It's terribly difficult and expensive to repair rivers in conventional ways, Brian says. You come in with heavy equipment, move thousands of tonnes of earth and rock, pour hundreds of cubic metres of concrete, and the day after you finish, a flood may wash away all your work. By contrast, he says, "We take time to read the river, to deduce what its aboriginal configuration was before Europeans came into the area and changed it. We're finding out what Chapman Creek would prefer to do, then we help it back into those natural channels."

This takes time: but it also uses less energy and money than the customary blast-and-build tack. And it creates a more stable river, one that's content to stay where it is even during periods of high runoff. It's knowledge-intensive rather than machine-intensive; and the knowledge is kinder, gentler, older.

"This isn't rocket science," Brian Carson says. "We're not developing new hydrogeological equations here. It's simply a matter of approach."

I would call it almost a matter of taste: more landscape gardening than engineering. And despite Brian's protestations—"I'm not much of an expert in anything"—I see that something new has indeed happened here. On a shoestring budget, in an area whose population is growing 5 per cent a year, with a team comprising mostly retirees and part-time volunteers, Brian has returned a battered watershed to near-pristine vitality in thirteen years. The originality of his approach involves not its individual components—Brian admits they aren't groundbreaking—but in how these are put together: in a word, attitude. Not novelty, not complexity, just finding the right knowledge and applying it in the right way.

It's about time that human engineering took on some kind of humility. The paradigm of science is to observe nature, infer a theory that tells how it works, and then test your theory by experiment. But in the past three hundred years, some people have come to believe that nature takes orders from them. *I don't need to observe: I'm the expert. Reality does what I tell it to do.*

Brian's team marches to a different drummer. They have that rare quality, humility. Rather than dictate, they listen. In doing so, they have achieved what whole departments of fly-in, fly-out, same-day experts have not: the cost-effective restoration of two huge watersheds.

Brian and his team rely on more than informed intuition. Scattered around Chapman and Gray Creeks and their branches are automatic sensors. The monitoring stations record water volume and muddiness in the watershed's tributaries and communicate their findings to Brian's home computer through telephone lines. An anomaly—say, a sudden spike in water opacity or volume—will trigger an alarm. This may have Brian out in his indestructible low-tech truck at any time of day or night, for those who listen to rivers are always on call. Their dedication is inconvenient, but it pays big dividends in understanding.

"In a bureaucracy, no one has the time or mandate to pursue things in this intensive way," Brian says. "If a turbidity plume appears along some creek at midnight, well, too bad: the observation is lost. That's the kind of data we've been able to capture."

In addition, Brian says, conventional wisdom tends to reject non-quantitative evidence as "unscientific." Yet Brian's team has found visual, anecdotal observations to be so critical that neglecting them would be the truly unscientific action. "When I started this project, loggers and old-timers who worked near rivers told me things I found incredible, mere tall tales," he says. "But when I observed the river continuously, I realized that the locals had been right all along. That increased my respect both for non-scientists and for nature."

The passionate humility of Brian Carson and his team has proven a perfect way to restore watersheds where big-money, equipment-intensive projects have stalled. The lesson is clear: often the knowledge economy is most successful when it's simplest. That demands clarity in concept, minimalism in how that concept is realized, and above all simplicity in use. Technology is a human enterprise. People won't use it, at least not in numbers sufficient for commercial success, if that use demands a doctorate from Yale.

The knowledge economy is partly scholarly and partly spontaneous; it borrows from low and high. Whatever its sources, it succeeds by using what works. Brian Carson's project shows that. He found unworkable complexity and replaced it with effective simplicity; he found a bunch of so-called experts trying to tell nature what to do and replaced them with a team sensitive enough to hear what nature is saying.

The Prototype: First Attribute

Our first attribute for the ideal knowledge organization is that its scientific, technical, and strategic knowledge should be as simple as possible.

About A.D. 1325, the English scholar-monk William of Occam proposed this rule: *Axioms should not be multiplied unnecessarily.* He meant that you shouldn't assume more than you must. The truest explanation is the simplest one that fits the facts.

So useful has this tool proven that it's called Occam's Razor. The image is of a scalpel, paring away the unnecessary.

Here's the application for the knowledge economy. Yes, you can contrive a steam-powered apple peeler or a weird and wonderful computer operating system. But the less elegant your solution, the further it is from the absolutely minimal, the less effective it will be. The most successful solutions, whether commercial or academic, are the simplest. The best people, firms, and departments never lose sight of Occam's Razor. This is the lesson of Brian Carson's watersheds.

My next port of call is Nanaimo—more precisely, an artificial research station floating in Nanaimo Harbour. To get there I will work my way up the coast to Powell River. I am glad of the drive: after a day with Brian Carson, I have some thinking to do. In particular I want to consider the ongoing land-use conflict, found almost everywhere in Canada, that's been nicknamed the War of the Woods.

A hundred years ago everyone, even lumbermen, considered forestry a form of mining. The vast aboriginal forests would be cut only once: the land so cleared would then be used for farming. It made sense to colonists, who were trying to repeat a process that had turned the Old World's woodlands into farms. But while Europe's deciduous forests had loam deep and rich enough for agriculture, most of Canada's conifers stood in thin, rocky, acid soil. Not only did the rocks eat steel plows for breakfast, but millennia of needle fall had also made the soil so acid that everything except moss and lichen died. In many of the clear-cut areas, hardly a thistle could grow.

About ninety years ago, the provincial governments that still control most of Canada's forests began to change their thinking. Since clearing and farming were untenable, why not treat trees like an agricultural crop? The idea made so much apparent sense that outside of a few fertile areas such as the Okanagan and Fraser Valleys, successive B.C. governments have restocked harvested forests with new trees.

Ah, if only it were that simple—restock, wait, and cut trees forever. Slowly, however, a different story emerged. Unless replanting were part of a larger policy, the planted seedlings might as well go in root-side up. Without proper site management, the light forest soils would often wash or blow away in the interval between clear-cutting and restocking. The precious soil slid down from hills and uplands, where it could do some good for seedlings, and gummed up waterways. This compromised a fishery that needed pristine streams for old salmon to spawn and young fry to head out to sea.

Fifty years ago, however, few people suspected the extent of these problems. For everyone else, especially big government, it was a time of unqualified optimism. Great plans were afoot. Newfoundland joined Confederation; Ontario Hydro planned enormous Candu reactors; the government of Canada established marketing boards to moderate the boom-bust cycles that strangled family farms. The Avro Arrow was the world's best fighter plane; B.C. Ferries had the world's biggest peaceful fleet; and in forest products, new knowledge was applied much less to the living forest than to the enormous mills that ate it.

A 1957 article in *Popular Mechanics* outlined the Sawmill of the Future. No one would be needed to run the place, the magazine said; the factory would be 100 per cent automated. Incoming logs would be sliced into lumber by "rays."

Wrong on one count, right on one. We're still waiting for laser saws, but automation did improve sawmill productivity, defined as the ratio of total output to all contributing workers.

Canada's lumber companies increased productivity in two ways. Partly they increased output, cutting down and carving up more stems of standing timber. Mostly, however, they simply shrank the fraction's denominator: that is, the human workforce. The mills spewed out two-by-fours by the trainload, oversupplying markets and holding down selling price. Worse, this high output gobbled up the readily accessible, fine-grained old-growth timber of Canada's ancient forests, squeezing the lumber industry's raw resource. Low prices, squandered materials: why shoot yourself in one foot when you can blow away both?

Today, the core skill of much of Canada's lumber industry is converting a non-renewable resource, or at least a resource it is not renewing adequately, into vast quantities of goods so cheap that they are nearly worthless. The eco-activists have coined a vivid term for a modern lumber mill: it is a lawn mower, chewing up public forests and spitting out low-grade chaff.

To a great extent, then, Canada's lumber industry is a classic case of working dumb. The knowledge economy is not wholly excluded from the forest sector, nor can it be, but in wood products, the introduction of better methods and more enlightened attitudes is often an uphill fight.

It's a shame, for there are many more things you can do with a cubic metre of wood than chop it into two-by-fours. Think of the beauty of wood, how restful it is to look at its grain or walk across a wooden floor. Even when it is restricted to structural uses, wood is an amazing material. Its strength-to-weight ratio approaches that of titanium, but unlike titanium, wood requires no expensive infrastructure to refine and extrude. Wood is workable on site, with simple hand-held tools. Titanium is not.

Considering wood's unique qualities, the commodity approach of Canada's provincial forest agencies—one can hardly dignify it with the term *strategy*—seems like giving away the forest in return for the promise to cut it down. This is a survival from clear and farm, but without the farming. It is not surprising, then, or at least not to those outside the lumber industry, that an unintended result of the industry's productivity drive has been to trash its own reputation. Higher productivity means fewer workers: that means fewer jobs, fewer votes, and less political clout. In this way the lumber industry has efficiently flushed itself down the political toilet in the past twenty years. It never fails to astonish a timber baron that politicians don't care about productivity per se and persist in seeing things in terms of votes.

And that's a kind construal. An uglier one is that of the radical Greens: that the forest sector is the exclusive preserve of a rich kids' club of self-satisfied, thumb-in-suspender atavisms that bugger the planet for a bigger dividend. I can't quarrel with this, for I've seen it myself at close quarters.

In the wood products industry, the most intractable opponent of ecological ethics is a certain type of industry CEO. A Green might think these people are cunning, ruthless businessmen, but they're really just as ignorant of innovations in marketing and manufacturing as they are in ecology. As Seminole Sam said in Walt Kelly's Pogo comic strip, "I don't think they're as diabolically clever as they are stupid. It's almost the same thing."

The old-line sawmill chief doesn't see himself as a briefcase carrier. He's a *lumberman*, cousin to Paul Bunyan. He treats forests as hunks of cellulose dumped on his doorstep to use as he wants. Most new knowledge, from any source and in any discipline, is for weenies. Like his father and grandfather before him, he (always *he*) grew up with sawdust in his blood. He isn't a businessman making a product; he's an apostle preaching the Wood of God. He resists presorting green lumber into wets and drys, a procedure made possible by new techniques of infrared-based remote sensing. (Now it's possible to kiln all-wets or all-drys together, rather than overdrying some and underdrying others. A kiln can be packed with wood within a predetermined moisture range, reducing energy costs and creating a more carefully controlled product.) When our reptilian CEO stacks his kiln with all-drys, it isn't wreathed in steam, the way it by-God should be. To our CEO this means it isn't working properly. Where's the *drama*, for God's sake? And so his mills lose millions of dollars, and he wonders why. He blames unions, or governments, or the mill in the next valley. He does not look for the culprit in his shaving mirror.

Like all wars, the War of the Woods creates self-righteous prevaricators on both sides. If hard-line Greens are right to condemn the timber barons, the barons are right in deriding some of the radical environmentalists' demands as unrealistic and inflexible. While I accept much of the Green platform, their insistence that all old-growth cutting be stopped at once is flat impractical. As I'll shortly show, it may not be a bad thing to cut down some old trees and substitute growing seedlings. And while Canada will certainly harvest more managed second-growth trees and spare more old ones, a full transition to this healthier state may take decades. If it were abrupt, $20 billion of export revenue, the value of our paper and timber production, would be sucked from Canada every year; whole regions might face ruin. In the extreme case, there's even a matter of sovereignty. Once every settlement within vast tracts of our country had been abandoned, the world community might be tempted to redefine millions of formerly sovereign hectares as uninhabited wilderness, up for grabs by whatever nation could permanently settle and develop them. We already find it tough enough to sustain our claim to the Canadian Arctic.

Caught in this paradox, what can we do? I believe the knowledge economy can create solutions. For it to do so, however, we must go back to basics and rethink our relationship with nature. Before we answer *What to do?* we must first answer *With whom do we work?*

The physical world in which humanity is imbedded has proven a tough nut for thinkers to crack. The Middle Eastern creation myths that shaped us imply that the human mind, expressed as technology, lifts us above brute nature. This is certainly how many forest-company CEOs see things: *Subdue the Earth!*

Lately, however, competing interpretations of the old myths have arisen. Dr. Roger Fouts, a professor of psychology at the University of Washington at Everett, and director of its Human-Chimpanzee Communication Research Institute, is one of the most humane thinkers I have met. He maintains that the ancient verbs that the King James Version translates as "subdue" and "have dominion" convey none of the cold, managerial dominance of the English terms—*it's yours, you own it, do what you like.* The Hebrew text, Roger maintains, conveys a custodial responsibility, an attitude almost of tenderness. A better word than *subdue* would be *nurture.* The world is ours not to violate for profit but to care for gently and hand down to our children. I find this an appealing concept: it replaces the head-butting of pro-development versus no development, with a more balanced view that accords equal dignity to humanity and to the rest of creation. Given this ethical context, new knowledge can help us immeasurably. Rad Green or simian CEO, each side currently deifies itself and demonizes the other. Any workable solution must incorporate ideas from both.

Let's look at the partners in this ancient dance. First, *H. sapiens.* We're merely part of nature, goes the Green cliché, an animal like others. That's a crock. Let's face it, we're different from squirrels and squid. Nothing else ferments antibiotics, writes poetry, or makes nuclear bombs. Besides, it's politically naive to think we could return to a state of nature, which is, after all, far from a state of grace. Our destiny is not to wear skins and scratch out twenty-year lifespans, dying early so that the rivers may run clean. We have known more. We will retain it.

Second, everything else in nature. If we share a planet with the dame, it must be as equals. She's older, true, but we've grown up; we've acquired a lot of power, and nature needs us as much as we need her. Our relationship must be a compromise, mediated by technology. The planet will never again be the unspoiled wilderness it was in the Pleistocene; but what is wrong with well-managed parks?

Don't mistake me. I am not saying that there's nothing more to existence than the Dow-Jones Average. Anyone who has walked through a grove of old-growth trees and listened to their silent eloquence cannot believe that. But remember that the past was not a golden age. When there were no jet contrails, no smoke, even, the world was terrible as well as unspoiled. The historical Eden was full of dead infants and *Dinofelis*. That we are here today at all we owe to our knowledge of technology. Even sparsely settled Canada has too many people to return to a hunter-gatherer lifestyle. A healthy child is worth a tree or two.

What's clear is that we need a new metaphor for the human-nature dyad. The Earth and its biosphere cannot be personified as a whimsical predator goddess with a cruel sense of humour and a taste for pain. Equally, they are not our subjects, like downtrodden field slaves. Perhaps we humans should treat nature as partner, lover, roommate—in other words, like a spouse.

Fanciful? Consider that the sum of information in Earth's non-human life is about a hundred quadrillion bytes—ten million species, times one billion nucleotide base pairs per species, times an uncertainty factor of ten. That roughly equals the sum of knowledge that we humans have amassed in science and literature, stored in our planet's digital memory. Our single species, in other words, may be as complex as all the rest of life on Earth, which is all the life we know exists anywhere. Yes, nature has rights: but so do we. And the marriage we make, like all healthy marriages, will entail sweat and blood as well as love and joy. Nature exists for us, certainly, but we also exist for her. As Rilke said, "Love consists in this: that two solitudes protect and touch and greet each other."

Man and nature are certainly equivalent in one thing: their adaptability. Both spouses here are profoundly resilient. Our own ability to change defines us: we are Earth's resident specialists in nonspecialization. Though we humans are the slowest of the intermediate mammals, we can run to earth all other species either via vehicular and weapons technology, or on foot through sheer bloody-minded persistence. And we are robust. We have bounced back from every war, from every plague. Now we are poised to leave our planetary crib and travel throughout creation.

Yet nature is robust and adaptable too—so much so that all our modern tampering with her is as nothing compared with what she has already survived. This is not to say we can be cavalier in how we treat our bride. Nature has a long memory; like all women of spirit, she will requite us fivefold if we are stupid or vicious enough to knock her around.

At the end of the Cretaceous Era, our ancestors the proto-mammals scuttled furtively beneath the feet of the planet's true masters, the dinosaurs. Fast, warm-blooded, and ferocious, these genera dominated the biosphere. In air, on land and in water, the terror lizards called the shots. Moreover, it appears they were on the brink of evolving intelligence. *Stenonychosaurus*, discovered by the Canadian paleontologist Dr. Dale Russell of the Royal Tyrrell Museum in Drumheller, Alberta, was a late-Cretaceous dinosaur with big, forward-looking eyes. Its large brain probably had stereoscopic colour vision like ours. *Stenonychosaurus* was bipedal; its gracile upper limbs ended in three-fingered appendages with an apparent delicacy of grasp—fingers, on hands. Given so advanced a dinosaurian, *Mammalia* might have been destined to end like the reptiles of today, as a source of chic handbags.

Then, in half a day, the world changed. A large cometary core, solid rock and ice, slammed into Earth from a counter-orbit. The relative speed of the two bodies was perhaps forty kilometres per second. At two km/s, a crawl by comparison, matter that is otherwise inert packs the punch of an equal weight of trinitrotoluene. Moreover, kinetic energy rises as the square of velocity. At forty km/s the power of inert matter becomes not twenty times greater, but four hundred times greater than a given mass of TNT. By some estimates the Armageddon comet weighed ten billion tonnes and packed four million megatonnes of explosive power. It punched through the Caribbean Sea east of Yucatan, excavating a crater the size of Ireland on the abyssal floor. As the thing descended, the radiant heat from its fireball ignited every bit of living tissue in the Western Hemisphere. As it hit, its impact raised a tidal wave five kilometres high. The comet vapour rose, condensed in the troposphere, and settled as white dust: a layer of iridium-rich ash that to this day enshrouds the whole Earth. Most of the dinosaurs died then, making room for us mammals. A few saurians survived, evolving into forms that we call birds.

And Earth endured; life endured. Despite the cataclysm, the death of four-fifths of the planet's genome, and a global twilight that may have lasted decades, life as a whole rebounded and flourished. Almost instantly in geological time, the strata show new forms, mammalian this time, radiating into the eco-niches vacated by the dead dinosaurs. This is the time of the great land mammals, ground sloths and beavers as large as elephants.

Conclusion: it takes more than a comet to kill Mother Earth. Our bride is one tough lady: she bleeds, but she pulls through. Individual species may go to the wall, but life itself is everlasting.

The moral is clear, if frightening. It isn't nature at risk from our pollution, it's us. Our wife will survive just fine as our widow.

If this marriage works, it will save our life and Lady Earth's composure. The contract must be dictated not by her (as occurred until we invented technology) nor by us (as has happened since). The dyad must be negotiated between equals. Equal does not mean identical; the human-nature bond, like most others, has a division of labour. The lady supplies raw materials, energy, room to live, and soul-restoring beauty. The groom must supply the wit to use wisely what his lady provides, with maximum benefit and minimum cost to each spouse.

This will require a set of meta-techniques, a technology to use technology. Nowhere do we need more insight and innovation than in the region adjacent to invention proper, the how and why of its use, the ethical and moral issues that we have so long left in neglect. Signs are strong that this will shortly change. I hope so; our survival is at stake.

The Prototype: Second Attribute

Our second attribute for a prototype organization in the knowledge economy is that it be humane.

By *organization* I mean not only a corporation but any group within the knowledge economy—firms, professional associations, and government departments. By *humane* I mean respectful of one another, of their clientele, of people in general, and of the environment to which humankind is wed.

This is more than good ethics: it is essential business practice. If a knowledge organization does not forswear the traditional ruthlessness that old-economy firms have so often exhibited, it will never attract, nurture, and profit from the knowledge workers it needs. A brutal company may satisfy shareholders in the short run, but in the long run it is unlikely to survive.

Compare the takeover artist of the 1980s, who specialized in raiding cash-rich companies so he could dismember them and sell their assets piecemeal. He treated wealth gain as a zero-sum game, moving funds from someone else's bank to his and creating wealth for nobody but himself. In a branch of mathematics called game theory, this situation is called *Win/Lose*.

By contrast, the well-run knowledge organization knows how to add to the world's sum of wealth—conjuring real prosperity where none had existed. In so doing, it pursues its affairs without being a scourge to us and to our planet. *Win/Win*.

Nanaimo. Bright spring sun, gulls on cold-water beaches, a rocky archipelago just offshore. While the knowledge economy is steadily dragging the forest industry into the present, resistance is high and progress is slow. But in another resource, even more ancient than the forests, new knowledge is about to vault production ahead ten thousand years at a single step. I have come to this small city to find out how this is being done.

Ten millennia ago, some forgotten genius had a transforming idea. Why hunt game and gather roots, seeds and berries? Why not stay put and help the next year's crop along—weeding, pruning, watering? Why not leave off grubbing and scavenging, and farm?

The process was hardly as abrupt as my summary suggests. Most likely our domestication of animals and grains, and our accompanying shift from hunting-gathering to cultivation, took place over centuries and required countless hands. It was sporadic and proceeded by fluke, but domesticated animals steadily came to replace hunted ones. In captivity the wild aurochs became *Bos*, the cow; wolf became dog, our companion and tracker; raven became our airborne spy. Since our species' birth we had been wanderers: now we exchanged mobility for a grounded life, toiling through the seasons for the promise of next year's food. Bit by bit most humans settled down.

Still, the ancient ways persisted here and there. Man as farmer? Not universally. Not the logger, not the fisherman: not in Canada, not even now. We still go down to the sea in ships and into the forest with saws, as hunter-gatherers of some of our most valuable resources. As far as our woods and oceans are concerned, the Neolithic is just something that happened to other people. Farming is limited to the treeless land.

That's finally changing. In forestry, knowledge that supports true farms of second-growth trees is at last being applied. Our descendants will shake their heads in wonder that as recently as the early third millennium, workers in advanced nations such as Canada routinely went into the aboriginal forest to log and onto the oceans to fish.

Enter the knowledge economy, which is now domesticating that last frontier, the sea. God knows it's none too soon. We have pillaged the sea, sucking out its life with over-efficient longliners. Vast wild stocks of edible fish—groundfish like cod, far-swimmers like salmon—have been gravely depleted. The time may come when cod exist only in aquarium tanks. On sea as in land, then, it's time to stop hunting and gathering. It's time to farm.

Clayton Brenton and his partners founded Future SEA Technologies because they were (in Clayton's words) "sick of seeing fish die in old-style fish farms." The SEA in the company's name doesn't mean the ocean. It's an acronym for Sustained Environment Aquaculture. Brenton *et al.* have developed a system that offers the benefits of fish farming with no apparent disadvantages. The SEA system keeps fish growing without severe environmental stress and the consequent need for constant medical intervention. It produces fish that are more alert when alive and more delicious when cooked.

To date, seawater aquaculture has kept fish in pens open to the ocean. This exposes the fish to the plankton, bacteria, and temperature gradients found naturally in seawater. Wild fish can avoid much of this, but the immobility of penned fish often leads to high death rates. The SEA system solves these problems.

A sharp onshore wind keens as I arrive at the Civic Biological Station of Fisheries and Oceans Canada. The station hugs the southwest shore of Departure Bay in Nanaimo, B.C. Clayton Brenton meets me at the dock with one of his technologists, a fresh-faced young woman with windblown hair. Cradling my computer, I step into their boat and we roar out into the ocean to Future SEA Research Station #1.

Halfway to our destination, a smooth wet head the colour of black coffee rises from the water and looks at us with soulful eyes. "That's Napoleon!" Clayton shouts above the outboard motor's roar. "He's our resident harbour seal. He's been hanging around the research station since we set up shop. He can smell the salmon but he can't get at them, and it drives him crazy!" Napoleon watches us out of sight with a face as reproachful as a starving dog's.

The boat slows as we approach the research station; our technologist-pilot lays us alongside with a practised hand. I step onto a floating dock that heaves beneath my feet in the boat wake, doing odd things to my balance. It's the first time I've felt seasick on a dock.

Ways to catch fish without running after them are not new. The natives of Micronesia built low stone walls across the mouths of ocean inlets. Fish swam over these at high tide and were stranded at low tide, prey to nets and spears. Fish weirs made of woven wickerwork, shaped like funnels, survive from Bronze Age Europe. The large end let the fish swim in; sharpened stakes at the narrow end kept them trapped.

But despite their ingenuity, these fish traps were not true fish farms. Real farming involves weeding, or removing alien species that compete for food; guarding stock from predators (rabbits for lettuce, wolves for sheep, seals and killer whales for fish); and culling puny or diseased stock to give the healthy remainder more food. But since Canada's waters swarmed with fish until a few decades ago, we have not farmed fish widely until today.

Initial essays at fish farming were anything but knowledge-intensive. Inland, freshwater ponds were stocked with trout. Periodically young fry were added and mature fish removed. Saltwater species were penned in bays and sheltered inlets that worked like Neolithic weirs. No attempt was made to remove dead fish or fish excrement. Fish farmers merely assumed that twice-daily tides would scour out their saltwater pens. Freshwater ponds were usually scooped into streams, whose running water performed a similar function.

Advanced knowledge came late to fish farming, and even then only as a Band-Aid measure. Since farmed fish stocks often had high rates of sickness, antibiotics were mixed with pelletized fish-food. Biotechnology firms such as Microtek, in Victoria, developed vaccines against the most common killers of farmed fish. But one fact persisted: the domestic fish was usually punier than its wild cousin. In captivity, even with medical aid and a guaranteed food supply, it grew more slowly and topped out at a lower weight. In addition, although restaurants clamoured for all the output the fish farms could provide, gourmets could tell at first bite whether the trout or salmon on their plates were wild or farmed. Free-swimming fish had firmer, tastier flesh than their jailed and listless cousins.

It's been observed that education and gardening produce miracles for the same reason: in nature, most forms are stunted. Evidently, the old pen-style fish farm was not living up to its potential. Under the right conditions, fish shielded from predators—seals, bears, orcas—and fed with perfect nutrients *had* to be superior to their wild relatives. The key lay in new knowledge—in finding and implementing the ideal conditions. Here in Nanaimo, it's finally been done.

Out in Nanaimo's windy shoal water, attached to the dock, float three enormous bright blue bags. They are the Future SEA fish pens, made of polyvinyl chloride and filled with seawater. Each contains several hundred coho salmon at the same stage of development. I peer into a bag. Each fish faces the same way, as if chasing the fish before it counterclockwise around the tank. The fish swim furiously, yet stay in one place. What's going on?

"The SEA system duplicates natural conditions," Clayton explains. "A high-throughput pump creates a clockwise current inside the containment bag. The smolt—that's what we call young salmon—automatically orient themselves and swim against the current." So they're *exercising?* "Oh yes. They grow up active, with good muscle tone. That keeps them healthier and makes them taste better when they're cooked."

The top of the bag is open: why can't Napoleon and his cousins get in? "The seals could jump into the bags if they wanted to," Clayton says. "But the bags are opaque, so the seals can't see what's inside, and they won't risk a blind leap."

What about the, you know, the, ah—

"The fish crap? It collects at the bottom of the bag. We pump it on shore and turn it into fertilizer. That makes something useful. It also drastically cuts the odds that any fish disease incubated here will be transmitted into the wild."

Precious little chance of that, in any case: these fish are vigorous. The water in which they swim is pulled from a deep, clean layer below the ocean's scummy surface, then double filtered before the pump circulates it. Conditions are continuously and automatically adjusted by solid-state instrumentation so that the water remains within optimum, predetermined limits of salinity and temperature.

Old-style fish farms in B.C. have recently been in the news because of mass escapes of farmed fish into the open ocean. Even assuming the escapees were healthy, many of them were not local varieties but an alien species, Atlantic salmon, whose release into Pacific ecosystems might cause chaos.

No fish has ever escaped from Future SEA's closed system. Thanks in part to this knowledge-economy success, the B.C. government recently lifted a five-year moratorium on fish-farm expansion. If any new technology can allay the fears of fishermen and MLAs for wild fish stocks—as well as the average diner's fears that the salmon on his plate may be the last he'll ever nosh—it's the sustainable-environment system from Future SEA.

"This technology doesn't depend on specialized legislation to make it economically viable," Clayton tells me, tapping a flow gauge. "It works. It's safe. It's good for the environment. It makes a profit for the operator. And it's healthier for salmon."

It's taken until the twenty-first century for the knowledge economy to extend the benefits of the Early Neolithic from land to sea. Better late than never.

My research has begun to reveal a pattern: the movers and shakers of the knowledge economy—those that originate and apply new information—to a disproportionately high degree work for themselves. Sometimes their self-employment is de facto. Brian Carson, while a nominal employee, endures few constraints to independent thought and action. But more often the innovator is a unique breed of scientist-entrepreneur like Roy McKee and Clayton Brenton. As I drive south along the new Island Highway, I consider why this is so.

Why do we work for others? Why are there jobs? Not work: that's easily defined in the functional sense, as activity done to achieve necessities and pleasures. But jobs? As my ten-year-old would say, *Weird!*

The Common Law, universal in English-speaking countries, uses as its employment model the master-servant relationship that has existed in practice since Mesopotamia and was legally codified in medieval times. The servant (employee, slave, serf) contracts to give his master (employer, owner, lord) sole benefit of the employee's efforts in specified places, times, and professional jurisdictions. The master reciprocally promises regular remuneration at agreed-on rates, plus other benefits that may range from part payment of medical-dental insurance to company housing and relocation assistance. It doesn't matter whether the work is planting or programming. To the law it's more than an exchange, a one-time transaction like a purchase: it's hedged about with abstracts of religious intensity. Trust. Duty. Fiduciary obligation. Diligence. Punctuality. Address. As John Law sees it, employment is more than an exchange of time for goods and services. It is a bond in which the master functions as a loving father and the employee as a faithful, obedient child. (This is the legal model: the ideal. Remember that Dickens's Mr. Bumble calls the law "a ass— a idiot.")

In accepting this eye-popping anachronism, the average worker implicitly commits to set aside the things that make— *made*, rather—him or her a free human being and a thinking, responsible citizen. Out the window go independent judgment, self-allocation of time and energy, determination of activity based on what is witnessed during work. Lurching in to replace them come acceptance of the boss's will above one's own, a trust in the boss's judgment, often despite the evidence of one's eyes. It's a matter of faith, defined by a cynic as what lets us believe what we know to be untrue. *Hey, you're the boss!*

One of the most striking properties of the knowledge economy is its potential to sever these chains: to reinstate workers as independent agents, with a full ration of intrinsic dignity. This has happened in two ways. First, the full-time worker within many knowledge companies has a recognized and lofty status. Second, over the past two decades an army of people in professional mid-management was given the bum's rush by downsizing employers. The bereft employees had trusted their bosses to return loyalty for loyalty. Finding themselves on the street but saddled with mortgages, children, and other long-term obligations of midlife, these professionals unwillingly became self-employed.

Then, astonishingly, they found they liked their new state. The pay was irregular, there were midnight worries over deadlines and cash flow, but something ugly had been lost: the choke chain. Suddenly the old way of doing things seemed, well, silly. The self-employed still have clients to satisfy, but those who have many masters have none.

Aesop tells about a dog who recounts to a passing wolf the advantages of being owned by a master: bed, shelter, regular meals. Then comes this dialogue:

"What is that around your neck?" the wolf asks.

"A collar and choke chain," the dog says.

"See you later," says the wolf.

———————

Late in the day I reach Victoria. If cities have personalities, Victoria is white, heterosexual, middle-aged, cautious, and fond of gardening. It wears tweed sportcoats and rumpled slacks. It drives a ten-year-old Volvo and votes in municipal elections; it considers other people's opinions before it speaks. In other words, Victoria is like government towns the world over.

In all this hotbed of propriety, however, some real innovation can still occur. A few years ago a young forest scientist in MoFo's Research Branch managed to co-ordinate production of a new cybernetic tool. The aim of his revolutionary software was to reduce B.C.'s reliance on old-growth timber, to hasten a shift to artificially planted second-growth stands. The software, called SYLVER, lets those who tend new trees forecast the results of their efforts in far less time than it takes an actual tree to grow. To do this, our MoFo scientist made use of computer modelling, replacing real wood with its conceptual equivalent in data and abstract algorithms.

This work was necessary because of something called rotation time. Despite governments' good intentions in restocking clear-cut land, trees are not your average crop. As Karl Marx noted, a big enough difference in degree creates a difference in kind. Something really huge is something else: a light rain waters your garden, a monsoon washes it away.

Now consider the difference between the life cycle of trees and that of other crops. Hay matures in ninety days, grain in five months, and trees take a century. "When a tree is wide its planter has died," goes the adage. It's true. If you plant trial stands of second-growth conifer, you won't live to table the results: your great-great-grandchildren will record them. By that time it's a little late for you, as stand manager, to adjust your tree-farming methods. If the forest is a crop, it's a radically different one. You can't treat trees like wheat.

Even in the coastal rain forests of British Columbia, where Douglas fir and hemlock may grow twenty-five metres tall and seventy-five centimetres thick in eighty years, second-growth regeneration is a long drawn out process. Even with productive soils and without too much heat, cold, drought, or wind, seedlings need at least three human generations to grow to harvestable size. How to get more data in less time—to fill the unforgiving minute with more than sixty seconds' worth of distance run? That was the task Tom Silke, our government scientist, set for his colleagues and himself.

The tree species they concentrated on first was *Pseudotsuga menziesii*, the Douglas fir. It is Canada's most important commercial wood species, measured by hard-currency export earnings. Tom and a few like-minded scientists in government and industry decided to understand second-growth Douglas fir in every detail. They would then use their new knowledge to assess the effects of stand-management techniques.

Fine. But how to do this in a reasonable time? Could the scientists find a way to accelerate the process—to test their hypotheses before everyone in the project died of old age?

In a word, yes. The forest scientists created computer models of tree growth, into which they put all their new data about the effects on Douglas fir of planting density, soil quality, and site conditions. They also input whether seedlings had come from random cones or from large, healthy "alpha" trees.

"Our computer models use the best available data to generate estimates of forest response and financial worth," Tom tells me in a cluttered office overlooking Government Street. "In so doing, they telescope the 'wait-and-see' period for stand managers from centuries into minutes." Thanks to Tom and his crew, when the electronic tree is wide its planter hasn't died. In fact, he probably hasn't finished his morning coffee.

SYLVER, the model's name, stands for Silvicultural impact on Yield, Lumber Value, and Economic Return. SYLVER's components examine each step of second-growth tree management. The software starts with planting seedlings, goes through various tending activities, and ends with revenue from wood products—lumber, panels, and so on—made from the stand.

One of SYLVER's subcomponents is a growth program, called TASS, for Tree And Stand Simulator. It lets you "farm" a managed stand while applying various silvicultural treatments. TASS then displays the results of your work in exhaustive detail.

It feels seriously strange to fill in SYLVER's data fields and turn the program loose. When you're as much of an amateur as I am, you make choices with a mental coin-flip. Site? Make it coastal and mountainous, west-facing, with rocky soil. Average yearly temperature? Say 12 degrees Celsius. Average yearly rainfall? Oh, 685 centimetres. Latitude? Fifty degrees north. Annual growing season? Twenty-two weeks. Planting density, stems per hectare? Try nine hundred. Enter. Go get 'em, TASS.

At this point the computer switches on its graphics. And when the SYLVER screen starts changing, you know what it feels like to be present at the Creation. There before you, speeded up until a year flashes by in seconds, a forest grows. SYLVER lets you inspect your virtual stand from various angles: front, side, top. I like the overhead view. With the screen set to show a stand one hundred metres to a side—that is, one hectare—seedlings are mere dots. Within two minutes they have become circles, representing the leaf reach of saplings. In five minutes their branches touch in the ancient struggle for available sunlight. When some trees die from Ambrosia beetle or root rot, their neighbours crowd opportunistically into the free space.

Suddenly the trees' growth freezes, and a computer prompt appears. Do I want to prune my saplings? If so, I'll have to pay for labour and equipment. If not, I may forgo the added downstream value of higher-value, knot-free wood. Right, no pruning. It costs too much. Carry on.

More minutes elapse. Then a chime sounds—TASS has run its course. The E-trees have reached a size where I can simulate their harvesting and processing.

What kind of wood have my decisions made? It's easy to find out: just position my cursor and click on any tree. Then SYLVER displays a circular (transverse) or longitudinal (triangular) cross-section of the stem. Heartwood, or mature wood, is dense, fine-grained, and relatively knot-free. Hence it's the most valuable wood type for high-end uses such as decorative veneer and furniture. To highlight the heartwood, SYLVER tints it yellow.

Another wood type, "juvenile wood," is a young fibre, as its name suggests. It tends to degrade in dry kilns, splitting and warping, and so is worth less. Juvenile wood is coded red, then, because it's commercially undesirable. Tree bark is brown.

Figures spring into life beside my cross-section, showing the absolute volume, relative volume, value in 2081 dollars, and net present value for each different type of wood.

As its name implies, net present value relates future benefits to today. At 10 per cent compound interest, for example, a dollar doubles in about seven years. If I grow my virtual trees to harvest in seven decades, my initial planting costs at Year Zero will grow nearly a thousandfold. To break even on a planting investment of $100, my stand must bring in $100,000 seventy years from now. While money may not grow on trees, it does grow—unfortunately—faster than trees do.

"We compare costs incurred today, costs incurred ten or twenty years from now, and revenues that may not be realized for sixty years or more," Tom Silke tells me.

Once TASS is finished, a mouse click invokes follow-on subroutines that buck, saw, plane, and kiln-dry my E-stems into virtual lumber. Other programs let me peel tree stems on giant lathes and glue up the resultant veneer into plywood. Leftover wood is chipped for pulp and waferboard; there is little waste. Even bark has value: it goes into a new type of waterproof panel called BarkBoard.

Now I watch as FAN$Y, SYLVER's Financial ANalysis $Ystem, computes the value of the virtual products that my choices helped create. The scientists replaced the acronym's *S* with a dollar sign to remind them that value, not volume, is the goal.

Here's my final report card, expressed in today's dollars. *And the winner is—*

Oops. I've blown it: my experimental stand has not repaid investment. In forestry as in marriage, small decisions have big consequences. I planted too few stems per hectare, pruned too little, and used nitrogen fertilizers that were unnecessary on a fertile site. Back to the drawing board. At least I can do that myself and spare my great-grandchildren the pain.

Overall, many of SYLVER's conclusions are surprising. The value of a good second-growth stand, i.e., one managed by Tom Silke rather than myself, peaks at only seventy years—even though its volume may increase 20 per cent in the next decade. The stand value gains nearly half as much again when it is harvested ten years earlier.

"By simulating silvicultural treatments before actual stands are planted," Tom says, "we can be confident that our new forests will give us maximum productivity."

I realize something as I walk back to my car: bit by bit, inch by inch, the knowledge economy is spreading through the forests. That's good news.

If you can't find enough resources, you can always make them—gemstones, for example. My next interview is at GemCorp, a small manufacturing business on Vancouver Island. Their specialty is creating flawless jewels as big as loaves of bread.

On my way there, I drive through parks and boulevards filled with enormous trees. When Shakespeare was a lad, these things could have been saplings; they certainly weren't planted by the Victoria Parks Board. It heartens me that even in our cities, we Canadians can nurture some of the magnificence our ancestors found when they first came here. Maybe—at least to a certain threshold—the world needs more people, not fewer. When we know we're going to stay somewhere, we take better care of its resources: after all, they're in our backyards. Nobody likes living in a clear-cut.

I think of Tom Silke and the intellectual audacity that let him and his fellow scientists put a growing forest inside a number-crunching machine. And I think back to when people first began to realize the immense power of pure information.

In the 1940s and 50s Norbert Wiener, Alan Turing, and other theoreticians decided reality and information were identical. From the Wiener-Turing viewpoint, *everything* is data. The behaviour of rivers, materials, weather systems, cities, life itself—all can be boiled down to information strings. And given the technology to encode, store, retrieve, decode, and display vast quantities of numerical facts, you can generate a detailed model of how nearly anything behaves. Since science assumes (so far without refutation) that what has been will continue to be, such a model not only describes, it also predicts. The quantity so modelled may be abstract:

sales trends, climate change, voting patterns. As I'm about to find out, there are even scientists who quantify the emotional force of words. But computer-based numerical modelling may equally well represent something tangible: the carbon locked in trees, the shape of a gene, or (à la Tom Silke) the growth of saplings.

In one form or another, *data*—the term is a Latin plural meaning "given things"—describe phenomena across a colossal, perhaps a universal, range. Mathematics has been called the queen of sciences, but *informatics*, the science of data, is the empress. Pythagoras was right: existence is the same as number. Everything but the soul has been reduced to bytes on a storage medium. And no doubt a researcher somewhere is on the track of digitizing the soul. Remember this: *It's All Data!*

Here is my destination for today, a parking lot beside a flat-roofed building. Despite the nondescript exterior, amazing things are going on inside. New resources are being made rather than discovered. The manufactured resources are not commodities but are highly valuable. Most amazing of all, they are born of an unlikely coupling. Their mother is knowledge, and their father is corrosion.

Things change, say the mystics. Life grows and decays, say the biologists. Metal corrodes, say the chemists. Each expert is right, but of all the types of matter, metal has the best claim to immortality. In theory, a bar of steel in interstellar space might last forever, unchanging while the ages roll.

Even in the highly oxidizing atmosphere of Earth, metals may last forever—some metals, anyway. Gold takes its ancient value from its ability to tolerate common hardships—burial in earth or immersion in saltwater—and come up shining after millennia. Iron, despite its usefulness in the short term, quickly forms oxides in the presence of oxygen and water. Unless buried in anaerobic conditions well away from O_2, in seafloor silt, for instance, even a cast-iron cannon will quickly crumble into scale.

Most metals have several types of corrosion: there's bad rust and there's good. Perhaps you've noticed a highway bridge made with unpainted steel. If it's on a regular route of yours, you'll see its plates go from bright to blue-grey as the months go by, yet the bridge stays up. Its metal conforms to the North American structural specification G40.11, for "weathering steel."

A high-strength construction alloy, G40.11 combines iron with traces of rarer metals, including molybdenum. The result is an immensely strong crystalline microstructure. A G40.11 bar whose cross-sectional area is only one square centimetre can withstand a stretching force of several tonnes. In fact, G40.11 was developed solely for its strength; its weathering characteristics were discovered only afterwards.

Normal low-carbon steel forms oxides on its skin that are permeable to oxygen and water. This lets the corrosion move steadily through the steel until the metal is eaten through. By contrast, G40.11 forms an impermeable rust layer that seals deeper metal away from such corrosion. It rusts only so far. If some runoff stain is tolerable, thousands of dollars in sandblasting and repainting can be saved over the life of a bridge.

In forming an impermeable corrosion layer, weathering steel acts just like aluminum, whose principal oxide, AL_2O_3, also seals off the parent metal. AL_2O_3 has the added advantage of being almost insoluble in rainwater, so that materials next to the oxidizing aluminum hardly stain. The protective corrosion film is so clear and so thin that it is transparent. This lets the parent metal beneath shine through.

And when it crystallizes in a certain way, AL_2O_3 is hard: much harder than the metal from which it sprang. The chemical name for it is corundum, and the only known substance that can scratch corundum is diamond. Certain forms of corundum are used as abrasives. Rarer forms, naturally coloured by traces of titanium ion, have long been valued for their transparent beauty. They are also long-lasting, being both hard and chemically inert. We call these forms ruby and sapphire.

Chemically, these gems are little different from the coating that keeps a folding lawn chair from rotting away. I have to admire the scientist who first did destructive analysis on a gem-quality stone; no doubt he was independently wealthy.

The story now proceeds beyond rubies, sapphires, and lawn chairs to more interesting stuff. The knowledge economy operates by replacing ignorance with fact, even at the cost of removing wonder. (This ring, dahling? Oh, just some aluminum oxide.) It then reverses things, applying knowledge to create things never seen in nature. In this case, our new knowledge lets us make perfect sapphires larger than anything found inside the Earth.

The Edwardes Ruby in the Great Crown of Britain weighs 167 carats, or thirty-three grams—about an ounce. Each of the sapphires made by GemCorp (for security reasons, not its real name) weighs twenty-two kilograms or more. That's seven hundred times the British ruby's size.

GemCorp begins its manufacturing process by importing pure AL_2O_3 in bags. It's a fine white powder, the consistency of dust in an alkali desert. This relatively inexpensive raw material is then put into an electric furnace the size of a large refrigerator. The lid is closed and the furnace is switched on until the corrosion powder it contains glows white-hot and melts into a thick liquid.

At this point the GemCorp metallurgists carefully insert a heat-resistant carbon rod into the molten mass, slowly turning it like a glassblower's wand. If the furnace temperature is exactly right, the honey-thick AL_2O_3 begins to crystallize on the seed rod. It hardens into pure, clear sapphire.

This is where the knowledge economy improves on nature. Even the best natural gems have imperfections. They contain impurities or voids. More important, they comprise a jumble of different crystals of various sizes.

When removed and allowed to cool under tightly controlled conditions, a process that may take days, a loaf-sized sapphire cures into something that resembles a lump of glass. At first its skin is slightly rough, like the translucent surface of a gin bottle. But inside it is perfectly transparent, without any voids, inclusions, or fracture faults. Each of GemCorp's sapphires is a single crystal.

At this point, GemCorp treats its synthetic miracles as an industrial raw material. Using fine-toothed diamond saws, it slices some of its enormous sapphire crystals into strips a few millimetres thick, then saws out coin-shaped circles. These become the practically unscratchable faces of expensive wristwatches.

A more interesting fate awaits other gems. Laboriously, again with diamond-tipped tools, GemCorp machines some sapphire loaves into hemispheres fifteen centimetres in diameter. The result is a polished dome, structurally strong and perfectly transparent to the emission spectra of military jet engines. GemCorp's sapphire hemispheres become the nose cones of heat-seeking air-to-air missiles.

The sapphire domes are tough enough to withstand high accelerations and abrupt course changes. They tolerate friction heating from velocities approaching one kilometre per second in dense, low-altitude air. During this time, they continuously transmit to the missile's onboard sensors the precise location of an enemy jet engine.

It's evident why infrared-guided missiles for air combat are so costly. In the nose of each is a flawless synthetic jewel whose only purpose is to destroy itself along with its airborne enemy.

Planes, trains, boats, automobiles. Part of me hopes that British Columbians never build a fixed link from Vancouver Island to the mainland, like the recent engineering miracle that took the I out of P.E.I. The ferries are fun to take, and the break from driving is relaxing. Not restful, however: I don't switch off my mind. There's something about a wine-dark sea, clouds of seabirds, and air as clear as GemCorp sapphires that sets me thinking. Soon I turn my back on the perfect April day and head amidships to Deck Five. Here B.C. Ferry Corporation has fitted *MV Spirit of Vancouver* with study carrels that have lights and grounded power outlets. Soon I'm deep in my computerized notes again.

The emergence of the knowledge economy solves the old puzzle of the Missing Computer Benefit. Before the computer took over, its advocates promised it would revolutionize work, school, and play. It would make all these easier, more enjoyable, and more productive. Or so ran the rosy predictions.

For most of us, that miracle has yet to happen. The average worker's leg iron simply shifted its attachment point from manual typewriters to VDT screens; the manacle's other end stayed firmly on the human ankle. Even with new owners, serfs are serfs.

There's little indication that humanity's new owners are any kinder than the earlier set. *It's All Data* has ushered in a raft of ills that are worse in kind, if not degree, then what went before. We have traded inkstains, eyestrain, and writer's cramp for rotator-cuff injury, VDT astigmatism, carpal-tunnel syndrome, and above all overwork.

Why is this? Management theorists call impediments to business *friction*. Computers take a lot of friction out of business, thereby accelerating society and shortening available time for reflection. This should be good: friction is bad, isn't it? Answer: not necessarily. Consider the material source of the friction metaphor, resistance to effort. When you push a rock up a hill, a frictionless surface means you have nothing to push against. No friction, no work. As well, there is much to be said for a more gracious way of transacting affairs—what William Blake called "Toil unsever'd from tranquility." Say this for business friction: it gives us time to pause, catch our breath, and ponder our decisions.

There are times when the technology-intensive workplace seems to consider such leisure archaic. By making it easier to redo a text, for example, word processors trap writers into perfectionism. We now feel compelled to do six drafts where previously we might have measured our words and derived good prose in two. A similar effect appears in the military, where automatic weapons and devices to track and lock on to targets have all but destroyed good marksmanship. Again, E-mail permits five or ten round-trip communications a day, up to sixty times the five-a-month maximum of snail mail. But precisely because E-mail is so easy to use, it has no energy barrier to it—no friction—and thus it gobbles time. What E-mail user has never compulsively checked his in-box ten times an hour? How many of us have never regretted sending an ill-considered E-message the instant that it vanished from our screen? Friction can be beneficial.

Again, electronic payroll and inventory software have reduced some of the routine procedures in human-resources offices. Pension calculations, for example, no longer require reams of hand-written forms. Yet when every competitor runs a similar system, where is the competitive advantage? We seek to modernize but only keep abreast; we're on a treadmill. In most tasks of our workday, computers have done nothing but make us run two kilometres where earlier we would have settled for one.

By the 1990s, informatics appeared to have reneged on its promised benefits. As a philosophy, *It's All Data* apparently did little to improve our lives. Instead, it threw whole classes of us—clerks, tellers, assembly-line workers, traffic cops—out of our jobs. Despite the propaganda, the benefits of this new knowledge seemed elusive.

But the great computer benefit wasn't an empty promise. Just as we surrendered all hope of seeing a payoff from informatics, it arrived. All of us—technological experts and laity alike—missed the epiphany because it didn't appear where we were looking. We expected it to show up incrementally, via standard jobs made easier one by one, but the revolution arrived as something vaster than we had imagined: a whole new economy, the knowledge economy. We looked for a shower and got a monsoon.

This happens in revolutions. Initially, people have no idea what they're dealing with. In expecting digital informatics to restrict itself to little tasks, jotting notes and filing tax returns, we tried to stuff it in yesterday's mould. Today, after four decades of fruitlessly trying to do so, we see the true scope of change. The decades of sweat and tears we invested in adapting to computers have yielded not just a new role for secretaries or a simpler way of doing home-work. They have produced a separate ecosystem: a radically differ-ent approach to work. That is the knowledge economy.

➤ I emerge with the blinking, blurry eyes of the computer user into a day even prettier than the one I left. I buy some fresh-made cappuccino—hey, it's the Coast—and carry it onto a windy deck. We're approaching the halfway point of our voyage, and the ferry makes a sweeping turn to transit Active Pass. We enter a spectacu-lar, rock-bound channel, named for a smaller ship in Capt. George Vancouver's eighteenth-century flotilla. The channel must be deep, or we wouldn't be within eight kilometres of here: but oh, man, is it narrow. A section through Active Pass must look like a knifeblade.

A sudden blast of the ship's whistle makes me jump and slop my coffee. Foaming toward us is a second ferry that looks exactly like ours. There's even a black-jacketed, sunglass-wearing idler on the starboard promenade who looks like me. Surely the captains can't mean to pass each other: the waterway's too narrow. But pass they do, saluting with another skull-melting blast of whistles. The big ships don't even slow. I notice some equipment on the other ship's superstructure; I look above me, and find the same equip-ment on ours. Two millimetre-wavelength RF transceivers swivel ceaselessly, a small paraboloid that spins at breakneck speed and a long rectangular strip that pirouettes with regal dignity. Marine radar makes our spectacular manoeuvre routine. Because of that knowledge, ferries on the Victoria-Vancouver run can take a shortcut through Active Pass and shave half an hour from each one-way trip.

Ah, speed. Human nature being what it is, nothing is ever good enough: big must be bigger, productivity more productive, speed speedier. In the mid-1990s Royal Sealink, a private firm, imported two fast boats from Norway and put them into service as high-speed ferries between Victoria and Vancouver. No cars, just passengers. But you didn't need a car, because the new boats went harbour to harbour.

And they were *fast*. I could board Sealink at the foot of Howe Street, Vancouver, at 7:00 a.m. and step onto the quay of the Empress Hotel at 9:30 for meetings in downtown Victoria. The voyage took no longer than a car ferry, once you figured in the drives to and from the deep-water docks. It was also more relaxing. Occasionally you'd hit some chop, but no worse than an airplane's. The boats were beautifully detailed. They were catamarans, with twin aluminum hulls, and they cruised at forty knots. The scenery that flowed by was lovely, and the boats had bars.

In his first term as B.C.'s premier, Glen Clark, a scrappy politico who grew up in Vancouver's working-class East Side, had a great idea. What if B.C. Ferries took one card from Royal Sealink's hand and one from its own and made a high-speed twin-hull boat that carried cars as well as people? That could shave half an hour off the Vic-Van run. But though the concept was sound, its execution was sloppy. Clark's zeal scuppered his own invention. Technical objections from outside experts were dismissed as whining, though the experts were right: the new ships needed more powerful engines and reinforced hulls to avoid cracking in use.

Just as bad, from an environmental point of view, was the lack of thought about the sea wakes that the fast cats might produce.

These proved so disruptive that speed limits came into effect whenever one of the new craft approached within four kilometres of shore. Since such conditions obtained over almost one-third of a typical route, the forecast time savings quickly dwindled.

Worst of all, Clark was so determined to have his new craft operational while he was still in office that he imposed an illogically severe production schedule. As the shipyards' labour rolls swelled to accommodate multiple shifts, as workers were trained at high expense in unfamiliar new technologies such as aluminum fabrication, costs nearly doubled. It's a maxim in business as well as in politics: when budget fudging and fast-tracking succeed, people forgive the shortcuts and forget the lies. When they don't, *caveat Caesar.*

After Clark was forced from office, his successor cancelled the fast-cat program and put the new ships up for sale. But even at a 50 per cent markdown, there have been few nibbles and no takers. It's a pity, for the fast cats, made about a kilometre from where I live, were gorgeous craft. One autumn day I stood on Spanish Banks and watched one of the new ships take a trial cruise. Lord, she was speedy. Her superstructure was raked aft for better aerodynamics, and her new paint made her as sleek as a warplane. But as she rounded Point Atkinson and disappeared north, I noticed something racing toward me on the surface of the sea. It was a line of bow waves three ranks deep, all of them so steep and fast that on dead-calm English Bay they showed whitecaps. I retreated up the beach as they broke; they were like storm waves.

At that point I realized there was far more to economic success than technical data. The most essential skill in the knowledge economy is knowing when to resist pressure, slow down, and think things through. That's what turns good ideas into great ones. For want of such knowledge, a fleet was lost.

———————

Vancouver has a buzz, a snap, a pizzazz. It's fully aware it has out-grown its origins as a resource town and has more in common with Calgary and Toronto than its own backyard. Vancouver wears work-boots and drives 4x4s, but not because it has to: it's a fashion state-ment. This city, like almost every Canadian city today, doesn't hunt or fish, doesn't own guns, and can't imagine why the folks in the hinterland think otherwise. For the next twenty years, until the knowledge economy squeezes corporations out of the cities, the most logical split in Canada will be urban-rural. Partitioning the country by province seems as absurd as sorting its citizens by eye colour. What do Vancouverites have in common with people from Fort St. John?

It's 11:00 a.m. when I arrive at the University of British Colum-bia on Point Grey. Not all of this sprawling campus is dedicated to undergraduate studies. Those two rows of brand-new buildings, for instance, house fledgling corporations, clustered in what's called a technology park. Every firm here is a start-up, commer-cializing new knowledge spun off from original research at UBC.

Like most Canadian technology parks, this one holds a range of disciplines. One company began with recently declassified com-puter modelling of U.S. nuclear explosions. That taught it so much about the fine-scale intricacies of oxidation, especially how a burn front moves through uncombusted material, that it can now run a diesel engine on natural gas. The modified engine has the full power and torque range of a standard sooty diesel, but what comes out of its tailpipe is cleaner than the exhaust of a brand-new pas-senger car.

But all that can wait. I want to finish looking at the knowledge economy in forest resources, and the big news there lies on East Mall, in a building completed in 1990. That's my destination today.

The Western Laboratory of Forintek Canada Corporation has nearly 20,000 square metres in a figure-eight design. Its laboratories and offices cluster around two central courtyards, which give every desk natural light. It's big and modern. But from my viewpoint, the story lies in what's invisible. The lab is built entirely of wood; its only metal is in nails, joist hangers, and decor. Its floors, which are solid and quiet, are underlain by fifteen linear kilometres of wooden truss joists. I park my car, enter the building across its medieval-style bridge, and meet Dr. Charles Szabo in the airy entranceway.

Charles Szabo is tall, slim, and bearded; he's an avid canoeist and outdoorsman. In addition to working as a Forintek resource scientist, he's an adjunct professor at the University of B.C. For the past twenty years he has helped Canada get more from its forests, squeezing so much value out of every tree cut that billions of other old trees can be left standing.

Forintek stands for Forest Industry Technology. The institute, what the British call a QUAGO or quasi-governmental organization, is Canada's national institute for R&D in wood products. It was born in 1979 when Joe Clark's short-lived federal Conservative government abruptly privatized Canada's Eastern and Western Forest Products Laboratories. This was a precipitate move, dictated by the Tories' pro-business wing. Lab personnel woke up one day and read about their privatized status in their morning papers. But Forintek survived this partisan surgery so well that the QUAGO is now healthier than the party that tried to strangle it. The institute is currently financed by contract revenue, grants from the Canadian Forestry Service and the wood-producing provinces, and—most important, because politically indispensable—self-levies from member companies that make wood products such as lumber, plywood, and waferboard.

The Forintek logo forms an upper-case F, which on close examination proves to be sawteeth cutting into green substrate. It's a perfect symbol. Forintek scientists investigate each of Canada's commercially important wood species, asking, How strong is it? What are its machining qualities? Is old-growth different from second-growth? Can we use wood that's waterlogged or damaged by fire or insects? And most important of all: How do we manage our great forests? What kind of wood should they produce?

In the past twenty years, Charles Szabo and other Canadian resource scientists have developed exhaustive answers to these questions. Their new knowledge supports an incipient industry shift from old-growth timber to managed second-growth stands. Whether or not the industry dinosaurs know it, Canada's trees are at last about to become a truly agricultural crop.

New knowledge is imperative to smooth out this resource transition. Now, after years of hanging fire, such change is coming rapidly. Already the eco-activists are defending the old-growth more fiercely as it diminishes; the tourist industry is raising its voice to require unbroken green vistas; the forest industry continues to automate, removing jobs; new jobs in biotechnology and IT will pull population out of the hinterland. Our forests will split into farms and parks, with the only true wilderness being parkland. This makes sense: if trees really are a crop, they must be tended in special areas. We wouldn't have much wheat to export if we let it grow wild and assumed it would self-seed.

Farm fields full of trees are called intensively managed second-growth woodlots. Once established, these stands must be planted, inspected, topped, pruned, fertilized, and continually cured of insect or fungus infestations. Nature did a fine job when she created old-growth forests, but she had a billion years to do so. The forest industry has about a millionth of 1 per cent of that timeline to get its act together. After that, our old trees will either be permanently off limits or already cut down.

It's certainly time for change. To produce edible grains, humanity shifted from gathering to farming ten thousand years ago. As I've just seen, even fish are being intensively farmed. We must do the same thing with trees: not tripping out a-berrying, figurative basket on arm, but intentionally and intelligently growing wood from scratch. Tomorrow's Canada may parallel today's Europe, where indigenous full-time foresters know their woodlots down to individual trees.

This makes Charles Szabo's job never-ending. Wood is a complex and variable material, and new data must constantly be derived to explain its behaviour. This knowledge will let future industry make the best use of its wood.

Human behaviour, however, is more complex than any material's. What motivates Charles Szabo and his colleagues? A detail I notice during our conversation gives me a clue. On Charles's office wall is a photo of an enormous lodgepole pine. The great tree stands alone in the midst of a flat plain of stumps, the last survivor of a massive clear-cut in the 1980s.

Charles explains the situation to me. The tree was so large that the lumber company's top fellers, the elite of its forest workforce, could not cut it. The company sent for larger saws, which at length sliced the giant through. But the tree had grown so perfectly vertical that it was rock solid: severed, it still refused to topple. The company had to truck in the heaviest hydraulic jacks it could find and use them to shove the tree over until it fell. It measured sixty-five metres in length. It weighed, by best estimate, over twenty tonnes. But when the work crews went to buck it into logs, they found the wood had grown in a spiral. It was as if a Titan had taken one end of the tree in each of his hands and twisted it. Its spiral grain pattern made the tree useless for lumber. The great corpse ended its days in a pulp mill, which hacked and stewed it into millions of rolls of toilet paper.

I asked Charles Szabo why he displayed the tree's picture. He thought a long time. "Because I'm ashamed," he said at last. You had nothing to do with it, I told him. "Oh, yes I did," he said. "I'm human." The thought that such a magnificent thing was slaughtered to wipe dirty backsides filled him with a lasting grief.

Charles Szabo was fortunate: his job gave him a chance to make amends—to beg forgiveness, as did the Haida and the Nu'u-chah-Nulth, from the spirits of the trees they felled. Charles and his colleagues have a vision for Canada: not replacing resource firms with multimedia firms but bringing the knowledge economy into the forest. One of the results of that transition will be to reduce or eliminate the tragedy of the spiral fir.

Charles's employer, Forintek Canada Corporation, is finally making progress in this. In the late 1970s Dr. Max Corngold, then Charles Szabo's boss and a Yankee ex-pat working in Vancouver, realized that Canada's lumber industry was judging the productivity of its forests by the wrong gauge. Traditional criteria for forest economics stressed volume: cubic metres of harvest, board feet of lumber a day, train flatcars full of two-by-fours. Corngold realized that measuring forestry by quantity in this way was futile. Instead, true productivity should by assessed by how much *value* industry adds to each cubic metre of unprocessed wood.

Even the unprocessed wood should not be judged on volume, Corngold saw. The goal to aim for was weight per unit volume. Denser wood, he said, is better wood—stronger and more stable. In products ranging from roof trusses to the dissolving pulp from which rayon is made, higher density increases wood's worth. In assessing wood by value, and value in turn by density, Corngold and Szabo helped develop the most important gauge in the history of forest products.

If this seems simple to the point of idiocy, think of the *Andy Capp* comic's repairman—"Tuppence t'whack th'telly, ten quid f'knowin' where t'whack it." Arriving at this new simplicity and clarity of understanding required vast amounts of new knowledge, and from Corngold and Szabo, that meant both conceptual brilliance and a hard scientific slog. But afterwards, wood scientists and forest managers had a means to accurately measure the value of managed second-growth stands. That also let them estimate the efficacy of the tending treatments. Successful forest management finally had a clear definition: it was whatever created denser wood.

Density is a key characteristic by which SYLVER evaluates its E-trees: it is the key index of silvicultural success. The greater a second-growth stand's average density, the more it's worth. My SYLVER run failed because my E-stand had insufficient amounts of denser wood.

The Forintek scientists also made use of a rating spectrum for wood products that was based on added value—that is, on added knowledge. On the low end are raw logs shipped to export customers with the bark and roots attached. (Believe it or not—and I wouldn't believe it myself without first-hand knowledge—there are still suited apes in some forest companies who do this.) At the high end are remanufactured items such as furniture. A log broker might get $1,000 for a big stem of old-growth; sliced into decorative veneer, the same stem might bring fifty times as much. If Canada exports the log, it gains no added value. The only beneficiaries are the companies that swindle us Canadians out of our raw logs.

Finding truth is one thing; convincing dinosaurs of it is another. Here's what the scientists are up against. A few years ago a huge B.C.-based forest-products firm reviewed its forest operations at Forintek. As a Forintek associate, I attended this closed meeting and sat flabbergasted as a company shill announced he had just sold $50 million worth of logs to customers in Asia. These trees averaged two hundred years old; they were ripped from the aboriginal forest and loaded onto boats without a penny of value added here. The profits, gloated the company rep, financed a capital expansion program that cut mill staff by a further 5 per cent. More productivity! Fewer workers! Lower wood prices! Wasn't that great?

The scientists who emerged from the auditorium were, like me, white with rage. "I heard of another business," one of them told me. "A guy lived beside a river full of this company's pulp logs and had an eye for good timber. He skimmed off old-growth pine and paid two bucks for each log. Then he took them back to his workshop, dried them, split them, and made violin backs. I've calculated that he got six thousand times more value per cubic metre of wood than the company did."

The scientist was Max Corngold. Today, more than a decade later, he and his colleagues have helped create a new kind of technology for wood products, one whose end is not sheer volume but the far wiser aim of product value.

It's still unclear how long it will take the more reactionary forest companies to listen. Canadian companies are still exporting logs; the firm I cite isn't the only stegosaurus in the woods. Will the benefits of new knowledge—technical, marketing, ethical—win out? Ultimately, I think so, but I place no bets on when. As my grandmother used to mutter, none are so blind as those that will not see.

By the time I finish with Charles Szabo I'm in a foul mood and decide to walk it off. UBC's Rose Garden is a good place to see beyond the problems of the moment; its view is spectacular, across English Bay to Howe Sound and the massive shoulders of Tetrahedron Peak. The sun is setting and the sky is rose quartz. Two hundred kilometres of my voyage, half of it to date, lies spread before me. And away up the coast, I see something that reawakens my hope.

See those cut blocks far ahead, where a forest company has harvested trees? Clear-cut used to be exactly that: a continuous space where nothing alive stayed standing. But here the chainsaws have left extensive treed areas throughout each cut block. From my viewpoint, untouched slopes and stream valleys stand out: big knots of old-growth that have been spared for no apparent reason. The areas seem halfway between old-economy clear-cuts and the select-cut practices of Carpathian foresters, who wait with endless patience to cull trees one by one.

Behind this new approach is the knowledge economy, whose reservoirs of data are infiltrating and transforming every aspect of our lives. It was said best in late 2000 by the CEO of what had been a typical old-economy firm, the basic-steel producer Dofasco: "From now on, everything is the New Economy."

The cut blocks I can see are done to a set of new standards called variable-retention logging. The technique was developed in

1996–98 by MacMillan-Bloedel and was retained by Weyer-haeuser Corporation when it bought MacBlo in 1999. VRL leaves sizable forested areas within a cut block. These too will be harvested, but not for a long time—as much as three decades in the future. Instead of scraping out a contiguous area of absolute desolation, VRL is selective and intelligent: it makes clear-cuts less clear.

Though almost unknown in North America outside coastal British Columbia, VRL marks what may become an irreversible shift by American and Canadian firms to meet tough ecological and public-relations demands. It's as if the chairman of General Motors had read Ralph Nader's exposé *Unsafe at Any Speed* and said, He's right! instead of his actual response: Bigawd! Communists!

Surprisingly, some businesses can understand and adapt to new facts rather than bad-mouthing critics by reflex. You can do well without circling the wagons. You can, in fact, earn more money, for a longer time, when you *don't* react with fear and loathing to every negative word. Maybe your critics know things it would pay you to hear.

This is still not widely recognized. A population, whether of bacteria or of business people, adapts in one of only two ways. By far the more common occurs when individuals better fitted to new circumstance survive and multiply while intractable ones carry their dysfunctional pigheadedness with them to the grave.

But at long intervals another change mechanism occurs: a person, or a fictional person called a corporation, alters behaviour in response to reasoned argument. The individual, rather than the population, makes the change. Weyerhaeuser may be this uncommon type of firm. Its shift to VRL is not yet complete; if and when it is, it will have been made out of realpolitik—that is, for reasons of marketing and PR image—at least as much as from ethics or ecology.

This is not to denigrate the company's change. The whole idea of morality may have evolved to foster actions beneficial beyond the moment. For most North American corporations, that moment is ninety days or less—the time till the next quarterly report.

I'm an optimist. I suspect that Weyerhaeuser will fully implement VRL. It will then recoup the expense of doing so many times over by vastly improving its company image with consumers. This success will then, belatedly, persuade rival firms to follow suit.

Of course if Weyerhaeuser's competitors remain as intractable as they have proven to date, they will simply perish and be replaced by better-adapted firms. Perhaps the dinosaurs, deep in the forest industry that is their final refuge, are at last about to meet their killer comet.

––––––––––

Despite both the rad Greens and the forest industry's reactionaries, sound scientific arguments are emerging in support of harvesting some old-growth. New knowledge indicates that cutting and replanting a mature forest may actually benefit the environment, provided the wood goes to long-lasting uses such as houses and furniture.

In this more long-term view, a forest is a greenhouse-gas tank; every time it's cut and replanted, it can accept a centuries-long top-up with atmospheric CO_2. In a sense, a clear-cut that's quickly restocked is no more blameworthy than the stubble that's left when wheat is harvested.

A bit of background. Cellulose, the main ingredient of wood, is a sugar polymer comprising oxygen, hydrogen, and carbon. These constituents are freely available, even though trees are sessile organisms that can't forage as animals can. Water provides hydrogen and oxygen; air supplies carbon dioxide, CO_2. The tree's genome tells it how to assemble its raw materials into wood. Sunlight provides the power.

Much power is needed, for a growing tree extracts an amazing volume of material from its environment. A willow, for example, drinks water from the soil, ducts it through roots and trunk, and wicks some of it into the atmosphere as water vapour. This is not a small-scale operation. On a summer day when its biological processes run quickly, a mature willow may breathe tonnes of water into the air. In flood-prone areas, conservation engineers often plant willows rather than build dams. Similarly, the growing conifers in a forest extract millions of cubic metres of CO_2 from the air, and lock it into wood.

Carbon dioxide seems harmless enough. It's a natural product of human respiration and non-toxic in normal concentrations. To understand why CO_2 has become a modern pollutant, scientists look back to Earth a hundred thousand years ago, when our biosphere's carbon budget was in stable equilibrium. Limestone, made of small sea creatures' shells, stored carbon until tectonic forces exposed it and let it weather. Earth's forests were also carbon sinks. As they grew, they bound atmospheric CO_2 into wood and held it there until they died.

The time of lock-up varies according to tree species. A spruce in a boreal forest may live for sixty years, a coastal *Metasequoia glyptostroboides* for two millennia. At maturity, a tree stops binding carbon. At its death, whether quickly by fire or slowly by disease, its carbon is unlocked to the air, and the cycle restarts.

This exquisitely balanced system was destabilized by old, old circumstances—human meddling. When we found that those naturally occurring carbon sinks called coal and oil made fine fuel, we extracted them to heat our buildings and power our vehicles. Later we used them as feedstocks for synthetic materials like plastics, fabrics, and pharmaceuticals.

Undeniably, these fossil fuels have improved our daily lives. But they also yielded a major, unintentional by-product: gigatonnes of carbon dioxide, released into the air at rates unprecedented since immense volcanic eruptions millions of years ago. This is unfortunate, because atmospheric CO_2 has another property. It is transparent to sunlight striking through it to the ground, but nearly opaque to re-radiated infrared trying to escape back into space. The net energy transfer inexorably heats the Earth.

Industries that generate a lot of CO_2, such as the oil and automotive sectors, naturally balk at any call to curtail their carbon output. Like the tobacco companies faced with similar unwelcome evidence, they propose further studies. But globally, science is rapidly reaching consensus on global warming: it's here. And unless we stop it, Earth and Venus—whose surface is as hot as a self-clean oven—will be twins in climate, as well as in size.

To control CO_2, scientists are making sober proposals that ten years ago would have been considered science fiction. These use a concept called carbon sequestration technology, or sucking carbon away from the air where it can't turn up the heat. Researchers from Norway, Switzerland, and the U.S. have recently proposed injecting CO_2 into sub-ocean holes, pumping it into dry oil wells on land, or bubbling it through the abyssal depths to create a kind of giant soda. One suggestion is as effective and much easier: plant trees.

Dr. Hamish Kimmins is a professor of forest ecology at the University of British Columbia. His specialty is forest ecosystems, both in the pristine state and in response to human disturbance. Among other techniques, Hamish Kimmins analyzes forests by means of their carbon budget.

"Any ecosystem," says Hamish, "has a maximum quantity of carbon it can store. Just as cars have different sizes of gas tank, various forests differ in their capacity for holding carbon. When a forest reaches old-growth stage, its carbon tank is full and the forest is in equilibrium. It takes from the atmosphere only as much carbon as it returns."

When an old-growth forest is harvested, Hamish explains, its carbon tank is emptied. Second-growth stands that arise to replace the old-growth then bind carbon for several hundred years, until carbon equilibrium is re-established. Whether this benefits the environment depends on what happens to the harvested wood.

"If the trees go to short-term uses such as toilet paper," Kimmins says, "their carbon returns to the atmosphere within a few weeks and there is no net removal of CO_2. But if the harvested wood goes to longer-lasting uses, its carbon remains locked away from the air while replacement saplings bind new carbon. This creates a net atmospheric removal of CO_2." Long-lasting uses for wood include furniture, which may endure for hundreds of years, and building structures. From construction to teardown, the average American house lasts sixty-five years; and its wood may continue to function as a carbon sink even after the house is demolished.

"In anaerobic landfill, wood breaks down at 3 per cent or less per year," adds Jamie Meil, who's visiting from the Athena Institute in Ottawa. "At these decay rates, it might not release all its stored carbon for a century or more."

Alternatively, says Hamish, wood from a demolished house could be used as a feedstock to generate engine fuels such as methanol. This would place no more carbon into the air than allowing the wood to decay naturally. At the same time, it would displace its BTU equivalent in fossil fuels.

The Athena Institute, named for the Greek goddess of wisdom, looks at the broader context of materials used in buildings. What demands would a proposed design make on the environment? How much of this eco-load stems from the creation of building materials, and how much from a building's lifetime impact on its surroundings? To what degree does this eco-load depend on what happens to materials when a building is torn down? In constructing computer models that address these issues, Jamie and his associates have unearthed some interesting facts.

"Wood is often less environmentally disruptive than other building materials," observes Jamie. "That is our inescapable conclusion. When you consider raw-resource consumption, energy spent on extraction, transportation, and manufacturing, global warming potential, and generated wastes, wood emerges as a clean, ecologically responsible material."

In resource extraction, the Athena models consider four dimensions: how wide an area is affected, how deep into the biosphere the disruption goes, the time it takes an affected area to regain its biological productivity, and the area's ecological significance. The computer model rates resource removals from coastal rain forest as more significant than from boreal forest and much more significant than from northern barrens.

The extent to which wood products are recycled in Canada, Jamie says, depends on use and region. "Warehouse pallets are made from low-grade wood. If individual planks are replaced as they wear out, a pallet may last for years. In big cities, a pallet that's worn beyond repair goes to a recycling facility that extracts the nails, then chips the wood for reuse as fibreboard. Outside the cities, worn-out pallets usually go straight to landfill." In each of these instances, however, the carbon stays in the wood and out of the air.

If such considerations sound insignificant, think about the numbers. Last year the U.S. imported US$8 billion worth of lumber from Canadian forests. That represents about ten megatonnes of carbon dioxide pulled out of the air and sealed up harmlessly into wood.

"Obviously, the best thing for us to do would be to have everyone leave our forests alone and cycle to work," Hamish says, laughing. In other words, the only pristine planets are those without people. "But since we aren't likely to do this, it makes sense to maximize our forests' carbon capacity by periodically skimming off their bound carbon. Harvesting lumber makes the forest a more efficient carbon sink."

Concludes Jamie: "The bad image that wood products get from eco-activists is rarely deserved. Building with wood can show a real commitment to the environment."

———

Some people prefer urban campuses, and it's true they're often exciting. A student can go from class into some noisy little bistro and argue about an idea just discovered. But to my mind, the perfect campus is the one I'm walking in. When I'm struggling to understand and integrate a concept, cities put me on overload. I like it where I am.

A short distance from Hamish's office I come across a structure that I haven't seen before. A sign at its door announces it's the Centre for Native Canadian Studies. It occupies a two-hectare glade shaded by enormous trees, in the lee of a little ridge. There's even an artificial waterfall and pond behind the building's main hall, around which offices cluster.

In half an hour I'll be back in the fray, but now it's inexpressibly sweet to sit and dream a bit. Beside the plash and sparkle of the falling stream, I wonder if the architects designed their oasis as a reminder of a world that once nourished our Native cultures. Now it occurs to me this little haven might predict rather than summarize—foreshadowing a tranquil new world that the knowledge economy has already begun to create.

———

➤ The UBC campus is the source of yet another means of cutting down on atmospheric carbon: cleaning up the diesel engine.

About 1900, the German engineer and inventor Rudolf Diesel conceived a new type of power plant. Like the standard auto engine of today, his system exploded a mixture of petroleum and air inside a hollow cylinder, forcing down a piston to turn a shaft. But the diesel engine has a key difference from other internal-combustion engines: it needs no electricity to detonate its fuel. Instead of a spark plug atop the power cylinder, the diesel uses a compression ratio high enough to heat its air-fuel mixture to ignition. It *squashes* its way to a burn.

Diesel's simple innovation gave his engine some major advantages over sparked power plants. First, it could muddle through on a lower grade of petroleum than what sparked engines demanded—

highly refined gasoline for autos, and kerosene, a still more rarefied distillate, for aircraft. Diesel's engine burned a petroleum derivative as crude as furnace oil. It practically lived on sludge.

As well, the diesel's dynamic characteristics make it ideal for heavy work. Sparked engines develop their highest torque, or twisting power, at higher speeds—about three thousand revolutions per minute. By contrast, the diesel is a kind of mechanical ox. The more slowly it turns, the more torque it develops, which makes it almost impossible to stall. When the going gets tough, the diesel gets going.

Over its century of use, the diesel has come to dominate the stand-alone production of heavy-duty power. Examples range from on-road (trucks) to rail (locomotives) to off-road (mining trucks) to mobile electric power generators. Over this time, the diesel engine has accumulated a considerable quantity of technology: learned papers are frequently written on its dynamic output, or the application of ultra-high-pressure injection systems to supply its cylinders with fuel oil. But the essential design remains as Rudolf Diesel imagined it: simple, reliable, powerful, and easy to maintain. Diesel has replaced the steam piston in the railways and the steam turbine at sea. It is as indispensable to the global economy as electricity or oil.

However, recent years have highlighted the disadvantages of this power source. Diesel is an environmental barbarian. Its emissions are loaded with oxides of nitrogen (abbreviated NO_x), plus a carcinogenic soot known to regulators as PM (particulate matter), plus the CO_2 that's linked to global warming. Strong and tractable though this ox may be, it reeks. Think how often you've put your car's air vents on RECIRC when stuck in traffic behind a diesel-powered truck.

Worse, the harder a diesel works, the more it reeks. The property that makes it so useful—its virtual inability to stall—means that at lower RPMs, a diesel burns very, very dirty. Temperatures fall inside the cylinder, combustion is less complete, and PM-CO_2-NO_x

emissions soar, with consequences both practical and ironic. Consider the dominant role that diesels play in public transportation. With the exception of the Montreal and Toronto subways, Vancouver's SkyTrain, and Calgary's elevated commuter system, nearly every vehicle in Canada's mass transit systems relies on diesel. AIR PURIFIER! proclaimed a recent poster on buses in Toronto. When the buses pulled away, they masked their own advertisements in noxious, toxic clouds. Just whose air was being purified?

For decades the manufacturers of diesel engines and vehicles and the vehicle drivers maintained that despite the foulness of diesel-engine emissions, diesels were so vital to the economy that they should be exempted from the laws that limit PM and NO_x in auto exhausts. Public-transit engineers added their own voice to the chorus. Sure, they admitted, diesels are smelly, but each bus holds a lot of people. If you calculate emissions per passenger, the bus still runs green.

Well, no. New research data done under the auspices of the California Air Resources Board suggest that on average, a diesel-powered bus emits over eighty times as much particulate pollution as a new, well tuned gasoline engine in a passenger car. Even fully loaded, most buses hold fewer than eighty passengers. If average use is 80 per cent (a sanguine estimate of transit use) and every car holds only one person (an underestimate), everyone taking transit still causes more direct pollution than if he or she drove a car.

Admittedly, this is simplistic because it reports only on-site, in-use emissions and neglects the environmental load of building all those automobiles and the roads they drive on. Some of those cars will be beaters, too, burning lube oil. But many manufacturing emissions are due to diesels: think of mining trucks, or stand-alone ore crushers. And emissions in remote locations, mines and inter-city rail lines, have more dilution and less human exposure than pollution vomited into congested urban areas. No way around it: in cities anyway, the diesel's long free ride must come to an end.

In fact, it will. The U.S. Environmental Protection Agency, the North American benchmark for emission reductions, has mandated major reductions in allowable pollution thresholds for NO_x and PM from diesel engines. The new regulations take place in 2002 across the continental U.S., the world's biggest market for commercial diesels. And don't count on delays. Even a pro-business federal administration will think twice before taking on the popular EPA.

That's the law, but how to follow it? There have been several attempts to clean up the diesel. It's possible, for instance, to make a diesel burn clean fuels like natural gas provided that the engine is "sparked"—that is, modified to accept spark plugs. Unfortunately, while it does reduce emissions, the sparked diesel also relinquishes a diesel's best feature: strong torque at low RPM. Test drivers routinely report poor response in hill climbing and sluggish acceleration away from stops. As a compromise, the sparked diesel fails.

California, so dependent on the automobile, has been lowering engine-emission thresholds. "California fuel policy is at a crossroads," writes John White, a state lobbyist on air-quality issues for the Sierra Club, in *The Wall Street Journal*. "The South Coast [of California] is setting a tougher standard for the state as a whole, and that is forcing the technology [of cleaner diesels] forward."

While diesel-powered vehicles make up only 2 per cent of California's total vehicle registration, they generate almost a third of NO_x and a staggering two-thirds of particulate material. Barry Wallerstein, district executive officer for the South Coast Region of the California Air Resources Board, cites a recent study that "implicates diesel exhaust in 70 per cent of airborne cancer risks in Los Angeles." Evidently something needs to be done well before 2010–15, the earliest that commercial fuel cells are likely to come on stream.

Enter a new Canadian firm. Ten years ago Dr. Philip Hill, a professor of mechanical engineering at UBC, was reviewing recently declassified data from the American nuclear weapons program. Powerful supercomputers had modelled, in extreme slow motion, how an infant atomic fireball propagates from the core of a newly detonated H-bomb. In a flash of insight, Dr. Hill saw how the data could be applied to making a diesel engine burn natural gas without any need for power-sapping spark plugs.

The solution was to inject a tiny amount of diesel fuel in a precisely predetermined spray pattern, at exactly the right time. Normal compression heating would ignite this "pilot burn," which would then ignite a second injection of natural gas a few milliseconds later. It all came down to knowing how a newborn oxidation front spreads inside a diesel cylinder.

Westport Innovations, the company Dr. Hill and his associates incorporated to develop his theoretical breakthroughs into a practical and cost-effective technology, is maintaining a fairly robust price on the Toronto Stock Exchange. More to the point as far as human lungs are concerned, Westport has entered into a co-development project with Cummins Engine Company of Columbus, Indiana. Cummins, the world's largest manufacturer of high-output diesel engines, is nearing completion of a new power plant for the eighteen-wheel rigs that lug everything from CD players to live cattle. The Cummins-Westport unit will be powerful and economical; more important, it will also burn clean.

Westport and Cummins expect their new engine will meet or exceed the stiff EPA regulations that are on the way. But their new engine carries an additional benefit. Besides cutting particulate and nitrogen-oxide emissions to a tenth of their previous levels, the engine will also have a greatly reduced output of carbon dioxide. Canadian technology is thus producing a first for the environment—a heavy-duty power plant with an exhaust cleaner than most cars, which anticipates greenhouse-gas restrictions still not written into law. The knowledge economy is the clean economy.

Important as the diesel is, it's only one part of a gargantuan world-wide problem. A vast quantity of resources goes into transportation, because people hate staying put. My own case illustrates this. As a writer I work from home. E-mail and the Web connect me with the world. No traffic jams or commutes for me, no rushing to appointments. I make contacts, do research and interviews, check drafts, and submit text without leaving my chair. By rights, I shouldn't need so resource-devouring a thing as private transportation. Yet somehow I not only own a car, I also log a thousand klicks a month on it.

Multiply my case by several hundred million other people in North America alone, all demanding the right of movement at will, and you realize how heavily humanity's wanderlust weighs on the world. It's fine to speak of less polluting alternatives, but public transit is adored only by urban planners who don't seem to comprehend its harsh realities. A half-hour car trip may devour half a day by bus. Few of us who don't live in ivory towers have that much time to burn. Despite countless planning studies decrying the private auto, it's here to stay: it's simply too convenient. And yet, all those pristine resources the auto devours in its creation and operation—metal, energy, oil, electronics, rubber, synthetics, even so humble a thing as gravel—are sources of pollution. What do to?

I believe the issue is not how can we kill the car, but how can we reduce the car's impact? Like all good compromises, this is workable. Expecting North Americans to vacate suburbia, squash together in densely packed communities, and queue up obediently for a crowded, smelly, foul-arsed bus is not.

Workable, however, is not the same as easy. Each knowledge option for cleaning up the automobile has costs as well as benefits. Let's start with the gasoline engine, the motive force of almost every car in use today. At first blush, there appear to be existing solutions to its shortcomings. You can run your car on gasohol, a mixture of ethyl alcohol and standard gasoline. The blend burns clean, creating fewer gaseous emissions out your tailpipe and less gunk dumped in your engine's guts. Closer inspection, however, reveals a more complex story. The ethanol used in gasohol is fermented from farm products—agricultural carbohydrates like those in surplus grain. But when (as with the Athena models) you add up all the energy and pollutant costs of growing and processing the plant material behind gasohol, they prove to be higher than those of gasoline.

In Vancouver, many people tank up with gasohol only once a year: the day their car must pass its annual emissions test. Since the inspecting technicians look at their instruments rather than at life-cycle costs, they give the gasohol-fuelled cars a pass. *On your way, good citizen!*

Such evasiveness cannot continue. The real hurdle for the family clunker's power plant comes from the American EPA, which now requires a declining output of both nitrogen oxides and particulates. Some pollution-prone states have mandates so stringent that they exceed those of the EPA. California, for example, requires an increasing percentage of new cars sold within its borders to be all-electric.

North of the border, only Vancouver and Victoria currently require private autos to pass a yearly emissions test. But similar programs are certain to come to a town near you. Such stringencies are only the beginning. Even though a new private car emits a fraction of the pollutants spewed by a gasoline lawn mower, EPA regulations will inexorably strangle the internal-combustion auto engine. The days of old bang 'n' smoke for transport are numbered, giving new meaning to the old terms *throttle* and *choke*.

Canadian knowledge to the rescue. One front-running candidate to replace the four-banger engine is the fuel cell, originally developed for the U.S. aerospace program. Astronauts in the Mercury manned program went aloft in small capsules, hardly larger than home freezers, which got by on battery power for the minutes or hours they were aloft. With the advent of larger craft—the two-man Gemini capsule, then an Apollo module the size of a Volkswagen—and week-long flight plans, electricity requirements rose sharply. A new power source had to be found. Its main criteria, what engineers call its design drivers, included supplying electricity continuously within specified voltage and amperage levels; having a power-to-weight ratio at least ten times higher than the best current battery; and producing little or no toxic gas or effluent.

The solution came from what was to that point a little-known laboratory effect involving the combination of hydrogen and oxygen. The reaction producing water (H_2O) from two elemental gases is exothermic: that is, it releases energy. Those who have taken high-school chemistry will remember igniting the two reagents, which combined with a loud bang and a *zap!* of blue flame. But there's another way of welding the gases into water, an alternative that avoids pyrotechnics. The gases are put close together, separated only by a catalytic membrane. This transmits the hydrogen nuclei, allowing them to mate with the oxygen on the other side; but the membrane denies access to the hydrogen's electrons. When the gases unite in this way, they exert an intense pull on those excluded electrons to join them and help them become neutral water molecules. The electrons cannot move to this rendezvous directly: they must travel a circuitous path. And since electrons in motion are known as electric current, the rerouted particles can be tapped for power.

Under political pressure and resultant government funding, this arcane laboratory effect quickly left the bench and became a compact, efficient, portable power source for spacecraft called the fuel cell. It was silent; it worked at room temperature; and it produced nothing but water so pure that you could drink it straight. This is the power supply that got astronauts to the moon and back.

At least it did so most of the time. As in all new knowledge, there were complications. On a week-long space voyage, a fuel cell uses several cubic metres of hydrogen and oxygen gas. To conserve space aboard Apollo, these elements were stored as supercold liquids. At intervals, the tanks holding the liquid gases had to be agitated by the astronauts. During one such "cryo-stir" early in the flight of Apollo 13, a tank failed catastrophically. The explosion tore apart much of the main crew module, forcing the three astronauts to round the moon and return to Earth using the smaller fuel cells aboard the two-man lunar module. The astronauts got back, but barely—proving that even in the knowledge economy, all innovation carries both risk and cost.

Though the quest for a problem-free power source continues, many people think the fuel cell is an idea whose time has finally come. R&D activity on fuel cells by both industry and government has reached levels not seen since the 1960s. Paradoxically, however, the same could have been said in 1984, when the Conservative government of Brian Mulroney cancelled a cherished Liberal creation, the National Energy Program. Although Mulroney's dislike of the NEP was largely based on its cap on Alberta oil prices, a collateral casualty was an extensive original program, based at the National Research Council in Ottawa, to develop alternative energy sources. At a stroke, the myopic government obliterated decades of world-leading work on wind turbines, active and passive solar technologies, and other non-polluting energy sources.

Yet one of the casualties, while crippled, was not quite killed. This was the fuel cell, which has now been resurrected, this time for good. In the mid-eighties, advocates of fuel-cell technology emerged from the Canadian military to keep the concept alive. They put seed money, in what was for original power research ridiculously small amounts, into a start-up firm in North Vancouver. Its founder, Geoffry Ballard, made fuel cells using a new technique called the proton exchange membrane. A proton is a hydrogen nucleus.

Month by month for fifteen years, Ballard Power Systems has boosted output of its fuel cells. They are now in full-sized demonstration buses across North America. And not surprisingly, the same agency that nurtured early work on fuel cells is back in the picture. In spring 1999, the National Research Council announced its intention to spend $30 million over five years to foster fuel-cell technology in Canada. The NRC program funds corporate R&D and demo projects, establishes an educational network, and lobbies for tax and regulatory environments favouring the clean power of fuel cells.

The NRC program supports fuel-cell R&D at several Canadian locales besides Vancouver, including Calgary, Toronto, and Quebec City. But the immediate benefit for Ballard Power, now a world leader in fuel-cell technology, was the establishment in July 2001 of a Fuel Cell Innovation Centre on the UBC campus, practically in Ballard's own backyard.

I talk to Dr. Ed Capes, the centre's first director, who has come to Vancouver to set up his new operation. Ed is grey-haired, well padded, and affable. He sits in the ultra-modern surroundings of the NRC Innovation Centre and discusses his research goals.

One of his aims, he tells me, is to determine the best fuel supply for the fuel cell. As it turns out, the cryo-tanks that failed aboard Apollo 13 are no longer necessary. Oxygen might come directly from the air, just as it does for gasoline and diesel engines. Hydrogen might be kept onboard as pressurized molecular gas (H_2), methane (CH_4), or inert solids called clathrate hydrates that store large quantities of hydrogen gas and release it when heated.

Hydrogen is plentiful in natural gas, but its use may pose a problem. Stripping H_2 from methane would liberate one atom of carbon for each two hydrogen molecules. And isn't minimizing carbon what the whole fuel-cell exercise is about? Ed agrees, but isn't worried. He thinks the carbon could be accumulated in a solid form rather than being released into the atmosphere.

Those who champion fuel cells as tomorrow's go-anywhere energy source frequently list applications other than transportation. Ed Capes hypothesizes that long-distance high-voltage AC transmission lines might one day be a thing of the past. Instead, today's huge centralized power grids could evolve into parallel networks where isolated communities, or even urban neighbourhoods, use fuel cells to meet local power demands. Other possibilities involve mini fuel cells tiny enough to power one-person scooters, lawn mowers, or even cellphones. These units might not need a hydrogen top-up more than every two hundred hours of use.

But just as with gasohol, there are limits to optimism. Fuel-cell disciples bridle when their darlings are called batteries. The fuel cell is (they say) an energy *source*, not a means of energy *storage*. Consider, however, that Quebec's main interest in the fuel cell is to use it as an energy dump, a kind of mega-battery. Although Quebec has made a multi-billion-dollar investment in hydroelectric production, its facilities often strain to meet peak demands on winter evenings, producing brownouts. It would benefit Hydro-Québec to use its surplus power production during off-peak hours to break down water electrolytically into hydrogen and oxygen. At peak hours, these gases could then be recombined into water in huge banks of fuel cells, releasing electrical energy. A fuel cell used in this way is simply a battery by another name.

Despite its promise as a future energy source for public and private transportation, the fuel cell is hardly poised to come off an assembly line. While DaimlerChrysler and Ford have announced their intent to market fuel-cell-powered passenger cars by 2005, more sober forecasts do not call for widespread commercial application much before 2010 or even 2015. Moreover, this is the timeline for public-transit vehicles, which have the brute strength to lug around heavy, bulky fuel cells. Fuel cells for private vehicles will take longer to materialize. More esoteric applications, such as mini-cells for personal phones and notebook computers, may remain science fiction for many years. In the meantime, public expectations of cleaner air will not abate.

The fuel-cell debate teaches the lesson of all technology: you cannot perfectly predict the shape of things to come. But a lot of knowledgeable people are betting that in some form the fuel cell will soon be commonplace in our lives. At the moment there seem few alternatives. Even Canada's forest industries (or at least the knowledge leaders in Forintek) have begun to admit the impact of greenhouse gases; and as for vehicles, the dirty old diesel is finally running out of time.

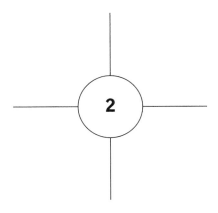

LIFE AS DATA:
THE BIOECONOMY

Today I begin to explore biotechnology, a part of the knowledge economy that is independent of geography. Although biotech firms have specific sites from which they work, these can be anywhere.

Biotech thus represents a radical departure from the old economy, which was chained to the land like a serf. Land supported investment because land was felt to be substantial. You could dig in it, build on it, mine and log it. Unlike airy-fairy intellectual property, land had value by virtue of its location, or by what it contained—ore, factories, trees—or even just by lying there. As Will Rogers said, "Buy land. They aren't making any more of it."

In Canada, the banks believed Will Rogers. Collateral, the clear-title property that debtors tender as hostage for a loan, was universally construed to mean land. Real collateral meant real estate. Of course markets did exist for things beyond boulders, dirt, and dry goods—sheet music, say, or the odd chemical process. But as late as the mid-1990s (!) a mature economic approach to intellectual property, or IP, was rare in Canada. To justify a loan, banks wanted to see factories and warehouses, bricks and mortar: land.

Not that this attitude precluded unsecured loans to fly-by-night firms. At certain times in post-war Canada, anyone with a farmer's tan and blackfly bites could convince a banker that he'd staked the strike of the century out back of beyond. But as recently as 1993 or so, Canada's knowledge economy was starved for capital. I used to lament this fact, asking how many great new companies and vital inventions had died in the womb from chronic cash deficiency. I finally realized the total was few or none. The capital starvation to which banks subjected knowledge-intensive industry had merely fostered ingenuity. In the face of tough or absent financing, the knowledge economy did an end run around the money establishment and created alternatives of its own. Far from slaughtering the fledgling knowledge economy, the big banks helped create it. This was unintentional and no credit to the banks. But their war cry, *Lend to Land*, sparked new approaches that transformed communications, pharmaceuticals, and data technology.

Although the banks' distaste for IP was a blessing in disguise, in the early days of the knowledge economy the blessing was, in Churchill's phrase, most effectively disguised. Lacking the cash to do otherwise, the CEOs of fledgling knowledge firms replaced ties and suits with shirtsleeves and sandals; corporate offices with rec rooms and garages; formal meeting rooms with kitchen tables; wages and salaries with shares in private firms. Instead of bank capital, they took second and third mortgages on their family homes. In place of forty-hour weeks, they worked whatever time the job required. All this was from necessity, not choice.

At least that was so initially. After working this way for a while, many knowledge workers realized they liked it. What's more, the absence of bank debt meant that capital for expansion and daily operations had sources that, while less deep-pocketed than the banks, were also less demanding.

The recent explosion of the dot-com bubble was set up by people who confused IPO funds with winning the lottery. They forgot that lottery corporations don't come back in thirty months and demand two bucks for every one they lent you. Investors do.

The most successful of the early knowledge companies had the motto Kill What You Eat—pay your way by what you earn, not with wads of other people's cash. It's a view that used to be common. Henry Ford, for example, regarded external investment as debt and hated it. Was he wrong? I don't think so, and neither did the nascent knowledge industries. The first cash purchase of the knowledge economy was its own freedom. No banks? No debts. Take risks? Reap benefits. Bill Gates *et al.* would have little of their present wealth had they not kept—indeed, been *forced* to keep—most of their own initial shares. They took the *public* out of Initial Public Offering. That's one reason why they're so rich.

Today's investment climate accepts as security both ideas and the people that conceive them. In fact, for a while the pendulum swung too far. Investors, wrongly thinking any firm that pretended to knowledge was worth bankrolling, spent several painful years hurling money at every dot-com that held out a tin cup. The investors assumed that since some knowledge firms without physical plants had good ideas, so did *all* firms without land-based collateral. Moral: there's no substitute for due diligence.

Harvard Business Review, a publication so conservative that it tends to predict only what is already entrenched, published in mid-2000 a special report on the Next Big Thing in Business: IP, intellectual property. Creating IP, acquiring it through lease, trade, merger, or purchase, managing it and leveraging it, said the *Review*, was central to every incorporated business, as of now. There wasn't a mention of a surveyor's stake.

This brings us to another kind of resource, one whose activity strongly influences a large part of Canada's economy, and which will soon affect the rest.

Biotechnology, or biological technology, is one of the knowledge economy's two main categories. Along with information technology, biotechnology is the knowledge economy's main engine.

In modern form, both IT and biotech go back fewer than fifty years. They fused into the nucleus of the modern knowledge economy only two decades ago.

By 1982 it had become apparent to official Canada that something serious was happening in the previously staid realm of the biosciences. At this time Canada's participation in the nascent biotech revolution was minuscule and limited to a few publicly funded labs. Irreverent NRC operatives shared a joke: on Sunday, the British find a cancer cure; on Monday, the U.S. turns it into a commercial pharmaceutical; on Tuesday, the Japanese undersell the Americans; on Wednesday, the Koreans undercut the Japanese; on Saturday, Canada calls a conference.

You can't blame the boffins for being cautious about biotech: its frenzied progress caught even its practitioners by surprise. For thousands of years, biologists had been content to describe living things by their appearance, behaviour, and putative medicinal properties. Meanwhile, other disciplines had had their revolutions. Chemistry synthesized new compounds called polymers, with trade names like Nylon and Bakelite. These replaced natural materials like ivory and silk. Physics was on the trail of incredible forces that could generate copious electrical power or create appalling weapons. Karl Steinmetz's technologies of AC transmission had electrified America. Civil engineers made vast dams and behind them huge artificial lakes.

And biology? Biology was dried leaves in a herbarium. Biology was counting hairs on centipedes' legs. Biology was dull.

Then came biochemistry, and the world changed. Like all great movements, it began with a simple idea: to extend the principles of chemistry to the still-mysterious workings of life. By the Second World War, chemistry had split into two streams: organic and inorganic. Organic chemistry was so named because at first it defined its study area as the substances produced by life. But as their knowledge deepened, biochemists realized these so-called life substances—isolated from urine, breath, or blood—were no more magical than inorganic molecules. Ammonia, found in bird droppings and diaper pails, was NH_3—one nitrogen atom bound to three atoms of hydrogen. Carbon dioxide, found in exhaled breath, was merely CO_2. Life remained cryptic to poets, but to biochemists it now began to seem known, even predictable. The biochemists were so successful that organic chemistry changed its definition. It jettisoned its previous title as the Chemistry of Life and became simply the study of carbon compounds.

By 1950 biochemists had even isolated the chemicals that governed heredity—and there they stalled for years. The inner workings of one particular chemical steadfastly eluded them. A molecule called deoxyribonucleic acid, or DNA, was found in both the cell nucleus and the mitochondria that powered non-bacterial cells. Scientists found that 99.999 per cent of life forms, be they human, hawk, or broccoli, carry DNA at their cores. DNA seemed to be the substance by which life reproduced itself, transmitting visible and invisible characteristics down the generations. And like other organic molecules, DNA comprised only a few atomic building blocks: oxygen, nitrogen, hydrogen, the odd trace element such as phosphorus, and the omnipresent carbon that supported all life.

But how did DNA work? Fifty years ago that was unknown. Some biochemists had a shrewd idea that DNA performed its replicative miracle by using its shape. Yet what was that shape? How could such an enormous molecule constantly split and re-form?

Enter two hotshot youngsters from Cambridge University, Drs. James D. Watson and Francis Crick, with a new theory. DNA, they said, is built like a ladder. The facts it transmits do not lie in the ladder's long members: these merely support and space the rungs. It is the rungs that hold genetic data, as a chemically written code.

Here's how it's done, according to the Watson-Crick model that's now universally accepted. Every DNA rung is a union of two simple compounds, called nucleotides or bases. DNA uses only four bases. Each rung comprises either base number 1 bonded to base 3, or 2 bonded to 4. Each of these two pairings can align itself in two ways, giving four rung types: 1–3, 3–1, 2–4, or 4–2. That's it. Life is a four-letter word.

It's also kinky. The pair of ladder verticals twists like the handrails of a spiral staircase. Mathematically, this twin spiral is called a double helix, and however twisted it becomes, it holds the ladder rungs in strict order. Since the genetic data are encoded as rung sequences, the process of deciphering genes is called sequencing.

To replicate, the DNA ladder first untwists. Then the midpoint of every rung, where its two base pairs meet and bond, snaps apart. The ladder becomes two half ladders. Each is shaped like a comb, with a vertical back holding a sequence of attached half rungs, the comb's teeth. These half rungs are highly reactive. Each hungers to replace its complementary base, left behind when the full ladder broke up. Biochemists say that each broken half rung has a "sticky end."

The sticky ends soon find what they need. Simpler molecules, free-floating in the water-based soup inside the cell, drop into place and complete each half rung: 3 finds its 1 again, and 2 its 4. This, incidentally, is why we need to watch our nutrition. If we don't eat well, our replicating DNA might reach for a calcium atom and come up short. And single atoms can mean as much in the language of life as single letters may in English. Chemically, calcium does not function quite like magnesium—just as *unite* is not *untie*.

Further DNA synthesis assembles two more verticals: and in place of the original double helix, there are two. Afterwards, a special enzyme cruises along the new strands checking for errors. The enzyme, called DNA repairase, is the original proofreader.

Watson and Crick's insight was one of the great scientific advances of all time. As an intellectual construct, DNA rivals Einstein's special relativity or Newton's universal gravitation. In 1999 researchers from around the world ranked it the key scientific achievement of the twentieth century.

The double-helix theory did more than give biochemical theoreticians a deeply elegant and satisfying explanation for observed facts. It also opened the way for the manipulation of the molecules of life.

The staid, sleepy, curiosity-driven discipline called biology was about to acquire a wild new engineering division called biotechnology.

What makes biotechnology workable is the way that DNA unscrolls its genes, reads them, and follows their plans to make organic compounds. It is an exquisitely complicated system that works without a hitch 99.999999999 per cent of the time.

This is what happens. Worker molecules decode DNA's ladder rungs in groups of three and use the data to assemble chemicals called proteins. *Protein* means "primal thing," a name that proteins fully deserve. The protein keratin makes up hair and fingernails. The protein collagen is in skin and scar tissue. Proteins move muscles, ferry around oxygen inside the body, and extract energy from sugar. No proteins, no life.

A living organism, especially one as intricate as a human, has thousands of proteins for which it needs construction data. Because of this, the complete human genome is about three billion nucleotides long. If this full sequence of nucleotide ladder rungs were printed text, it would fill three thousand five-hundred-page volumes at two thousand letters a page, each letter representing one ladder rung.

The most astonishing conclusion of Watson and Crick was that DNA is a data-storage device. It functions like a computer's hard disk. In essence, life is the same as information. Life as *data*? Absolutely. The information coded within DNA's rung sequences does not merely encode life: it *is* life. The hot new uses for supercomputers these days are all in biology. IT is the royal road to understanding every living thing.

This fact is one of the keys to the knowledge economy. Scientifically, life is information. Technologically, life and its substances can be assembled from off-the-shelf chemicals.

The double-helix model set off a thousand-watt floodlight in the mind of nearly every biochemist in the world. Hesitantly, then in a vast flood, a new discipline called molecular biology began inventing ways to stitch together live, functioning DNA.

Dr. Michael Smith, a young Australian working in an English laboratory in the 1960s, was one such researcher. He devised a molecular editing function that isolates any given rung sequence on any DNA chain. Mike's method let him and his fellow molecular biologists snip away gene fragments as small as a single atom. Such tiny changes can radically alter a gene's biochemical functions. Call it experimental life: find calcium, substitute magnesium, see what happens. The technique, with the mouth-filling name of *site-specific mutagenesis*, permits fine-scalpel surgery at the submolecular level. It won Mike Smith, by then a Canadian citizen working at the University of British Columbia, the Nobel Prize in Chemistry.

Chemistry? This is biology, isn't it? Yes, but a branch of biology that has opened up radical new types of chemical knowledge and of medical treatment too. One of the first of Canada's new Networks of Centres of Excellence (NCE), whose first scientific director was Mike Smith, has the acronym PENCE. The first two letters stand for Protein Engineering. The federal government began to establish the NCEs in 1990; at last count there were eighteen. Each NCE unites several existing sites of commercially vital research into a virtual R&D institute.

Previous societies' defining artifacts were roads and aqueducts; our society's key discipline, biotechnology, designs genes and the proteins for which they encode. We have reached the stage that we can manipulate things we have never seen directly and may never see at all.

Farewell, formaldehyde: biology has changed forever. IT has infiltrated the previously sacrosanct areas of the dissecting table and herbarium. Today, genetic base sequences are assembled automatically by machines containing sensors, manipulators, and of course computers. Similar machines take unknown genes apart in a process of analysis. The gene sequences that these machines decode are extracted as data, written to magnetic media, transmitted via optical media, verified and cross-correlated by statistical algorithms, compared to findings from other laboratories around the world, and finally posted on the Internet or released on laser-readable CD-ROM. Dr. Craig Venter, CEO of a big American biotechnology firm, puts it this way: "From now on, all biotechnology companies are in the information business."

———————

While all this may seem abstract, its consequences are direct and practical. As an example, consider the sponge. For years this creature belonged to the pure biologists, to the classifiers and describers. Now, because of biotechnology, the sponge is a source of unheard-of new drugs.

While a sponge is a sessile organism, spending most of its life anchored to one spot, its meekness may conceal quiet pride. Sponges have a hidden talent: they produce and stockpile a wide variety of cell poisons, or cytotoxins. They probably evolved this knack to deter mobile creatures from munching on them, much as some trees fill their leaves with poison when attacked by insects.

Before the knowledge economy, all this would have begun and ended in a series of learned footnotes in a biology text. But the knowledge economy defines life as data, data as money. A viable pharmaceutical company can begin with something as commonplace as a sponge. "Basic research has shown that many sponge species produce high percentages of secondary metabolites with interesting carbon structures," says Dr. David Burgoyne. "It's no coincidence that many of these molecules also exhibit cytotoxic activity."

David is vice-president of research for Inflazyme Pharmaceticals of Richmond, B.C. As such, he's an expert on the surprises that sponges have in store. What David is saying, with a scientist's usual caution and precision, is that sponges produce many molecules that hurt cells outside the sponge. This makes the sponge a biological hunting ground for scientists interested in discovering new compounds applicable to human medicine.

Poison as medicine? Absolutely. In my father's California boyhood, local dentists stopped bleeding after tooth extraction with rattlesnake venom, which coagulates blood. And anaesthesia involves using poisons—ethyl ether, chloroform, alkaloids such as opium and its derivatives—to lower metabolic rates, permitting surgery. One anaesthesiologist defined her discipline's role as preserving life by taking it to the brink of death.

Back to sponges. After David Burgoyne's basic research had identified certain poisonous sponge metabolites, applied pharmaceutical research began assessing these compounds as possible killers of human cancer cells. In the early nineties, David, leading a team from the Universities of B.C. and Alberta, isolated a cytotoxic agent from sponges. When David examined this substance, it proved to be a molecule that wasn't a protein. The shape of this molecule suggested how it might work.

The key principle behind DNA applies to other molecules: shape affects function. So one of the things that David and his team did to his new sponge metabolite was examine its structure. The more they did so, the more David suspected this molecule might exhibit some biological activity beyond cytotoxicity (cell poisoning) and onconecrosis (tumour death). It might, David thought, also function as a naturally derived anti-inflammatory agent. To his trained eye, it was simply shaped that way.

It was a shrewd intuition. Further laboratory work showed David and his team how to copy the newly discovered molecule synthetically, using bottled compounds available from chemical-supply houses. Further nips and tucks—I've strayed into commercial confidentiality here, and can't be more specific—led David to a patented compound called IPL576. This synthetic molecule is now undergoing trials that David is confident will show it to be an even more clinically efficacious anti-inflammation treatment than the original sponge metabolite. The progression is typical: *Pure data -> Applied data -> Wealth.*

For prospective applications of IPL576, Inflazyme is focusing on asthma, which in humans involves chronic inflammation of the bronchial passages. There are also secondary indications that the drug might work topically—for example, on psoriasis. While not life-threatening, this genetic skin disorder causes a lot of misery.

After completing toxicological examinations in 1999, Inflazyme took IPL576 into clinical trials. These showed that IPL576 is at least as effective as the steroids that now dominate asthma treatment. However, the Inflazyme molecule avoids steroids' common side effects. For one thing, IPL576 has no major impact on the human adrenal organs or spleen. Nor does it make skin thinner, or demineralize bone after prolonged use, or lower the body's natural steroid levels. Exactly how does IPL576 work at the molecular level? David and his fellow scientists aren't sure but suspect they are close to finding out. Indications are that the modified sponge molecule targets proteins deep inside the cell nucleus. It does *not* bind to the same cell receptors as steroids do: its mechanism of action uses totally different biochemical pathways. But although chemically distinct from steroids, IPL576 duplicates their best effects.

To date, pharmaceutical research on IPL576 has been largely empirical. What's certain is that IPL576 is not just an anti-inflammatory: it's also an inhibitor of late-phase asthmatic bronchoconstriction. In other words, IPL576 provides both rapid-relief and sustained-relief functions. That may well mean that tomorrow's asthma treatment will require only one agent instead of two or more.

"IPL576," says David Burgoyne, "may soon compete directly with standard pharmaceutical treatments. I think it will go head-to-head with prednisone as the treatment of choice in many types of bronchial inflammation."

All this from the humble sponge. If there are still some Canadians who don't support a shrewd duality of basic and applied research, there's a one-word comeback: biotechnology.

Today's biotechnological momentum took time to build. Nearly three decades separate the theoretical construct of the double helix from the modern flowering of biotechnology. The delay partly stemmed from the conceptual difficulty science had in shifting its research from one type of data gathering to a drastically different kind.

➤ About a century ago, a distinction arose between two kinds of research: "pure" or "basic," and "applied." Lately it has been vogue to blur this distinction and treat all data as equivalent, no matter for what purpose they were derived. I would like to champion the old, unfashionable position. Facts developed with an end use in mind are innately different from those developed for the pure joy of knowing. This duality is a powerful way to explain what has happened in biotechnology.

Pure data comprise facts that have been found entirely to satisfy scientific curiosity. These data are often surprising and sometimes astonishing. Every few decades (Einstein 1905, Watson and Crick 1953), they stand the world on its ear. Dr. Larkin Kerwin, president of the NRC in the mid-eighties, put it best: "When you know in advance what you're going to discover, your work doesn't merit the name of research." Pure data are telemetry from the Undiscovered Realm: notes scribbled in breathless haste by people who hardly believe what they see. The almost sexual excitement of this process must be experienced to be believed. Even then, it seems unbelievable—part gambling, part game playing, part sensuality, part wide-open adventure. Scientists, unless they are married to other scientists, often have lousy relationships. Like Confucius, they forget to eat when working. If their metabolism were voluntary, they would die when they forgot to breathe.

Applied investigations, however interesting their findings, belong on a less celestial plane. A CEO of a high-tech company must constantly wrench employees back from Knowledge for Its Own Sake, to Knowledge for the Good of the Firm. Since the quest for pure data is one of the ultimate human highs, the CEO's task is not an easy one. He must harness his addicts while feeding their addiction.

Pure and applied data correlate with what analysts call *technology push* and *technology pull*. Technology pull is a vivid, accurate metaphor for the constant, frantic need of a working company for new facts, products, and solutions.

As a workable concept, technology push is much less useful. Granted, the metaphor sounds inviting: a tree laden with luscious fruit, a cornucopia spilling over with goodies. Scientists like to speak of their results as "solutions looking for problems," and they are nothing of the sort. Pure researchers who wake from a data-search binge, blinking about them with gummy eyes and five-day stubble, use the term technology push to convince their managers that facts found for their own sake are throbbing with potential applications. Even supposing this is so, it takes people other than those who derived the data to determine economic usefulness. Pure data are found; their use must be created. That is the province of applied, or commercial, research.

Years ago city planners stumbled onto equations, buried in the arcana of theoretical hydraulics, that perfectly modelled certain types of traffic flow. Traffic, it turned out, could act like a fluid. Traffic jams resulted when cars en masse acquired a syrupy thickness, like a viscous liquid. Other traffic problems arose when the traffic-fluid became turbulent.

Well and good, but these discoveries were actually the work of the technologists who applied them. It would have been ludicrous to ask the hydraulics scientists to shop their equations around till they found a paying customer. *Differential equations-o! Who will buy?*

In their Web sites and printed literature, however, government and academic laboratories constantly proclaim that they are repositories of knowledge that need only be applied to produce fabulous wealth. It is a futile concept. Pure data must be kept available for public use; they cannot be *pushed* anywhere. As vital as knowledge is, you can't peddle it door-to-door. For it to create wealth, some business must come and find it.

In the past, it was easy to tell the difference between basic and applied research. Although they had the same subject matter, years or even decades would elapse between academic research and industrial development. Now, at least in the ultra-hot pharmaceutical areas where billions of dollars stand to be made, that time lag has vanished. By 1990, development began so soon after research that D breathed down R's neck. Drug multinationals hired full-time professionals to scan the world's scientific literature. The instant they spotted a journal paper with industrial promise, they arranged to meet the paper's authors. If they thought it advisable, some of these company scouts were empowered and encouraged to sign the scientists to ironclad contracts. In return for the scientists' IP, the drug-company operatives offered stock options, cash, and residual payments. All might be increased as and when the research led to marketable products. Sometimes this bait was dangled before the scientists, sometimes before their institutions, for as Robertson Davies once observed, "Universities are unceasingly avaricious in a high-minded way."

But the drug operatives' ace in the hole was to offer what all scientists lust for: further research funding. Few researchers on Earth can resist such temptation, even when the funder locks the resulting knowledge in an iron cage.

It is difficult to overstate how ruthless some multinational firms can be. The Vancouver science-fiction writer William Gibson imagines a future in which these companies dominate the world, castrating universities and suborning whole nations. At times I think he's optimistic.

In the past ten years, the drug companies' subversion of publicly funded academia has grown both worse and better. Worse, because throughout the world, D is not merely breathing down R's neck: it has caught up with R and swallowed it outright. I'd be surprised if one young bioscientist in a hundred hadn't considered the commercial potential of his or her work. In 1990 pharmaceutical development was content to circle academic research like a vulture; now it's nesting on the bench. Industry is in the lab, influencing what is studied, how, and when.

Yet in another way the situation has become much better. This ethical improvement is largely due to the largest scientific endeavour ever undertaken: the Human Genome Project. The project's audacious goal was to sequence the complete human genome—all three billion nucleotides of it. The thousands of bioscientists around the world who contribute to this immense undertaking affectionately call it HUGO. To a writer who's begun to think that *Science and Business Morality* is the shortest book on Earth, HUGO is enough to renew a cynic's trust.

HUGO wasn't conceived by some hidden elite for top-down implementation: it was open and democratic from the start. In HUGO, anyone's results are everyone's results. The process of openness is so strong that one or two multinational pharmaceutical corporations, normally bastions of paranoiac secrecy, have been inspired (or more likely shamed) to release their own proprietary data into the public domain. For example, when the Wellcome Foundation wanted to encourage research into malaria, which kills far more people throughout the world than AIDS, it funded academic scientists to sequence the complete genome of the trypanosome that causes the disease. These data were then published for all to see. (The Wellcome Foundation is a charitable trust established by the drug manufacturer Burroughs-Wellcome.)

Dr. Judith Hall, a world-renowned clinical geneticist and head of pediatrics at two public hospitals in Vancouver, has voiced the hope that medical law may one day even reverse its recently acquired position that genes are patentable. This would reopen the Book of Life to all.

———————

This week I'm in Vancouver to cover HUGO's fifth Annual General Meeting. This meeting is the last before HUGO publishes the complete nucleotide sequence of the human genome—humanity's greatest step to date in understanding life.

The great hall at Canada Place is buzzing like a beehive as I take my seat. The lights dim, and a slim figure walks to the podium. It is the incoming president of HUGO, Dr. Lap-Chee Tsui, geneticist-in-chief at the Hospital for Sick Children in Toronto.

Dr. Tsui cautions us that the human genome sequence that HUGO is about to publish is not a polished and final data set, but merely a starting inventory. Biology today, he says, is like physics in 1900: on the brink of its most profound achievements.

At coffee break I chat with Judy Hall, who agrees wholeheartedly with Dr. Tsui. Despite HUGO's immense scope, she says, the project is merely groundwork. "When it's finally finished, we'll take a night to party," she says with a laugh. "Next morning we'll start the real work—discovering what all those genes do."

Even more important than the vast technical issues are the ethical problems that the new knowledge generates. Who owns the human genome? Should we imitate the Vancouver-based futurist who patented his own genome lest some private company claim it? Perhaps the ancient Romans' test question should be ours: *Cui bono?* Who will benefit from this revolutionary knowledge?

The next speaker offers some reassurance. He's Dr. Michael Hayden, a bioscientist from UBC and chair of HUGO's local organizing committee. Mike is investigating ways to raise the levels of high-density lipoproteins in human subjects. HDLs are "good cholesterol." They are found in the blood of top athletes and are associated with fitness and good health.

I corner Mike after his talk. He tells me that Celera Genomics, an American company based in Maryland, is also sequencing the full human genome. Mike sees this not as competition for HUGO but as confirmation. Celera, he says, has acknowledged its debt to the gene-sequence data that HUGO makes freely available via the Internet. Further, he tells me, the company has promised not to patent the full human-genome sequence that it has derived.

Morality, sanity, and balance may be about to win a few rounds.

If further proof were needed that biology = data, consider that every one of biotechnology's recent spinoff disciplines is data based. Collectively they are called *bioinformatics* and are one of the meeting's hottest topics. Bioinformatics comprises—

- *Genomics*—identifying and sequencing genetic material
- *Functional genomics*—determining how identified and sequenced genes work in the living organism
- *Pharmacogenomics*—identifying unique traits in the individual human genome that modify drug action or that suggest new molecular targets for drugs
- *Pharmacogenetics*—tailoring medication to the individual genome
- *Proteomics*—understanding the chemistry, shape, and function of proteins (much tougher than it seems)

For the bench scientist, HUGO's goal is understanding; for the clinician, it's advanced therapeutics. "The Human Genome Project will give practical medicine a battery of new treatment options," Judy Hall tells me. "Since every human cell holds all the data needed to make a complete human, one day we might be able to take a cell from your skin and grow you a new kidney. In the near term, there will be far less hit and miss. We'll be able to diagnose germs in a doctor's office without waiting days for a laboratory culture. We'll tell you on the spot, by finding a single bacterium, if your sore throat is from *Staphylococcus aureus* with tetracycline resistance or some other cause."

That's all for the future; in the meantime, there's a lot of work to do. As the meeting breaks up, I realize its mood has changed from celebration to sobriety. The attending bioscientists have received marching orders for their next half decade of research. Just as important, the meeting has faced up to the moral and ethical consequences of its new knowledge: these people aren't in any firm's hip pocket. As a citizen of both Canada and the U.S., I feel profoundly glad.

————

As I sprint through Vancouver drizzle in search of a coffee, I am unaware of something important. Michael Smith, the Nobel laureate who made biotechnology possible and who has just spoken to welcome HUGO delegates, has just been diagnosed with leukemia. He will die before I finish my research trip.

If you seek Mike's monument, look about you: his work goes marching on. Perhaps $1 billion of the Canadian knowledge economy rests on what he did, for Mike was a consummate scientist—brilliant in hypothesis, rigorous in logic, impeccable in technique. But that's not why I mourn him. Mike was a *mensch*—strong, good-humoured, generous, long-suffering, and kind. He never forgot that everyone's first profession is to be human. Rest in peace, my friend.

————

➤ Dr. Frank Tufaro, professor of microbiology at the University of British Columbia, is an academic's academic. He publishes frequently in his discipline's most prestigious journals and at the time of our interview was the youngest full professor ever to be appointed by UBC. Frank is also CEO of NeuroVir, a firm he spun off in 1997 from his basic laboratory work. His two roles are so wildly different that they require two different minds, which at the moment both occupy his one beleaguered body.

At first I find Frank hard to decipher. He doesn't show much stress: he's . . . well, *nice*. Eloquent, friendly, able to adjust his answers instantly to his interviewer's knowledge base. This is not the profile of a hotshot academic who has turned a benchtop breakthrough into a formally approved therapeutic in a breathtakingly quick four years. Such people are almost always Type A—tense, aggressive, derisive of questions, constantly implying that you're wasting their time. Then I recall where I've seen Frank's serenity: in Mike Smith, and in every Nobel laureate I've interviewed. Frank doesn't have to be arrogant. He knows he's good, and so does everyone else in his scientific community.

There's an immediate reason for Frank's confidence: NeuroVir has developed a new clinical protocol that kills tumours using *Herpes simplex* virus. HSV is a common micro-organism; many of us carry it in our bloodstream. It's relatively innocuous, often remaining quiescent in our cells or causing nothing more serious than cold sores. But in concentrated doses, delivered directly by injection, HSV hits cancer cells like a high explosive. Used in this way, HSV is an advanced medical treatment, a form of gene therapy.

A word of background. Gene therapy, or GT, hasn't had good press lately. For one thing, it's so novel that its definition hasn't jelled. At one extreme are proponents who say all disease is genetic and predict GT will soon dominate medicine. Other clinicians define GT more narrowly and are more cautious about its future. So far the only consensus among scientists is that GT uses genetic material to address the symptoms or root causes of human disease.

The bolder scientists have one point on their side: every illness has some genetic component. In cancer, this is particularly high. Many cancers arise when something in the environment stresses the genome, reactivating a fetal gene that had been mothballed. This is a harmful result, yet only some people succumb. Why?

Current theory calls cancer a matter of statistics. Each human has fifty trillion cells. Many of these divide fifty times each in an average lifetime, so that whoever reaches threescore and ten undergoes 2,500,000,000,000 cell divisions. That's the number of stars in ten Milky Way galaxies. If only one division in a million slips up and leads to carcinoma, the average person spawns more than two million cancer cells in his or her lifetime.

But while all of us are constantly getting cancer, our genome has also evolved methods to blow it away. Some genes encode for chemicals called tumour necrosis factors which poison cancer cells. Other genes create substances that attract TNFs or that starve tumour cells for blood. Only when this complex, effective system gets overwhelmed—perhaps by the onslaught of carcinogens in tobacco or by a defect in a cancer-fighting gene—does the scale tip. Then someone "gets cancer." The disease is therefore more a matter of statistical probability than of linear cause.

The new NeuroVir protocol, says Frank Tufaro, is a treatment of last resort for those whom a particularly virulent cancer—a malignant brain tumour, say—would otherwise kill in weeks. The protocol first weakens *Herpes simplex* virus by removing some of its critical genes. This makes the virus unable to replicate unless it is inside a cancer cell. One natural gene left intact, called gamma 34.5, keeps the host cancer cell alive long enough to permit replication of the HSV that kills it and its nasty brothers.

"We don't fully understand how HSV works," Frank says. "But HSV appears to have no toxicity to normal organs. It's not even an opportunistic pathogen in patients whose immune systems have been compromised. HSV seems selectively toxic to cancer cells."

Because of this, Frank tells me, HSV dosage appears to have no upper limit. "Since there are no adverse effects on normal cells, there may be no such thing as a maximum dose." How about lingering effects in a patient whose life has been prolonged? That's unlikely, says Frank. "When HSV kills a cancer cell, it also destroys itself."

For all the promise of the new NeuroVir protocol, Frank Tufaro is very cautious in making claims for it. "I'd even be tempted not to call it gene therapy," he says. "It's a precursor to the true GT that will occur when we stitch a gene for oncotoxin [cancer poison] into the natural HSV genome. Now we're just using naturally occurring genetic material for therapy."

That's all, then—only a better way to kill cancer? I for one am grateful that Frank has undertaken to move his discoveries himself from laboratory to clinic, instead of being content to publish in learned journals and leaving the applied research and technology transfer to others. To do this, he had to go beyond science and acquire the skills of a CEO. That transition is as rare as it is necessary.

Other Canadian biotechnology start-ups are also helping gene therapy find safer treatment options. On a damp and chilly morning after my NeuroVir interview, I drive east to see one.

Eileen Utterson, vice-president of corporate development for Chromos Molecular, and Dr. Carl Perez, the firm's director of projects, greet me with brisk handshakes and broad smiles at their new office and laboratories in Burnaby, B.C. They have much to smile about: Chromos leads all other public and commercial laboratories in the world in its core competency. Chromos makes artificial chromosomes, inserts them safely into mammalian cells (mice, bovine, and human), and uses them to produce therapeutic proteins. The helpful proteins are not churned out haphazardly but are produced as long as needed, then immediately neutralized. It's the only GT developed to date with a foolproof on-off switch.

For individual humans, Chromos's technology will provide gene therapy, both for acute illnesses and for chronic conditions with a strong genetic influence. For society as a whole, it may well produce key therapeutic proteins at greatly reduced cost, making drugs such as interferon and human growth hormone no longer laboratory curiosities but readily and inexpensively accessible to all.

Within a living cell, the DNA double helix is kinked beyond belief. To make a functioning gene, cell machinery winds DNA's simple spiral into super-spirals, then winds those into mega-spirals. The final coiling takes place on natural skeins called chromosomes.

As structures, chromosomes are as complex as apartment buildings. They have spacers called centromeres in their middle; other structures called telomeres round off their ends. On these amazing spools the life data DNA is wound by the metre, like thread.

Chromos's core competency is to make synthetic duplicates of chromosomes, structurally and chemically identical in every way to their natural models. The copyright name for Chromos's main product is SATAC, for satellite artificial chromosome.

The first investigations into the possibility of SATACs took place in the research town of Szeged, Hungary. In 1995 Dr. Gyula Hadlaczky's work at the Hungarian Academy of Science came to the attention of Dr. Henry Geraedts, an entrepreneurial young Canadian scientist who was first administrative director of CBDN, the Canadian Bacterial Diseases NCE. After leaving CBDN, Geraedts took Chromos through its initial public offering and continues to serve as one of the firm's directors.

The SATAC synthetic chromosome promises to have a variety of uses, including producing commercial proteins on a large scale. Hoofed animals like horses and cattle, and cloven-footed creatures like goats and sheep, can output proteins dissolved in milk, urine, or even semen when injected with SATACs. Semen? Don't laugh: a full-grown boar can churn out litres of the stuff each week.

Why use animals as assembly lines? Alternative methods of making biologically interesting molecules require ultra-clean conditions. Flecks of contaminant—chemical, metal, microbiological—and tiny temperature variations, can void entire batches of drug output. On top of all this, the purity of any water used in the process must be continuously maintained at seven significant figures, i.e., 99.99999 per cent fine. Production criteria for some rarer compounds are more exacting still.

Chromos believes its SATAC techniques can replace such complex artificial systems with four-footed factories that need only shelter, water, and hay. This would lower present production costs by ten or a hundred times. Molecules now produced by the billionth of a gram, and thereby limited to infrequent small-scale use, could enter clinical trials and become as common (and as inexpensive) as Aspirin. It's worth noting, too, that the living factories in this technique are not harmed. To the contrary, they are cared for as the valuable entities they are.

A more spectacular application for SATAC techniques is in human gene therapy. Again, Chromos intends its technology to replace existing techniques. Many standard GT protocols now use a virus as a vector—that is, the means of delivering beneficial gene into target mammalian cells. Though ingenious, this method is fraught with difficulties and dangers. First, a viral vector, even a virus "gutted" of most or all of its own genes, can deliver no more than forty thousand nucleotide base pairs (ladder rungs) of therapeutic gene. Even to do this, the virus must be injected throughout the entire human bloodstream in quantities approaching *a hundred trillion*—that's 100,000,000,000,000—particles per dose. Most of these viruses never deliver their payload to the appropriate cell, yet there's no use delivering a virus with a replacement liver enzyme to a brain neuron. Not only does the Chromos SATAC have a genetic payload of millions of base pairs, but it is also far more target-specific. It can be inserted directly into the cells that lack a gene and then produce its needed compound only there.

Second, whatever genes viruses do deliver, head right for the pre-existent DNA in the human cell's nucleus and bind with it. Instead of helping, these added genes may foul up the workings of the normal nuclear genome.

Third, viral vectors have a nasty habit of reversing their attenuation and reawakening. They may then attach extraneous and harmful viral genes to the therapeutic payload, with serious consequences.

The Chromos SATAC avoids all these problems. The only vector it needs is a standard stainless-steel microsyringe with an inner diameter of 0.7 microns and wall thickness of 0.1 microns. (One micron is one-thousandth of a millimetre. Yes, engineers really do make needles that small.)

During injection, the SATACs—including centromeres, telomeres, and nucleotide sequences—are tightly coiled and mechanically rigid. Thus the artificial chromosomes behave like stiff rods, passing undamaged through the microsyringe into the cell. Once in place, the SATACs do not seek to combine with a target cell's nuclear DNA. They remain distinct protein factories that act in parallel with the original genes and do not attempt to interfere with them.

Fascinating as the science is, it would be a mere curiosity unless Chromos could commercialize it. Happily, the firm has this talent as well. Its announcement in late 1999 that its SATACs are heritable—i.e., they have been passed on intact and functioning to a second generation of test mice—made scientific and business headlines around the world. Since then Chromos has been inundated with queries by potential investors and commercial partners.

While some commentators fear that Chromos's technology opens the door to therapeutics like human fetal engineering, raising questions of ethics, the prevailing medical response is highly positive. Gene therapy that dispenses with viral vectors, can be turned on and off with one injection, and produces natural compounds in a natural way is likely to help patients all over the world.

Since optimal treatment for a disease rests on knowledge of its cause, some of medicine's greatest discoveries have been in causative agents. The flu does not stem from the influence of astral bodies (Italian *influenza*) but is caused by various types of virus. Cholera does not proceed from infected water alone but from a bacterium within that water. Scurvy comes not from bad air, as sailors once believed, but from an absence of ascorbic acid in the diet.

Unfortunately, some human scourges still have unknown agents. One of the worst of these is Alzheimer's disease, a progressive physical deterioration of the brain that causes first memory loss, then senile dementia, and finally death. No one knows what agent causes Alzheimer's—bacterium, virus, heavy metal, or something never before seen. We know only that this modern scourge rivals HIV in its effects. Like cancer, no one is too rich to be vulnerable to Alzheimer's; First World nations feel its effects like all others.

In the nineties, a scientific team at the University of British Columbia established a link between Alzheimer's and a new protein that they designated p97. This protein targets and binds with the element iron.

The UBC scientists detected p97 in "senile plaques" found in the brains of people who had died from Alzheimer's. The protein also appeared in the cerebrospinal fluid of live Alzheimer's patients who had advanced forms of the illness. No other known brain disease correlates with p97. The UBC team began to wonder if p97 were a tipoff for this baffling cause of human senile dementia.

If so, there were major consequences. Current tests for Alzheimer's extract cerebrospinal fluid via spinal taps. These tests are invasive and painful and carry a risk of infection. They also tend to confirm Alzheimer's only in advanced cases. A commercial market exists for a simpler test, especially if it uses samples that are readily obtained. For all these reasons, UBC incorporated Synapse Technologies Inc. (STI) with a mandate to investigate the links between Alzheimer's and p97.

"This is a protein that seems highly specialized to Alzheimer's," says Mark Thomson, STI's director of business development. "We think p97 is an index of the disease. Levels rise as the disease progresses and may fall off when the disease is treated with therapeutics. There's also a direct correlation between p97 levels and the virulence of the disease." Mark believes the new protein could be a useful monitor that keeps Alzheimer's treatments from being mere shots in the dark.

When I spoke with Mark, STI had just developed a serum-based test that requires only a small sample of human blood. Obtaining such a sample is routine: it is certainly less risky and painful than a spinal tap. As well, blood is easier to store and analyze than cerebrospinal fluid.

Mark stressed to me that Alzheimer's disease goes beyond patient symptoms. "There is an immense human cost, not only in the suffering of individual patients but also in the devastation that occurs to their families." One of the worst aspects of this is the uncertainty over who has Alzheimer's, for senile dementia may have other causes. STI, Mark says, wants to remove this diagnostic ignorance. "SDI's p97 serum test won't replace standard cognitive assessments," he tells me. "Instead, it will supplement them. If our serum test for p97 strongly correlates with some cognitive element such as word recognition, this would greatly improve diagnosis." The p97 blood-serum test may thus confirm the disease earlier than current tests, giving physicians a head start on more aggressive and effective treatments.

STI has applied for pre-market approval of its new blood assay from the U.S. Food and Drug Agency (FDA), a world first for any Alzheimer's test.

The new STI test technologies have a potential for detecting pre-symptomatic Alzheimer's patients in the general population. Until now, mass testing for Alzheimer's has been medically impossible. But soon an assay for the disease may be as much a part of your standard medical checkup as a blood test for low-density cholesterol.

———

Driving south toward the U.S. border along Highway 99, I find myself thinking about the tenuousness of human existence. We are complex creatures, and any number of things can go wrong with us. I find relief from my memento mori mindset in a completely different application of biochemical research: the world of pheromones.

Reading a 1955 *Collier's* magazine recently, I made one of those ghastly discoveries that remind the most nostalgic of us that the past was no bed of roses. "He turns his back on his wife's tears!"

shrieked an advertisement in the magazine. If this maudlin house-wife wants to attract her man, the copy explained, she should—are you ready for this?—*douche herself with Lysol.*

Science has, thank heaven, progressed since those dark days a half-century ago. We now know our bodies have a highly effective biochemistry designed to attract and involve the opposite sex. Blast-ing delicate organs with industrial-strength disinfectant knocks this subtle system right off the rails.

Take copulins, a family of molecules that Swedish scientists recently isolated from human vaginal secretions. Copulins in-crease male sexual interest during the female's monthly days of fertility. When male test subjects inhaled airborne copulins, they rated a woman's photo as more alluring. A biochemist friend in Montreal characterizes the basic human response to chem-ical attractants as a piercing blast on a klaxon. Broad-spectrum, industrial-strength disinfectants, however useful for spring clean-ing, destroy this seductive complexity. Our fictional husband would be more attentive, not less, if his wife reserved her Lysol for the toilet bowl.

Other species share our reaction to love's sad sweet song. *Buck fever* describes the male deer's reckless behaviour in mating season. When the chemical klaxon sounds, it overrides the normal imper-ative to self-preservation in the stag's brain. It claps chemical blink-ers on the stag and orders the hapless animal to pursue his lady love despite all obstacles—hunters, wolves, or truck traffic. Such behav-iour puts the stag at risk and often leads to death or wounding. But the genome knows what it has to do. Individual welfare be damned: the species must go on. As the Romans said, *Amor vincit omnia*: Love conquers all.

Birds do it, bees do it, even educated fleas do it. Even insects are subject to this effect, which is mediated by organic compounds called pheromones. These serve as airborne couriers whose orders tell individuals when to swarm, disperse, or mate. Quantities of pheromone as small as a nanogram (0.000000001 g), and in airborne dilutions almost below detection threshold, instruct mountain pine beetles to congregate. The insects home in on the pheromone source, following what molecular entomologists term a chemical gradient and we laity call a stronger smell. When the attractant is a sex pheromone signalling the sexual availability of females, male insects flock to the chemical source from kilometres away. *Hey guys! Lulu's back in town!*

This leads to a simple concept with highly effective results. Take insect females, isolate their pheromones, and determine the chemicals' makeup and structure. Synthesize these pheromones in millilitre quantities. Put a tiny drop of the synthetic chemicals in traps spread over an area of insect infestation. Then wait. The males, few of whom have studied organic chemistry, will follow the irresistible odour of fresh female right into the traps. When they arrive, things happen to them that they didn't expect.

Option one: incarcerate Romeo. Take him completely out of circulation. Imprisonment drastically drops the number of studs available to service the ladies, thus preventing an insect baby boom.

Option two: sterilize the males, then send 'em packing. Steril-ization makes the men shoot blanks, but the ladies don't know that. They are satisfied and won't copulate with more robust males. Result: an insect population that plummets drastically.

This is the logic behind PheroTech, a knowledge company in Delta, B.C. The officers of the company, including president Dave Walkerchuck, are graduates of a chemical entomology program at Simon Fraser University. In the past five years they have pared pest populations in British Columbia's biggest public forests by chemi-cally imitating insects' siren songs.

In an average year, insects in B.C. kill as much prime timber as everything that people cut. The land involved is immense. One beetle infestation can turn millions of cubic metres of choice conifer into deadwood. To add insult to injury, insect kill of this extent is dry and extremely liable to fire.

Even if standing timber escapes death by one type of insect, other pests can come along after harvest and degrade the wood's value. Stems in a log yard may be colonized by Ambrosia beetles and carpenter ants. The bugs treat the stems like condos, carving homes or "galleries" throughout the wood. Often these galleries remain invisible until the initial saw cut, by which time it's too late to solve the problem. Given enough of these holes, an otherwise expensive piece of dimension lumber may be useless for anything but chipping into low-grade flakes.

When it started operations a decade ago, PheroTech found the forest industry sceptical of its claims. Fellers swore the trees weren't infested when they harvested them. Stackers saw no insects in the log yards. Even if sawyers noticed the damage, they had no idea what caused it or how to forestall it.

Accordingly, Dave Walkerchuck says, "we decided to visit the log yards. We brought along immobilization traps that we'd baited with our pheromones. In one yard, an entire bucket filled up with Ambrosia beetles as the workers watched. They had no idea the problem was so severe." Did it stay that way? "Our traps swept the area free of beetles in a week."

Note the power of one idea. No artificial pesticides. Less wood spoiled, so that fewer trees need be cut to reach a given value. The compounds used are harmless to all life, even the target species, and are as natural as water. Moreover, they're used in amounts and dilutions as minute as spit in the ocean. No toxic residuals move up the food chain and accumulate in human brains or bones.

PheroTech has recently begun to characterize and synthesize pheromones from cougars and wolverines. These, it hopes, will protect garden crops more effectively than fences and scarecrows.

"You would not believe," Dave Walkerchuck says, "the reaction of a squirrel or rabbit who encounters one tiny whiff of these chemicals. They void their bowels, then they flee so fast they're almost airborne. Of course any prey species that didn't have that reaction would have been killed off long ago. That's why our

products are effective. They work with nature, not against her."
This is more than just science: it's elegance.

———————

Biotechnology, the identification of life and information, came
from research that began pure and became applied. The revolution occurred in science, spread to technology, and finally entered
the evaluation mechanism that we call the market. There it had
the same explosive effect as Einstein's equivalence of matter and
energy. Physics said $E = MC^2$, and the world trembled. *Life is data*,
said biotechnology, and the world grew rich and healthy.

Redefining life as data freed scientists to imagine new areas of
investigation. It also freed technologists to embody the scientists'
results in novel ways. Along with IT, biotechnology helped persuade banks to unlock capital for intellectual property as well as for
land-based industries. More than any other idea except the digital
computer, the equivalence of life and data created the knowledge
economy.

Not only is the biotechnology revolution well under way: it is
still gathering momentum. Many commercial processes in medicine have already changed their core approach from chemical to
biological. The list is rapidly being extended from medicine into
materials science, manufacturing, and even engineering. Economists have coined a word for this: the *bioeconomy*. We cannot foresee how it might transform our world. We only know that it will.

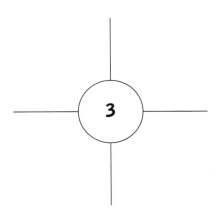

KNOWLEDGE

MACHINES

Manufacturing is the process by which hi-tech companies move products from mind to market.

Sometimes the products are pure idea, as in computer software. Technology analysts in the business magazines have some justification for their ongoing love affair with IT: algorithms cost almost nothing to encode onto magnetic or optical media, ship, store, and modify. Yet at the same time, pure information may cost more to create, test, and debug—that is, to manufacture— than material goods. Because of this, much of Canada's knowledge economy involves more standard manufacturing, which concerns itself with adding value to objects.

Not all Canadian manufacturing technology begins in Canada. Designs for products and processes are often imported. But knowledge isn't a commodity you own outright; you can't just uncrate new technology and turn it on. Whether you buy it, rent it, or devise it in-house, you must adapt it to your needs, which takes time and sweat.

Once Canadian manufacturers get a process up and running, however, they squeeze every dime out of it. Technology-intensive manufactured goods earned Canada over $20 billion in 2000, more than two and a half times the value of lumber exported that year.

Here are representative examples of Canadian manufacturing technology. Some are being produced in quantity, others are experimental; some are consumer goods, some are less tangible.

Although knowledge-based manufacturing may involve gigawatts of artificial power, it may just as easily involve the ancient elements of water and wind. Here is the best example of this I have encountered.

What a day for sailing! Steady ten-knot west wind, bright sun alternating with low scudding clouds, whitecaps on English Bay. Already there's a forest of sails on the ink-blue water: Lasers for the learners zip among the big sleek ketches of the rich. Flags and guns and pennants dipping. Everybody loves the shipping. I walk through the glass doors of the Royal Vancouver Yacht Club. Standing to greet me wearing the regulation white slacks and open-necked shirt is Don Martin, the commodore of the RVYC.

Don, as the old sea shanty has it, looks every inch the sailor. He is tall and gangly, with sea wrinkles framing friendly eyes, and is just what he appears to be. Don is no pomp-and-show commodore but an expert sailor and yacht designer who coaches Canada's challengers for the America's Cup. He's also CEO of Martin Yachts and has designed and made more than five hundred yachts up to twenty-three metres in length. I'm here to find out more about his newest design, the *Martin Sixteen*. It's a racing boat with a big difference: you don't need arms or legs to sail it.

Here's the tale. After Rick Hanson, the Canadian wheelchair-athlete, completed his cross-Canada marathon, he was commanded to the Court of St. James's. There Queen Elizabeth gave him a small sailboat called the *Sunbird*. This boat had been adapted for solo operation by a paraplegic athlete. Rick shipped it to his home on the West Coast and donated it to Don Martin's club, where the boat was operated by the Disabled Sailing Association of B.C. The *Sunbird* proved a mixed blessing. It let paraplegics sail, but it was complex and labour-intensive for RVYC volunteers to rig, launch, and maintain. The *Sunbird* seemed less a sailboat than a first cousin of the Royal Barge.

In 1994 Sam Sullivan, a Vancouver city councillor, executive director of the Disabled Sailing Association, and a quadriplegic, suggested to Don Martin that Don's firm build the *Sunbird* locally. Don was receptive to the idea but wisely decided not try to modify the cranky *Sunbird*. Instead of trying to rejig a craft originally meant for able-bodied seamen, he would start afresh.

"The *Sunbird*'s detailing is often unfriendly to the production boat builder," Don tells me in his big bright office overlooking English Bay. "For example, a boat should have a strong, simple, watertight edge where the hull joins the deck. The *Sunbird* does not. I thought there might be a place for a boat conceived from stem to stern for the disabled."

As Don looked into it, he became convinced that Sam Sullivan's request was more than a local need: it was a technical challenge and a marketing opportunity of global scope. A new boat could be created, far easier to sail and maintain, that could open up new markets everywhere. "I realized that this was a chance to create a new category. To start with a blank piece of paper and end up with something that was the best in the world," Don says.

His financial risk partly offset by a $102,000 grant from the Science Council of B.C., Don set out to rethink the concept of the paraplegic daysailer. His first decision was to go beyond a craft for paraplegics, who have lost use of their legs but can still use their arms. He decided to build a boat for solo operation even by high quadriplegics, people whose spinal cords are injured above the branching point of the nerves that control arms and hands. Don's new daysailer would use technology to let these people compete as equals.

"I've taught many people to sail, and it's a thrill to see them take to it," he says. "But the pleasure is even sharper for the disabled. When they sail, they're at no disadvantage. They're in total command of their environment. They find real freedom."

Sam Sullivan was Don's inspiration. "Sam was injured in a ski accident when he was nineteen," Don tells me. "In that, he's typical of high quads. These people get hurt because they're thrill-seeking and action oriented, so it's all the harder for them to adjust to life in a wheelchair. They can respond in one of two ways: give up or overcome. The majority of them refuse to be beaten. They retain their love of risk and adventure and redirect it to rise above their new situation."

Don's new design has a fibreglass hull. It's 5 metres long and 1.3 metres wide. Its total weight is 300 kilograms, of which keel ballast accounts for an astonishingly high 136 kg. This boat is 43 per cent counterweight, a ratio made possible by Don's use of an advanced alloy of antimony, calcium, and lead in the keel. This alloy, denser than pure lead, is cast into a teardrop-shaped pod. A hydrodynamic foil, like a vertical airplane wing, connects the pod to the boat's underside. Like a traditional centreboard, the foil keeps the craft from slipping sideways in the water. The heavy pod keeps the boat upright in nearly all conditions. Even if the boat capsizes, it rights itself in no more than a second and a half.

Don designed the hull using simulation software developed by Autoship Systems Corporation, another Vancouver company. Autoship software has helped sculpt Canada's entrants to America's Cup races as well as state-of-the-art warships for Australia.

Don wanted his new hull to move through the water with little resistance—in designer's terms, to be "easily driven." This would permit the use of smaller sails, which in turn could be manipulated more quickly and easily with battery-powered servomechanisms. The resulting hull is long and narrow, almost canoe-like. It is extraordinarily seaworthy and forgiving.

"I designed it for some pretty rough water," Don says. "I wanted it to handle whatever could be expected in North American day-sailing. It's been out in high seas and forty-knot winds and behaved handsomely." Don would not recommend such extreme conditions to inexperienced sailors: 40 knots is 75 km/h or #9 on the Beaufort scale—a full gale.

Another of Don's criteria was to keep his new craft as dry as possible. There were several reasons for this, the foremost being safety. Ocean sailing in the average boat has been compared to standing on a steeply pitched roof while someone hoses you with salty icewater. Yet many of the disabled have breathing problems that worsen in cold water, making standard sailing conditions unacceptable. Another reason to keep things dry was the presence of electric motors and controls. These included "sip-and-puff" electronics, which let a high quad use his breath to manipulate sails and rudder on a solo run. To get the levels of dryness that he needed, Don detailed a deck that projects out over the hull around the boat's full circumference. This keeps most waves and spray where they belong, in the water.

In addition to being dry, the hull has positive flotation. Each of its internal compartments has been made permanently buoyant with synthetic foam, making it unsinkable even when awash. "You could run over this hull with a tugboat," Don tells me, "and it would stay afloat."

When asked the most difficult part of his design exercise, Don immediately answers, "The seat." The standard approach in a small composite sailboat, he explains, is to mould a seat directly into the deck. But given the various operator types that the *Martin Sixteen* must accommodate—one leg, no legs, one arm, no arms—a one-size-fits-all mould was impossible. Don is proud of his solution: a plain-looking seat that changes the rake of its back with a rope and pulley and that can easily be removed and replaced with custom seating.

Technology is full of inventions made for one goal and then applied more widely; Don's new design is one of these. A boat tractable enough to let a high quad sail with confidence has also proven ideal for able-bodied beginners, seniors, and children. Within weeks of its official launch in 1996, inquiries about disabled and non-disabled use flooded in from Japan, South Africa, South America, Israel, and the U.S. In the same year, *Sailing* magazine gave the design honourable mention in its Boat of the Year awards.

Larry Boden, a quadriplegic sailor from Vancouver, has sailed an early production model of the *Martin Sixteen*. He is raising funds and public awareness for a solo Nanaimo-Victoria-Seattle-Vancouver voyage he intends to take. "I'm an adventurer, not a risk-taker," Larry says. "I trust this craft."

Don Martin agrees. "It's a snazzy, high-performance boat. It's tight and responsive, yet extremely easy for a learner to operate. It's full of technological innovation, most of which is invisible. It's for people who can't, or won't, lean to windward when they're on a tack."

———

One February afternoon my phone rang. My caller, a business-woman, had heard about a local knowledge firm called Connotative Reference. These people were out to quantify the emotional charge of language, she told me: to weigh the souls of words. Mrmph, I grunted—impossible. Oh? said my contact. I hear they've already succeeded.

This put me in a bind. I believe in technology; after all, it made us top dog when we'd been tiger food. And technical knowledge has the happy habit of returning to what it's messed up and fixing it. Think of the catalytic converter for autos or the chlorination that kills waterborne germs. Driving to Connotative, however, I felt less like *Dinofelis* than its dinner. This time, that wonderful new technology was threatening *me*.

Nuance, emotion, fit: that's the soul of writing. It's an activity for humans, not machines. Lexicons and thesauruses merely support this emotional-rational dance. Simple-minded software like current brands of grammar check do not threaten the dominance of the human writer. They exhibit the blunt, blundering honesty of a brain-damaged dog. But to strip the *sense* of words and quantify it! If that really had been done, as my friend thought, I was out of a job or soon would be. Software would quickly follow that accepted an input keyword, chose the *mots justes* that perfectly expressed it, and in seconds spat out crisp, clean, minimal, convincing prose. Or alliterative Old English iambics with a caesura, for all I knew. For forty years I had championed technology. Now it was about to bite off my nuts.

Twice on my journey I nearly drove through a red light, but I made it to my destination in one piece. I emerged from my car girded for battle, mentally preparing to toss both wooden shoes— the *sabots* for which the *saboteur* is named.

———

Connotative Reference occupies one of those offices that you immediately wish were yours. It's on Granville Island, a commercial-retail area of Vancouver that until the 1980s was a grimy industrial slum. This office has a view of boats at anchor in False Creek and the North Shore mountains beyond. It's warm and friendly, full of wooden beams and Navy prints. Standing to welcome me are the chief technology officer, Wayne Chase, who developed the technology over the past twenty years, and John J. Swift, VP business development and general counsel.

In five minutes I'm so far into their audacious, ingenious project that I forget to feel threatened. No enemies here: just two very happy people who have found the causes of things. Connotative has created a language-based technology that gives the connotative meaning of words and phrases in all known contexts.

I'd better explain. In writing, putting words on a sheet of paper or a VDT screen is just the iceberg's visible tip. Most of my work involves finding someone with interesting ideas, prying these out, understanding them, and putting them in context.

Context is vital. Words without understanding are empty; understanding without words is so nebulous that it may as well not exist. "Like a poem I meant to write," says Paul Simon.

A writer must understand two things: the literal meaning of words, called their denotation, and their emotional weight, or connotation. Take the Anglo-Saxon word *girl*. Its denotative meaning is simple: "young woman." Medical jargon carves the term into smaller slices—fetus, neonate, toddler, child, adolescent—but the denotative meaning remains "female + human + young."

Denotation is logical, rigorous, mathematical: a linear mind can master it. Connotation ushers in a whole new world, one that's hazy and indeterminate. Writers who use only denotation fall on their faces in the first sentence. For example, an eighteen-year-old female fielding incoming phone calls is, denotatively, a young woman—a girl. Call her a *girl* in a news story today and your phone will glow white-hot from protest calls. Connotation dissolves the firm ground of demonstrative meaning and substitutes the intangible. Reason gives way to emotion; sure becomes unsure. Connotation was risky even before the advent of political correctness. Here's an outspoken sixty-year-old woman: is she a *widow*, a *dowager*, or a *lady of a certain age*? A *harridan*, a *Xanthippe*, or a *Katisha*? Or merely *forthright*? Think before you type: you won't like letter bombs. One false noun and you're dead.

The *mot juste*, the perfect description, does an impossible balancing act with this riot of demands—accurately conveying strict denotative accuracy, emotional nuance, and even insult. (Usually writers want to avoid slagging someone; now and then we do it intentionally.)

Any writer worth the name must reconcile these pressures. First he learns a host of rules and regulations; then he forgets them. E. B. White, one of the great stylists, summed it up. Good writing, he said, is "all a matter of ear."

A supreme genius, a Dante, a Chaucer, a Molière, forges his own new language, inventing and discarding words and idioms at will. We lesser souls require help from various sources. Our first help was the denotative dictionary. Now, fishing for that elusive perfect word, we could consult Johnson, Webster, or Larousse.

Yet for all their helpfulness, denotative dictionaries left untouched the whole area of context. All a dictionary could do was list alternatives: choosing one still required human judgment.

To assist the writer here too, the next aid to come along was the thesaurus. This list of synonyms and antonyms, arranged by category, was pioneered by Peter Roget, a Genevan by birth, who spent most of his life in London. Roget's book was wildly popular from the first, going through twenty-eight editions in its author's lifetime alone. He compiled his reference because he was what we'd now call an ESL student and wanted to improve his "new native tongue." How well he succeeded is indicated by a single comparison. My publisher will faint from joy if any book I write for him sells ten thousand copies. Roget is at fifty million and counting.

Roget was explicit that his book was not a dictionary, but "a collection of words arranged according to the ideas which they express." A later editor of Roget's said the book's business "is with contexts, not with definitions." It operates, he added, like "a speaker or writer. . . . It images the working of his brain when he mentally scans his stock of words for the right expression."

And yet for all its intricacy, the thesaurus, like its elder sister the dictionary, is only a tool. Reference works list possibilities, what logicians call a universe of discourse. The writer must make the ultimate choice for every word or phrase. The lexicon, the thesaurus, are amazing vehicles, but they still require a human being at the controls. This is what Wayne Chase decided to change.

Wayne calls his method an infrastructure technology. Beneath the technical elegance of multivariate statistical analysis and IT processing, it parallels the century-old consensus technique that developed the *Oxford English Dictionary*. Oddly enough, Wayne tells me, it's the simplest terms that have the most contexts. Friend, for example, has shades of meaning that range from intimate ("soul-mate") to nodding acquaintance ("friend of a friend") to disinterested third party ("friend of the court").

Now the Luddite in me jumps out. What happens to this 'database engine' when language changes, as it must? In Augustan England, *artificial* meant "full of laudable artifice." Now it means "fake." And every twenty years, *presently* switches between "now" and "soon." That's denotative evolution. What about connotative evolution?

"The process we use is inductive," Wayne explains. "It takes a snapshot of a language at a specific time. We can take other snapshots whenever we want to—every five years, if we like. As language changes, the connotative engine that we generate from it will change too."

Connotative plans to base a variety of products on its newly completed database engine. "We want to be in the licensing business," John Swift says. "Our clients would buy time-limited rights to our technology, then use it to develop their own retail products." These products could include "connotationaries" and "connosauruses." These would give words' emotional freight, just as denotative dictionaries give words' literal meanings.

Another product would group together "connonyms"—words from wildly varying sources that share an emotional connotation. Connotative has already compiled preliminary connonym lists, and the results are fascinating. Even a Luddite like myself has to admit this opens a new window on language.

Volkswagen Beetle, for example, is a connonym with *pumpkin*. Both carry a whiff of lightheartedness, of something neither absurd nor threatening, but amusing.

The database engine taps deep currents in our English cultures. Connonym with both *pumpkin* and *Volkswagen Beetle* is a name: *Bill Clinton*. *Genius linguae* sees Clinton not as Republicans do— that is, as an adulterous Commie Antichrist who betrayed America—but as an amusing clown: Ronald McDonald with his pants off. It explains why the U.S. public never supported a Clinton impeachment. Nixon had to go: he was scary. But the Bill & Hill Show was merely a soap opera with an eight-year run. If Ronald Reagan turned the presidency into theatre, Bubba was Ron's follow-on act.

Fine so far: Connotative's technology seems amusing and non-threatening itself. But who will buy their engine? Who is its retail end-user?

Chase and Swift say their immediate target markets are two-fold: the publishers of reference works, and Internet portals. This seems a shrewd business move. Reference works outsell every other book but two: the Bible and the Quran. As for end users, Chase and Swift also foresee a major market in advertising agencies. These can give products names that appeal to target markets by invoking traits such as health, wealth, and pleasure. The shills do this already; with a connotative engine, they can go beyond intuition and focus groups and make the process more exact. Parents-to-be will be able to buy reference texts, both printed and software based, that let them locate children's names with set connotations—strength, friendliness, intelligence, success. (Monica's out, dear: it's become a connonym with "faithless" and "naive.")

Wayne says his company's connotative engine will work equally well in every language. Connotational reference works could be developed for Mandarin, Arabic, and French as well as for English. In addition, he says, the World Wide Web has opened a vast and growing market for simultaneous, machine-based translation among Earth's major tongues. Today's translation software founders on connotation: *Out of sight, out of mind* goes into French as *invisible et fou.* This would appear to open the door to yet another application: the Universal Translator, long a staple of space operas.

With a small shock, I recall a recent theory of artificial intelligence. Mind, it says, requires emotion. If this is correct, intuition may occur not only in humans but in an emerging generation of their machines. The day may come when you take your balky server to a psychologist.

A final question from a mollified Luddite. What could writers do with a connotational product? What might it offer that a writer's own intuition could not do as well or better? Chase and Swift have ready answers. One: new software could launch a connotative adjunct to a word processor at the touch of a key. Shall I call this character *strong* or *aggressive*? What nuances might each word convey? Two: other software could analyze text and rate its emotional intensity. It could even predict readers' probable emotional involvement in a text and the degree of sincerity they see. Why does one author sell and another not? Publishers may stand in line to find the answer.

But, I protest, Shakespeare had no such reference works, not even a denotative dictionary. Didn't he produce some decent stuff? Wayne and his VP business development exchange a smile.

"How many writers," Wayne asks gently, "are Shakespeare?"

————————

Connotational technology is a serious area of study that provokes the odd joking observation. But there is an area designed for amusement that has serious and far-reaching consequences for the knowledge economy: the use of information technology in video and computer gaming. A lot of praiseworthy innovations owe their origin to the apparent folly of games.

First, the innovations. Computers are not only big business in themselves, but "they" have also transformed all business to the core. Forty years ago payrolls, sales orders, and customer lists were kept on file cards. Sales people noted leads with that state-of-the-art recording instrument, the ballpoint pen. Presentations were made with felt pens and flip charts, backed up by that reliable standby, the restaurant tablecloth.

So utterly have computers usurped business that yesterday's

methods seem as remote as cuneiform today. Imagine a modern firm without Web servers and workstations for its office staff, or Palm organizers and projection pallets for its mobile workforce.

In 2000 Canada's economy broke the $1 trillion barrier for the first time. Most of this wealth was created, stored, borrowed, and lent via digital computers. Business is now so computer dependent that Y2K warnings about cybernetic meltdown threw otherwise stolid bank executives into gibbering fits.

Second, the apparent folly. It may come as a surprise that the driving force behind the cybernetic revolution in business is neither corporate demand nor basic university research; instead, it is that lowbrow, superficial waste of time: computer gaming.

"Business software is not driven by business," says Frankie Mann, a software engineer in Vancouver. "It's driven by games." Games, she says, explore the real-time nature of computers better than anything else. "Business people didn't know what to ask for until games showed them what was possible," she notes. "Business did not even demand colour monitors until games showed business what colour could do."

Barry Carlson, president of Internet service provider Parasun Technologies, agrees. "The games market has always pioneered the development of better software and higher-capacity computer hardware. Everyone who carts around a corporate video in a laptop or relies on presentation software to configure slides and overheads is paying tribute to some 'impractical' computer game."

Barry believes that games will become even more powerful for future cybernetic development. "When a truly instantaneous Internet appears, a real-time Internet, I expect it will have largely been driven by interactive games."

"One of the biggest mistakes made by Apple Computers was its deliberate decision to abandon computer games," one high-profile games developer told me last year. "Instead, Apple pushed itself as 'educational.' That sounds high and noble, but in practical terms it isolated the company from its creative wellsprings."

The games developer was Douglas Adams. More than twenty years ago he wrote the immensely successful *Hitchhiker's Guide to the Galaxy*. Just before his untimely death last year at 47, he turned his talents to the design of computer games. One computer magazine described his CD-ROM-based Starship Titanic as "the most imaginative game yet."

"Most species," Doug told me, "use their energy only to feed, flee, fight, and fuck. But if you look at the higher animals, you see play behaviour everywhere. Play drives computer evolution, just as it drove human evolution. So for a computer company to try pushing education while resisting games development is like trying to drive with one foot hard down on the gas pedal and the other foot hard down on the brake."

Confirmation of Doug's assessment comes from Robert J. Sawyer, one of Canada's most honoured writers of science fiction. "Gaming has driven the development of computers," Rob writes by E-mail. "The most avid game players I know—indeed, the only adults I know who have time to play games on a regular basis—are computer programmers. Writing computer code is like playing a game of strategy: you're always trying new approaches, new gambits, while racing against the clock. It's little wonder that long before computers got mouse ports, they had joystick ports."

"Business people pay top dollar for better graphics and higher speed," Doug Adams said. "But they did not insist on these things a priori. They chose from a menu that had first been created by games. While it may be true that technology ends up driving the business software market, games drive the technology in the first place. Business is where technology goes to, not where it comes from."

Despite the evidence, some business people resist the notion that money, mega-mergers and PowerPoint demos stem from adolescent pastimes. I once knew a CEO who said in his annual report that his company's employees had fun. His CFO flipped his toupée at the F-word; within months he finessed the CEO into retirement and took his place. The ex-CEO, however, had the last laugh.

Despite millions of dollars invested by governments and Asian investors, the company under the fun-hater is hemorrhaging money. It has been in the red every quarter for the past six years.

It doesn't surprise me that those who don't play don't profit. If humanity has one central trait, it is to leave off Improving Itself and go frolic in what Isaac Newton called the Great Ocean of Truth.

The Prototype: Third Attribute

If it isn't fun,
Don't do it.
– D.H. Lawrence, "Work"

It's the great Canadian game: Find the Disappearing Spring. Today, the recent warm weather has retreated. A cold wind sweeps across the North Shore peaks and blasts the exposed campus of Simon Fraser University on Burnaby Mountain. I have to believe it's temporary; otherwise this is Ragnarok, the Norse myth of the summer that won't come. At least the campus is clean: every scrap of litter has been lofted into orbit. The northwesterly is that strong.

Silly me, I'm dressed for warmer weather. My laps around the SFU four-hundred-metre track are so slow that I've given up timing them; I'm shuffling, not running. At least I'll get a good cardiopulmonary workout, assuming I survive. I imagine how I look from one of those windows overlooking these playing fields, where warm people in snug offices are inventing new technology. To take my mind off the weather, I turn over what I'm learning from the world of video games.

Games, I realize, are one instance of a larger trend in advanced IT called multimedia. Multimedia fuses two aspects of the knowledge economy: it is information technology displaying information. Multimedia presentations have both sound and graphics. Each time you access an Internet Web site, you employ multimedia technology. You also see the key trait of multimedia: its interactivity. Unlike traditional media, from live and recorded music to radio and TV, users can dictate the sequence and form of what they hear and see.

The Canadian writer Peter C. Newman calls the approach of standard media "fascist," and he's right. The cabal that plans, assembles, and disseminates radio and TV also predetermines their content. And as another Canadian writer, Mavor Moore, wrote, the real content of commercial media is advertising. Everything but the ads is just a sugar coating.

Peter Newman is more sanguine about multimedia-based IT such as the Internet. Yet even he fails to see that those who put together multimedia and post it on the Web still govern content. Those who browse the Web control little more than sequence. They can take any candy in any order—as long as it's from the box they're given.

➤ *Multimedia* is both a buzzword and a misnomer; a better term for this type of IT is *new media*, used as a singular. Media *are*; multimedia *is*.

Multiple media, i.e., communications that address two or more human perceptive faculties at once, have been around for decades. Perhaps the earliest example is live theatre, which may go back three thousand years. Even old black-and-white TV carries picture and sound. Radio plays have music, sound effects, and speech; and although all three outputs are aural, listeners process each stimulus in a separate area of the brain. All these older media are therefore multiple.

There is also the hidden essence of better radio: the ideas it evokes in those who pay it close attention. In this it is like all story-telling, whether in the flesh or in sequential phonemes encoded visually for high input—that is, in books. I got a better education listening to CBC *Ideas* while painting walls than I did listening to the droning mediocrities who infest Canada's university lecture halls.

By contrast, most television today is devoid of thought. Purporting to see all and tell all, mainstream TV is really so starved for ideas that instead of inserting them into its viewers' minds, it vacuums them out. To be a TV addict is to have your brain sucked dry ninety thousand times an hour—the number of discrete images displayed and then obliterated in that time.

The aims of new media are more ambitious than those of older communication methods. In information type and data density, new media wants nothing less than to exceed reality. From the geeks' point of view, reality is the original multimedia presentation, the standard to beat. I heard a story about some new-media developers who emerge from their studio after a three-day production blitz. They walk through south Toronto's Kensington Market on a summer evening and stand gaping at flowers in a lamp-post basket. "Cool," one says. "Fabulous pixel density."

Though probably urban myth, this encapsulates a truth about new-media geeks. Their goal is not better CD-ROM encyclopedias or more lifelike games but life itself. They won't rest until people can no longer distinguish between a studio production and the direct testimony of their senses. Again, the consequences of this are disturbingly painted by the Vancouver author William Gibson. Those entering 'cyberspace,' he imagines, will have realistic sensations directly created in their brains by IT machines—false memories and fake experiences that range from a full-course meal at Maxim's to group sex with the College of Cardinals. Viewers—participants, rather—will even be able to sense mathematical abstractions: they will *see* distributed networks and data depositories.

Gibson thought cyberspace might take two or three centuries to come about; yet some of the predictions in his 1984 book *Neuromancer* were commonplace four years after he published them.

One of the application areas most frequently touted for new media is schooling. In 1995 Canada established the Tele-Learning Network, a consortium of firms and colleges trying to apply new media to distance education, including what used to be called correspondence courses. Tele-learning hopes to substitute real-time interaction for written and mailed exam papers. A good example of such an approach is Forintek Canada's software package KDX. This trains operators of lumber dry kilns where they work, often in areas remote from brick-and-mortar classrooms.

But this is incidental. The main scholastic target of new media is K-12, the public system from kindergarten through the end of high school. Soon children and adolescents will be exposed to a variety of new-media tools. Researchers say this will be to our children's inevitable betterment, but I wonder if their assumption is

(a) Possible   (b) Desirable

(c) Productive   (d) All of the above

(e) None of the above   (f) Some of the above (*specify*)

Here's my worry. Though I wish the Tele-Learning Network well in its use of new media to improve public education, I wonder if it hasn't drawn an overhasty conclusion. New media is a means, not a goal—a distinction that today's public education often forgets to make. Too many educators mistake support techniques for learning. As Robertson Davies states in his novel *Leaven of Malice*, "pedagogical method" is a meaningless abstraction. Real learning needs only a master with a burning love for a subject and a student with an equally burning curiosity. Learning comes not from texts instructing about instruction, nor from new-media graphics and sound effects, but from a shared joy in discovery. That's what carries master and student through the necessary drudgery of memorizing times tables or learning machine code. *Conrider'et conloqui*, St. Augustine called it—"laughing and talking together." *That* is how we learn: no other. We evolved for such a style. It's that simple.

That mysterious, too. Like all great loves, the love of learning is complex in its simplicity. For one thing, it blurs learning and amusement in a way that dry scholars may dismiss as undignified.

"Shakespeare has the right idea," two boozy playwrights lament in a *New Yorker* cartoon. "People just want to be entertained." Of course, "deep entertainment" is the exception. Even in such exceptional times and places as Shakespeare's England, most entertainment has consisted of, in Will's own words, "a jig, or a tale of bawdry."

If most entertainment is trivial, the same is true of public education, most of which smothers the natural flame of learning like a big wet blanket. Schools that are too eager to copy the technical means of entertainment, whether these are couched as new media, games-platform self-instruction, or tele-learning, risk becoming as trivial as pop entertainment. True education is a what, not a how.

Modern education is perilously close to falling into the amusement trap. It has cognitively positioned itself to do so by trying to "scientificize" something that is humanistic and, at least to today's best science, still fundamentally unknown. All this being said, new media might yet lend engaging support to teaching, as long as both processes remain stoutly humanistic. Until otherwise indicated, we must keep the IT bells and whistles on a short leash.

I still remember two or three times in half a century when my education was all it should be. One of these was a history course taught by Dr. James Daly at McMaster University in 1966. Gown flapping, looking like a frowsy crow, Professor Daly would stride to his battered lectern and start speaking the instant he braked to a halt. And that's all he did—speak. No handouts, visuals, maps, overheads, CADCAM, fireworks, or on-line graphics. No new media, no tele-learning, but by God, it was enough. James Daly was an Irishman. To him the Word was heart's blood, breath, and the Will

of God. He needed nothing more, and neither did his students. I
pay the highest tribute to the eloquence of the man by saying that
when he spoke, I gave my complete attention to him and not the
class's young women.

According to Dr. Daly, good historians are incorrigible gossips.
They learn the dates and treaties only as backdrop for the real
stuff—the human activity that is always history in the raw. Dr.
Daly never bothered to give facts; he merely commented on texts
he assumed we'd read. When he spoke, the lecture hall became a
time machine. Out the windows were not rattling sleet or spring-
time blossoms; instead, there was a grassy field on the Welsh border, with Dickon Gloucester announcing to his armed carls: "We
ride for Henry Tudor." There was a Norman keep, with John
Angevin Lackland offering justice. There was Restoration London, with anti-Papists rioting in the streets.

Some of these anecdotes stick in my mind like real experiences,
which I suppose they were. Charles II, the Merry Monarch, was a
consummate politician who liked to please all factions. His delicacy extended to his appointment of two mistresses, one Protestant and one Catholic. When the rioters caught one of these (Nell
Gwyn) returning from the royal palace, they loosed her horses,
overturned her coach, and started rocking it, intending to rip it
open and lynch her. "Papish whore! Papish whore!" they chanted.
Suddenly the coach door—now a hatchway, since the coach was
on its side—creaks back; out climbs our Nellie. "Good people!"
shouts she. "I am not the Papish whore. I am the *Protestant* whore!"
The crowd roars approval, reharnesses her horses, and cheers her
on her way. You won't find that in the history books.

As the months went by, Dr. Daly added story to story, depict-
ing a world undisciplined, random, arbitrary, and anarchic—and
completely convincing. *This* was how the world worked: just
barely, and certainly not as trumpeted in politicians' speeches. The
laws, the rules, the ought-to-be, were for the textbooks. What
really governed history was what governed my twenty-year-old

life: ethanol, hormones, a little goodwill and kindness when they didn't cost too much, and a spark of intellectual curiosity.

Dr. Daly was the supreme embodiment of what good teaching is about: eliciting and then satisfying a visceral delight to learn. It's an ideal more honoured in the breach than in the observance.

Marshall McLuhan was right to say that those who distinguish between education and entertainment don't know the first thing about either. But those who *equate* education and entertainment know less, even when they apply spectacular advances in the hardware, software, systems, and theory of new media. Just as pedagogic method tacitly admits that teachers lack passion and students lack interest, so *edutainment* means "dumbed down." Three-D graphics are no substitute for a meeting of minds.

Learning, like gold, is where you find it. Wherever someone says "Aha!" with fire in his eyes, it walks among us. That is not a quantitative science and never will be. It is a miracle.

From games, multimedia, and education, I turn to new research on the brain. I make the transition in a five-minute walk across the Simon Fraser campus. It's a metaphor for the closeness of the disciplines: they're two sides of a single coin. Educators describe the brain by what it does, including learning and emotion. The scientist I'm interviewing today, Dr. Hal Weinberg, has developed equipment that directly inspects how the brain works. Hal's instruments treat the skull like glass and look through it at the bright sparks of thought that the conscious mind emits.

> I'd spill their hot program without remembering a single quarter tone. . . . The Yakuza would know about SQUIDs, for one thing, and they wouldn't want to worry about one lifting those dim and permanent traces of their program out of my head.

Yes, it's Gibson again. In this 1981 story "Johnny Mnemonic," the writer sketches a future in which messengers store software in their heads. Fifteen years after his story, and twenty kilometres from where he wrote it, a university laboratory is using one of Bill Gibson's imagined techniques to look inside the human brain as it lives, thinks, and operates.

Thirty years ago, scientists first picked up magnetic fields emitted by the heart, the first sign of the "biomagnetism" that, theory predicted, all nerves and muscles generate in small amounts. These cardiac fields were ten thousand times fainter than the weak magnetic field that surrounds the Earth.

The magnetic effects associated with brain activity are more than a hundred million times fainter than the geomagnetic field that deflects a compass. To sense these ghostly traces, scientists use an odd effect called superconductivity, which like most quantum phenomena usually lurks only in the subatomic realm.

The SQUID that Bill Gibson refers to is an acronym for Superconducting QUantum Interference Device. With niobium wires cooled by liquid helium to 4.2 degrees Celsius above absolute zero, a neural magnetometer using SQUIDs can sense the tiny magnetic fields emitted as a by-product of brain function. This instrument is known as a magnetoencephalograph, or MEG for short: "that which records the magnetism of the brain."

In SFU's Brain Behaviour Laboratory, Hal Weinberg and his colleagues seat human test subjects on a comfortable upright chair. Then they raise the subject's head into a MEG helmet containing three dozen SQUID detectors. The helmet eliminates the need for magnetic shielding, which would otherwise add another $0.5 million to the MEG's $2.5 million cost. The MEG is made by a spinoff firm in Port Coquitlam, a few kilometres away.

The sensing process is both painless and remote: the supercooled SQUID coils never come closer than half a centimetre to the subject's scalp. Desktop computers process the MEG's output signals and provide the attending scientists with magnetic contour maps of the subject's brain. These maps report on as many as sixty-four areas within the brain and can be updated every one-thousandth of a second. Through such delicate indirection, Hal and his colleagues not only glimpse what the brain does but can even pinpoint the precise areas where its data processing occurs.

Unlike older methods of sensing brain function, SQUID systems work in real time. The older methods require long scans that muddy what should have been a series of instantaneous snapshots into a single, uninformative data smear. But according to Hal Weinberg, "You have to know what's going on at every instant throughout the brain to deduce what it does." Otherwise, you're constantly sampling a different brain, Hal tells me.

Hal's laboratory has achieved some striking successes. For instance, a common optical illusion presents a shape like a white wineglass on a black ground. When looked at steadily, most observers see this shape suddenly become two black human profiles facing each other across a white ground. In test subjects, Hal's group can see with high accuracy the exact instant when the brain makes its perceptual flop—up to one second before the subjects realize it themselves!

"We look at two things in this laboratory," Hal says. "First, we try to identify which physical areas of the brain relate to which [brain] function. Second, we examine how the brains of different people employ different capabilities to process the same stimuli. This is important, because the brain's data processing depends on its previous processing of similar or identical input. At different times, everybody's brain may do the same thing in different ways."

The brain, Hal explains, is amazingly plastic, by which brain physiologists mean how the brain distributes its various data-processing tasks within itself. Not only different genetics, but also different backgrounds and even different training make differences in how two brains handle exactly the same task.

Weinberg *et al.* continue the long-established process of deducing how healthy brains work by examining unhealthy brains. Epilepsy, schizophrenia, and accidents all produce magnetic-field anomalies that the MEG can pick up. These anomalies cast light not only on the disease that caused them but also, by inference, on the workings of the normal brain. This means that Hal's investigations, including how brains process information and memorize and retrieve facts, mesh with practical applications that earn hard cash for the laboratory.

For example, Hal's laboratory examines people who have made claims on an auto-insurance company. The MEG looks for the possible effects of head injuries, helping verify or contradict reports of migraine, motor dysfunction, and memory loss. Another experiment tests a group of airline pilots.

"In North America, a seniority system ensures that older pilots fly the longer routes," Hal says. "But physiologically, these senior pilots are more affected than their junior colleagues by sleep deprivation."

Hal's laboratory looks for variations in what is known as a thalamocortical resonance loop, or TCRL. It's an internal brain scan that occurs forty times a second; Hal thinks it primes the brain for high-level data processing. When both alert and drowsy subjects process specific types of information, the alert subjects show higher levels of TCRL.

"We can scan pilots, locomotive operators, and air-traffic controllers to assess their states of alertness and so determine their fitness for extended duty," says Hal.

Beyond all practical uses of the laboratory's new knowledge is the infinite mystery of the brain's complexity. It is the quest for this pure knowledge that most motivates Hal. "We know more all the time about the brain," he says. "But the more we know, the more questions we face. We've proven that the brain has no one library. It stores its memories of, say, recent changes in hand positions separately from where it stores memories of changes in musical tones." But *how* are these data stored? The truth is that no one yet knows. "At this point we have far more experimental data than we have ideas to organize and explain them," he says, sighing. "We need a breakthrough in thinking about thinking." Brain science awaits its Isaac Newton.

Whatever concepts finally organize and explain the facts, they will have to take time into account. Hal Weinberg has a strong intuition that there's no such thing as a static way to describe the brain.

"Thought is dynamic," he says. "That means research on the living brain is like listening to a symphony. If a theme does not make sense to an observer, it is probably because he missed hearing it from the outset. In the brain, nothing makes sense unless you consider what went on immediately before and after."

Hal takes his glasses off, looks out the window to the cold grey day, and rubs his chin. "Maybe," he muses, "there's no more a start or end to consciousness than there is to a river."

We've heard about the human brain and the new inventions that explore it. Now here's a story about an invention that explores the brain's inseparable partner, the human body.

When I wrote my science-fiction novel *Sun's Strong Immortality*, I wanted something that did not exist: a workable way for IT to depict the dancing human form. I broke my brain imagining a technology to do this and came up short. Three pages of description ate up four brutal months of research and redrafting. Now I find I have an excuse: human movement, it turns out, is ridiculously complex. It has defied all attempts by software engineers to model it.

Even the obsessive geeks who create digital video games containing human forms are often driven to an inelegant method called motion capture. In this technique, a real live human is photographed in slow motion against a three-dimensional grid. Then the software engineers create a computer model that tries to catch the human model's static postures and dynamic moves. So far this has never produced more than a very rough fit, in which the fluid stalk of a dancer becomes a jerky, mechanical stagger.

"Four things there be too wonderful for me," says the biblical proverb. "The way of an eagle in the air. The way of a serpent upon a rock. The way of a ship in the midst of the sea. The way of a man with a maid." Solomon might have added a fifth example: the way of everyday human movement.

Technical attempts to refine motion capture can get baroque. Designers of a recent video game imported an action superstar from Hong Kong and tried to digitize him. They made him climb walls, leap hurdles, and kick imaginary villains, videotaping him all the while. But though the final results on the VDT screen are better than anything done to date, they still seem puppetlike compared with the living, breathing actor. Reality, as well as exhibiting a higher pixel density than a video screen, also has a smoother action.

The shortcomings of most digital systems explain why Pixar, the undisputed king of such purely computerized movies as *Toy Story*, mostly limits its imaginary stars to bugs and toys. *Homo sapiens* spins, tumbles, runs, fights, and walks in too intricate a way.

All this is about to change. Dr. Tom Calvert is a transplanted Englishman who over the past quarter century has worn enough hats to fill a prop box. Full professor at Simon Fraser University; Simon Fraser's VP research; president of the B.C. Science Council; vice-president of B.C.'s new Technical University—the list goes on. Now a new company, recently spun off from Tom's research with his graduate students at the SFU Centre for Systems Science, is about to revolutionize the analysis, synthesis, and display of human motion.

Tom is an IT expert specializing in computer graphics. Early in his career, he developed the first full-scale computer animation used in a commercial movie, the starship-docking sequence for *The Last Starfighter*. The frames seem crude now: they comprise simple geometrical shapes, spheres and cylinders, with the strong sunlight and unsubtle, knife-edge shadows characteristic of airless space. Today's Grade 10 kids do better on their iMacs. But in 1983 this work required hours of rendering, or image processing, on Cray supercomputers. It defined the state of the art in machine-based animation.

In the past twenty years Tom Calvert has further advanced computers' realistic generation of human movement. This time he has proceeded not via the universities but through his privately held firm, Credo Interactive.

Credo is based in Seattle, Washington, but it does its R&D 250 kilometres north, in Vancouver. The word *Credo* is Latin for "I believe." What—whom—Credo seems to believe in most is Terpsichore, muse of dance. Life Forms, Credo's most advanced software, is probably the best way in existence to capture, store and reproduce the movements of dancers.

"Life Forms is extremely simple to use," reports Nathan Reeves, reviewing the software in a trade journal for professional graphic designers. "You can create animations in literally seconds. This is fantastic for long animations and custom imported models. No other tool in its price range provides as much power for your money."

Nice words, yet a picture is worth a thousand of them. Seeing Life Forms demonstrated is an eye-opener. Sanford Kennedy, an American computer-graphic artist with more than a dozen movie credits, recently revealed how he is illustrating Julius Caesar's first landing in Britain. Caesar himself describes the scene in *De Bello Gallico*; Kennedy supplements this report with his own historical research. Writing in *3D Artist*, he explains: "Life Forms makes it possible to have twenty or more figures all moving on the stage at one time, while playing back the animation in real time." A competing graphics program, he says, "choked even on a dual-PII 450 MHZ with 256 Mb RAM and a 16 Mb display card [i.e., graphics hardware that was state of the art in 2000]. Life Forms, even with large groups of figures . . . makes it easy to see each character's body and limb location. I am using Life Forms to choreograph my entire battle scene."

Kennedy uses Life Forms for more than overviews. To develop individual figures, a figure editor on the Credo software provides close-up manipulation. Stylized figures can be moved in any joint not only along a plane but also toward or away from the observer (engineers call this *3-space*). Figures' joints can be rotated; the whole figure can be moved, posed and turned. Artists can examine the finished shape from any angle in 3-D. The result is an amazingly lifelike movement.

Bill Reid, Pixar's technical director for motion pictures, is a Canadian who started off using computers to model heart function at the University of Toronto and got a doctorate in mathematics and computer science at the University of Waterloo. Next time you marvel at Hollywood's computer animation, reflect that much of it—from *Toy Story* to Credo—is the brainchild of behind-the-scenes Canucks.

———

We're in a remarkable age, at once an end and a beginning—a watershed. We're right to be glad of it and to celebrate the triumphs of our knowledge economy. But to the future, today will be ancient history. Just think! our descendants will say. They *died* in those days: permanent, irreversible death. They suffered poverty and disease. They needed *vehicles* to move around, vehicles powered by *fire*. Were there dinosaurs back then, too?

When we sneer at the past, we forget two truths. One: technology created us; before technology, our species did not exist. Two: we have always been defined by our technology. Though today's innovations do constitute a kind of technical firestorm, in one sense we have lived with a knowledge economy since we first invented tools. New economy, be not proud: you differ from antiquity not in kind, but only in degree.

Oh, our arrogance is understandable. Society neatly splits into those who think the Golden Age is gone irretrievably and those who think it's here, and the knowledge economy is in the clutches of the latter group. More, better, faster, and to hell with yesterday; we're tomorrow oriented. The past is kerosene lanterns, vacuum tubes, stone tools. The very self-confidence that lifts us to the moon, lowers us into the abyssal trenches, and sends instruments to Neptune makes us think we're smarter and more accomplished than the oafs who went before.

Yet that's only from our viewpoint. Look at Europe's great churches, said Charles-Édouard Jenneret, the Swiss architect who practised as Le Corbusier. Today you see cathedrals as mementos from the past: dim, grimy, long since superseded by more advanced engineering. But there was a time when the cathedrals were white. You cannot judge that past time by its modern remnants. You must imagine what it was like when cathedrals first took shape, guided by the newest technology; when the Freemasons, an international elite of self-employed designers, daily advanced that technology; when technologists allowed for such arcana as the tendency of stone to flow like cold molasses under enormous dead-loads; when nations, newly awakened, moved unanimously toward audacious goals.

Now extend your imagination back to other ages. See them not as the dust they have become, but as they were in their heyday: before their achievements became the artifacts and grimy curiosities of today. The Enlightenment, when statesmen were philosophers. The Renaissance, when the white space on the maps filled in. Imperial Rome, which gave the known world one strong, humanistic law. Ionian Greece, which W. H. D. Rouse said "first showed us what the human mind is for." The Hittite empire, whose iron weapons sliced through bronze to end an era. The Paleolithic, when all language lay coiled within the first word and all technology lay implicit in the first stone tool. "All these were honoured in their generations, and were the glory of their times."

The key processes of prehistoric technology—ceramics, weaving, leatherwork, button fasteners, food storage, knives, spears, atlatls, bows—are in their way as complex as computer machine code. Few among us can tune a car engine. Yet considered as an empirical process, engine mechanics is simpler than the technology of the Old Stone Age. To tune an engine, you follow the steps in a service manual. To flake a laurel-leaf point, as the Paleo-Amerinds did twenty-three thousand years ago, you must feel stone as a living thing. Two hundred and thirty centuries in the past, a good obsidian point was as much a technical triumph as the World Space Station is today. Back then, too, the consequences of failure were greater. Botch an engine tune-up today, and you take the bus. Botch a spear point, and you risk losing wife, children, and yourself to battle or starvation. Yet laurel-leaf points have been found imbedded in mammoth bones, still in one piece and still as sharp as razor blades. *That* is technical success. What will remain of all our works in twenty-three thousand years?

High utility often accompanies surpassing beauty. Whether it is a weapon c. 23,000 B.C., a cathedral c. 1190, or a long-span bridge c. 2002, great technology doesn't just perform well: it looks wonderful. As the form of pure idea, the material shape of intent, it could not be otherwise. Respect the past, then. In every age, our ancestors knew a lot.

Take an apparently simple thing, wheat. Some of my readers will know how to plant, cultivate, and harvest it, which I do not. But—and this is not generally realized—wheat itself is an invention, a synthesis of pre-existent seed-bearing grasses. It's an early example of empirical biotechnology. Faced with a sea of natural species from rye to rice, who among us could make the plant crosses that led to frost-resistant Durham Hard? Build a cathedral? Plan an aqueduct? Chip flint into a flawless laurel-leaf point capable of killing mastodon?

No. Most previous technological advancements, from blacksmithing to the calculus, are not just triumphs for their own times, they are amazingly complex by any standards. Even now, only specialists can duplicate them, and that's mere mimicry. To make any key discovery—weaving, sailing, speech—someone had to conceive a thing that had never been done before. All advances reveal the defining characteristic of genius: the shaping of reality in new ways.

To a high-energy physicist, time is a function of events. When nothing happens, no time passes; when much occurs, time rushes by. Thus to change, to find knowledge, is to acquire great age; accomplishment equals time. Seen in this way, we humans are among the oldest things on Earth.

My next-to-last interview in the West Coast university community takes place neither in a campus office nor in a laboratory. This morning I am visiting a police station.

While much of society's IT effort seems directed toward frivolous games or sober education, IT has also progressed in another area. Games affect our pleasure, education our awareness, but crime affects our lives.

Consider the serial killer. His are not crimes of passion, committed by someone well known to the victim. The serial criminal is typically a stranger to those he rapes, abducts, or kills. The very randomness of his attacks makes him harder to catch, which increases our fear.

Serial crimes must be investigated without the police officer's customary start points, chiefly a short list of the victim's relatives and friends. Serial-crime investigations must compile and sift through vast quantities of data, most of which prove useless. In serial-crime cases, suspect populations can run into the thousands. Given too few officers and too many facts, an investigation can slow or even stall.

To help the world's police forces solve such crimes, applied mathematicians have developed a new field called geographic profiling. From one viewpoint, geographic profiling is an academic pursuit. It generates journal papers and conference proceedings, and creates a set of practical techniques embodied in computer technology.

The technology's aim is catching bad guys who are still at large.

The duality of geographic profiling reflects the dual nature of its creator, Dr. Kim Rossmo. By day Kim Rossmo is a mild-mannered academic, an adjunct professor at Simon Fraser University's School of Criminology. A second business card reveals his other profession: Detective Inspector, Vancouver Police Department.

Kim defines his geographic profiling as "an information-management system using data from a connected series of crimes to determine where the crimes' perpetrator is likely to live." As such, the discipline offers police forces and security agencies a new weapon in their ongoing war against the serial arsonist, rapist, and killer.

Kim says such criminals, Paul Bernardo being an especially chilling case, share certain characteristics. "Seventy-five per cent of serial killers hunt in their own community," Kim tells me. "Even a 'poacher,' defined as a criminal hunting far from where he lives, may return to a former residence to commit his crimes. Geographic profiling is designed to track these people down."

GP uses principles of mathematical association, embodied in the algorithms of computer software, to link a series of crime sites to where the criminal lives. Is this susceptible to specious questions? If fed data on unconnected crimes, might Kim's new GP system assume a connection and provide a likely residence site for a nonexistent man? Kim says it isn't likely.

"The central mathematics of geographic profiling are robust," he says. "One or two wonky inputs won't affect the result too much." This is partly because more than geographical data are used to link incidents. VICLAS—the RCMP's Violent Crime Linkage Analysis System—correlates crimes via dozens of separate factors, including victims' age and sex. If it's still not clear that a given incident belongs to a given series, the questionable crime can be statistically weighted. Giving an incident a weight of 0.8, for example, reflects the analyst's 80 per cent certainty, or 20 per cent doubt, that a crime fits. This mathematical correction adjusts the software's conclusions.

Kim Rossmo began his academic career taking mathematics at the University of Saskatchewan. At one point, he interrupted his undergraduate degree for a year to join a private-investigation firm. To connect his studies with the excitement and action of PI work, Kim took a sociology degree in crime and policing.

Kim joined the Vancouver Police Department in 1980. Once there, he took a master's degree, examining how fugitive criminals move around. He also developed mathematical models of how offenders relocate to avoid penalties. That thesis, and further work in Vancouver's Skid Road, brought home to Kim the supreme importance of geography to crime.

"Police officers are comfortable with geography," he says. "If you've spent any time in a squad car, you know that being in the right place at the right time is half the battle."

During his academic research, Kim discovered that 80 per cent of Canadian police records have an address component. Increasingly, geography seemed to connect nearly every other aspect of crime.

Kim searched the world for a university where he could under-take doctoral studies to explore his ideas. He settled on SFU, where the husband-and-wife team of Paul and Patricia Brantingham had developed mathematical crime/geography models. These began with the residences of known offenders and predicted where new incidents might occur.

Kim asked the question in reverse. Could he take crime sites as his start point and derive areas where criminals were likely to reside? No one knew.

For months Kim didn't know if his primary question was solvable. One day he was in Japan, looking idly out the window of the famous Bullet Train, when a possible solution occurred to him. After what he calls "a mad hour of scribbling on train napkins," he had found his mathematical approach.

But back in Vancouver, examining his idea more closely, Kim realized that only computer software could handle the vast number of calculations required. He then learned a programming language and wrote a program that enabled desktop computers to run his model. As a test, Kim used a serial arson case that had been prosecuted to a conviction. From the facts, his new model correctly determined the arsonist's home address.

Now, several years after obtaining his doctorate, Kim is the only detective inspector in Canada with a professorship. He spends most of his time testing and refining his new system, for which there has been a steady growth in interest. He recently presented a paper at the International Conference on Forensic Statistics in Edinburgh and has turned down job offers from the FBI. He's even been offered a visiting fellowship at Cambridge.

Asked to demonstrate his system, Kim swivels his chair to a computer monitor behind his desk. The screen's first image is a white-on-black street map of Vancouver. (Trivia lovers will recognize it as Gotham City from the first *Batman* movie.) A click of a mouse superimposes white circles, the sites of actual armed robberies with a single perpetrator. Next the system shows the crime sites by contours. Each line, an isopleth, links points with a similar likelihood of being the offender's residence.

So far I find the system cold and remote, an exercise in bloodless logic. That changes with the next mouse click. The system colour-codes the spaces between the contour lines from a cool blue, indicating low probability of offender residence, to a high-probability red. And when the system translates its isopleths into peaks and valleys, with the illusion of a third dimension, its full power appears. There it is: the topography of a serial offender's most likely residence. *Crimespace.*

Crimespace is as real to a police analyst as the streets it's superimposed on. Perhaps it isn't a coincidence that a 3-D correlation of this sort is called a jeopardy.

To turn his academic work into a practical desktop system Kim formed a company, Environmental Criminology Research. The commercial system, under the trade name Orion, runs on hardware whose power equals that of a mainframe computer of 1990. The hardware uses "middleware," software whose specialty is to integrate different databases. The middleware was written in an advanced programming architecture by Facet Data, another Vancouver firm.

Orion's operators can undertake high-level search tasks with ease. Once the system identifies probable areas where a criminal might live, it compares them with millions of names and addresses stored on its CD-ROM. I can imagine a future Orion unit with voice access automatically telephoning the prime suspects in a serial-crimes investigation and politely inviting them to the local con-stabulary for a friendly chat.

Whether or not this happens, both the science and technology of geographic profiling are spreading from their Canadian birth-place to the police forces of the world. Sgt. Christine Wozney of Vancouver RCMP, a developer of the Mounties' ViCLAS, sees Kim's system as "one piece of a puzzle," the other pieces being ViCLAS itself and a personality assessment of the unknown serial criminal.

"Wherever traditional methods of police investigation no longer work, we need new systems," Christine tells me over the phone. "GP is one such system. It tells us where we should go to start knocking on all those doors."

The Prototype: Fourth Attribute

Our fourth attribute for a prototype knowledge organization is that it exploit a niche market using unique technology. This minimizes competition and maintains prices strong enough to let the organization thrive. Uncommon knowledge is uncommonly successful.

In our use of oceans, forests, and the genomes of life, I have seen projects whose potential consequences are immense, but on my last day on the West Coast, I enter the realm of the microscopic. My interviewee is Dr. Ash Parameswaran, a professor of engineering at Simon Fraser University and director of its Micromachining Institute.

Ash is compact and broad shouldered, with a flashing smile and streaks of silver in a jet-black beard. He shows me around his basement laboratory with maternal pride.

Ash's specialty is machinery. That's not unusual in mechanical engineering, but Ash's concentration is hardly run of the mill. It's called microtechnology, and it deals with machines with working parts too small for unaided eyes to see. Working with colleagues in Alberta, Ash's team designs and builds operating machinery on the scale of a few microns, a micron being 0.001 millimetre.

After he fetches me a coffee, Ash rummages in an enormous briefcase and pulls out photos of his pet inventions. One of them catches my eye. It glistens metallically in the black-and-white picture, its edges razor straight, as if it were the size of an my hand. But a bracket superimposed on the photo marks off fifty microns. That's the size of a human white blood cell.

"What is it?" I ask.

"A weigh scale," he says.

"Weighing what?"

"See that blob on its sensor arm? It's a mammalian cell."

"My God," I say. "You're weighing a living cell?"

"Oh no," Ash responds, with a laugh. "We're far more accurate than that. We're weighing changes in the cell's mass when it absorbs nutrients or gets rid of waste. A few hundred molecules at most—about a billionth of a gram."

The weigh scale, Ash explains, doesn't use gravity. Instead it relies on resonance, which lets it work in the water, where most cells prefer to live. The heavier the object on the scale's microscopic sensor arm, the more slowly it vibrates. The vibration frequency, measured in Hertz (H_z) or cycles per second, lets the engineers easily compute the cell's weight at all times.

The scale, Ash tells me, is not some miraculous one-off. Instead, it is designed to be mass-produced. Ash and his colleagues base their manufacturing on techniques that make computer micro-chips. But where semiconductor factories mould in only electrical components and conducting pathways, Ash's lab uses photo-mechanical masking methods to insert incredibly tiny machine parts into the chip. Result: an engineering technology that's smaller than your wildest dreams. Instruments, even whole test labs, can be put on one chip.

Ash smiles at my amazement. "This kind of thing is routine for our lab now," he tells me. I then find out the most astonishing thing about microtechnology: it's on the brink of being replaced. A story is circulating that a workshop in Alberta will explore an engi-neering discipline whose subjects are so small that they're invisible. Its artifacts are the size not of a silicon chip but of a molecule.

I thank Ash Parameswaran and walk back to my car. I realize that what he's told me about molecular engineering is something I should explore. It's time I made the long haul to Alberta.

―――――――

It's a good day for driving: cool and clear, with spectacular scenery. Here is what defines Canada: forest, mountain, river. At Hope, the Coast Range rises abruptly. Highway 3 takes a pass among peaks that soar two and a half kilometres above me. Behind me is the Fraser, swollen with snowmelt. I'm the only car on a twisting road. My driving tweaks a memory. I recall my first encounter with the knowledge economy, long before I ever heard the term.

On New Year's Day 1985, our car broke down as we drove through Kaladar, Ontario. My wife and I were returning to Ottawa after spending the holidays with her parents. Clouds of vaporized coolant announced we were going to be late—probably very late.

Kaladar, a village halfway between Ottawa and Toronto, was nearly shut down. One place was open—a combination laundromat, snack bar, and garage. We went inside its smoky, steamy interior and asked if a mechanic were around. Well, they'd give him a call, though he'd be at dinner. Ten minutes later, a man came into the store looking like the day outside: short, dark, and dirty. Three of his fingers ended at the second joint. He looked under my car's hood and diagnosed a ruptured water pump. Was the part fixable? Nope. It was die-cast and couldn't be welded or sealed. Did he have a part for a 1980 Honda five-speed? Nope, but he'd call his brother. Another ten minutes produced a spitting image of the first mechanic, and the two men went to work.

In the attached café, my wife and I read old magazines and drank coffee. An hour later, the first man put his head through the door. "She's done!" he said. "We cut down another pump and fitted her up."

I was astonished; I'd assumed I'd have to tow the car to a dealer. "You mean it works?" I said.

"Sure!" he said, grinning. "She's fine." And so it—*she*—was. We were on our way within the hour: full cost $59.50, plus tax.

In retrospect, I should have known I was in the presence of a master mechanic when I saw his damaged hands. Our mechanic was a holdover, a modern anomaly. Years ago, skilled workers of his calibre used to live in every settlement. Like software engineers, they made a living not by juggling expensive black boxes whose guts they didn't comprehend but by making skilled judgments and doing delicate work. They were artists, minimizing their expenditure of effort and time. They were what the American management scientist Peter Drucker calls a knowledge worker. That's whom we were lucky enough to find.

A hundred years ago, a lot of workers were like my competent Kaladar mechanic. But then the great trusts—Andrew Carnegie's steel mills, Cornelius Vanderbilt's rail lines—began to standardize labour. A workforce made of faceless, interchangeable men squeezed the knowledge worker from his sole proprietorship.

By the 1960s, this process had spawned a supporting philosophy, *reification*: the opposite of personalization. When you personalize, you put a human stamp on something. When you reify, you depersonalize. It's no coincidence that my Kaladar mechanic called the cars he worked on *she*. He interacted with them; he befriended them. But big industry's reification treated workers, and finally even customers, like so much inanimate waste.

In the business journals of the thirties and forties, managers began speaking of themselves impersonally: managers became Management. Individual human quirks and skills were compressed into lockstep conformity, with appalling results. There's no better example of this than the Chevrolet Vega, a compact car that General Motors sold in the early seventies.

The company's first attempt at a compact auto had been the Chevrolet Corvair, introduced ten years before the Vega. While the Ford Edsel got the ultimate bad rap, the Corvair did more damage to its parent firm. The Edsel was a money pit and an eyesore: the Corvair was a death trap. For years, Detroit had shifted blame for traffic safety from itself to the driver. Our cars don't kill, said the automakers, speed kills. But as Ralph Nader argued in his book of the same name, the Corvair was *Unsafe at Any Speed*. In one horrific example, a little girl sat in a Corvair's front passenger seat as her mother drove through a parking lot at walking speed. The mother braked; the slight jar popped open the glove-compartment door, which sliced off the little girl's head as she fell forward. She was unrestrained, of course: at the time, American and Canadian cars lacked even the anchors for seat belts.

Although the Vega thus had some bad history to overcome, from the viewpoint of GM's cost accountants and engineers, the newer car seemed a good design. It could be loaded onto rail cars nose down, cutting shipping costs. Even better, the Vega assembly line was an engineering wonder. No human on it was required to do anything complex: workers had been reified into a workforce, a sort of meat-based machine.

But by the mid-seventies, all this perfect logic had inexplicably gone wrong. Reified GM bean-counters began to log incredibly high rates of worker absenteeism and turnover. The reason, we know now, was that the work the humans were forced to do was so trivial, so God-let-me-die boring, that their minds were shutting down. They left before their work drove them insane.

Management could not admit this effect or even perceive it. The only solution it could accept for its workforce problems was to simplify assembly-line jobs still further. In this way, management told itself, the replacements shuffling in to succeed their boredom-crazed brothers could be trained in minimum time, making every-thing more efficient. Rather than addressing absenteeism and turnover at source, management accepted the statistics as givens and worked around them.

GM found its solution so to its liking that it stepped up the reification process. Reification was soon taking place on five fronts. First, jobs were dumbed down to bedrock. Second, work was shifted en masse to Mexico and other countries that had cheap, compliant labour. This threw tens of thousands of Ameri-cans and Canadians out of work and gutted whole cities. Down-sizing: God's gift to share price. The third area of reification was the unions, who bought into the philosophy as fully as manage-ment. The unions' seniority system treated its own members as things. Education? Attitude? Energy? Learning ability? None of it mattered: seniority did the trick. Brother Jones was essentially the same as Brother Brown. Everyone was interchangeable.

As a coup de grâce, GM management even managed to reify its customers. They were redefined as the Consumer, a faceless mass without mind or will. Marketing was confident it could sucker the consumer into buying anything, anytime: all it took was chrome and glitz.

And finally, in a concerted attempt to dispense altogether with troublesome human workers, GM developed and installed computer-controlled robots. As Stalin liked to say during his purges, "No man, no problem."

Strangely, the last two points shattered reification as a viable philosophy. More than that, they nearly toppled GM, a corporation whose immense earnings and market capitalization exceeded the gross domestic product of some nations.

In the late sixties, GM analysts calculated the company could save money by drastically cutting the range of car parts it made. The part types that survived the cut could be combined and recombined in a handful of slightly different autos. While the models made in this way looked and were almost identical, they could be differentiated (marketing assured management) by trim, permitting retention of auto marques. This would work because the consumer had brand loyalty. Children would buy Pontiacs, just like their parents.

To buy a Pontiac, however, the consumer—in reality, the human customer—had to know what a Pontiac looked like. Car-crazy North America had grown up learning to tell an Olds from a Buick for any model year. Under the new regime—which was made of, by, and for the bean-counters—you couldn't tell two GM models apart even when they were parked side by side. As late as 1991, no one on the GM board of directors could detect any difference between adjacent Pontiacs and Chevrolets.

The tale is shortly told. Within three years, customers took their money to other manufacturers whose models, while perhaps made less efficiently, looked less undistinguished, and mighty GM nearly went to the wall. "What's good for General Motors is good for America!" crowed Alfred P. Sloan, GM's chairman in the twenties. Half a century later, America stood up to reply.

––––––––

Another force that saved humanity from reification was a most unlikely ally: the robot.

As GM bean-counters efficiently pursued their firm's near-demise, head office was funding research and development on robotics. The aim of reified management was to get troublesome humans out of factories altogether, making them production machine-perfect. But in a wonderful paradox, robotics helped re-establish human values in modern work. They did so by resurrecting that all-but-vanished breed, the knowledge worker.

The robots didn't replace all humans, as management had planned. Only *some* humans lost their jobs. Ironically, robots made other humans high priced and indispensable—the people who developed cybernetic theory or engineered robots or repaired them. Suddenly, production again needed irreplaceable human skills.

Here's the lesson, which the old economy learned just as it began to disappear. *The wealth of the knowledge economy is not in physical labour: it is in the minds that direct that labour.* Intangibles such as skill and judgment earn the wage; the sweat, like an athlete's, is of no consequence. Whether of robots and supercomputers, or of nuts and bolts, knowledge pays your way.

GM and its industrial clones had worked toward an old-economy Promised Land, where a few human workers earned minimum wage for minimum effort and zero understanding. But in trying to drain all knowledge from its jobs, GM unwittingly hastened an economy that rewarded the unique knowledge of the individual specialist. As reification perished, the old economy birthed the new.

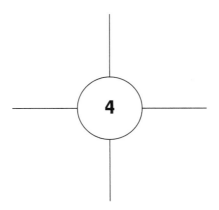

RAVENS, GEEKS,

AND ALTERED FOODS

My highway climbs up out of the Okanagan, back to a land of grandeur and extremes. At 5:00 p.m. on my second day in from the coast, the mountains change to foothills. Then I'm outside Calgary, facing the wide blond Prairie. I gas up at a roadside station, look skyward, and smile. Far above me wheel a pair of ravens.

I like these birds. When my second son was born, a mated pair took over a tree outside our house. They nattered all day, then disappeared; I never saw them again. Five years later, another pair nested in a big Douglas fir at the edge of my property. I learned to imitate the territorial call they use to tell other ravens, *Bug off!* I can't describe a raven's curiosity when I run by him making this sound. I suppose it's as if he hailed me in Italian.

For a long time, scientists wouldn't believe that ravens are as brainy as they seem. But in time, everyone who studies ravens is forced to admit that the birds seem brilliant because they *are* brilliant: they're feathered Einsteins. In the Yukon, ravens stand on photoelectric switches on city streetlights. That masks the switches and turns the lights on, warming the ravens' feet. Other ravens tease eagles by pulling their tail feathers, then doing barrel rolls to evade the enraged raptors. Ravens have been observed working in tag teams to filch food from intellectually outclassed dogs.

Though the presence of ravens here in Alberta seems a good omen, I hope these two are careful. Recently some Alberta live-stock farmers complained that ravens were swarming and killing newborn calves. The provincial government then amended a law to let ranchers shoot ravens on their own land, which ignored two things. Scientifically, the overwhelming evidence is that ravens near a kill are opportunistic scavengers, not killers. Legally, it vio-lates an international treaty that protects migrating birds called passerines. This includes *Corvus corvax*, the raven. Evidently there are rural myths as well as urban ones.

I shake my head and get back in my car. The province will never modernize as long as it nourishes attitudes like these. Knowledge, Alberta, knowledge. A person without it is nothing.

In fairness, things may be changing. Alberta has consciously moved toward a diversified economy in the past twenty years; nearly a third of the B.C. biotechnology companies I interviewed have some connection with Alberta. Edmonton has strengths in biomedical research and cancer genomics. And Cameron Chell, founder of a new subset of the IT industry, is an Albertan.

The ASP industry (application service provider) lets you down-load computer programs over the Internet without having to go out and bring home software in a package. "You don't need an IT background to do this," Cameron says. "You don't need to know how to upload and download, or *reconfig* and *deconfig*. It's ludi-crous that in today's North America, we have to know how to do all this simply to access information."

The province's shift to a knowledge economy is greatly helped by what's known as the Alberta Advantage. This starts with a gov-

ernment committed to minimum regulation and maximum entrepreneurial advantage for private business. Alberta has the lowest
overall taxes in Canada, with no general capital or payroll taxes and
no provincial sales levy. It was the first province in Canada to have
deficit-free annual budgets and leads the rest of the nation in
planned annual reduction of its total debt. There has even been
talk lately of eliminating the provincial income-tax surcharge.

But that's only part of the A-Advantage, a statement of how
flush Alberta is. The rest of the story is in how the province spends
its bounty. Alberta hosts key nodes in the federally funded centres
of excellence for new R&D, including the Protein Engineering Network—the only NCE so far to generate a Nobel laureate, Michael
Smith.

Alberta's transportation, housing, and education are all sound.
And in 2000, Alberta announced a $0.5-billion fund for research
in science and engineering. This new money is not some press
officer's invention, a ragtag collection of existing programs. It is
new, stable, and long term. Depending on provincial revenues, it
may increase by a further $100 million a year through 2005, the
year of the Alberta Centennial. Even the federal government can't
match that big a per capita investment in new knowledge.

All this has made Alberta a magnet for knowledge professionals. Other provinces have brain drains; Alberta has a brain *gain*. In
biomedical sciences, the province siphons off top talent from both
Canada and the world.

In resources, Alberta has proven more open to the knowledge
economy than B.C.'s forest industry. The most striking example
lies in the new technical knowledge that has steadily expanded the
oil-sands development in Fort McMurray. This is the most knowledge-intensive part of the Alberta oil patch.

The accepted maxim, repeated as recently as February 2001 by
the CEO of DaimlerChrysler, is that "you can't cost-cut your way
to success." Yet the experience of Syncrude, the firm that mines the
oil sands, flatly contradicts that conventional wisdom. By 2012,

Syncrude plans to produce two million barrels a day of light crude oil. By contrast, DaimlerChrysler is struggling.

As I drive south of Edmonton, the business news on my car radio quotes sweet crude at US$28 a barrel. The knowledge that halved Syncrude's production expenses in the past twenty years means that Syncrude now pays only $12 to produce and ship that $28 barrel. The $16 balance goes into capital expansion and share dividends. In the century's first decade, new oil-sands investment may reach $40 billion. Who says you can't succeed by cutting costs? In the knowledge economy, all things are possible.

———

At six-thirty I find a motel on Calgary's Trans-Canada bypass and turn in to it gratefully, having logged eight hundred kilometres in one day. A shower, clean clothes, a meal, and life loses some of its stress. The beef is great, the gas is cheap: Alberta's land-based economy may have something going for it, after all.

Back to my room. Only ten o'clock: I have time to check my correspondence. I unlimber my notebook computer, plug its modem into the room's phone jack, and log on to my Internet service provider. Strange to think of the days when I had to leave my office at home.

Aha! Answers to my interview questions. My messages have a double significance, because I'm using E-mail to research a story on—what else?—E-mail.

Wired magazine calls E-mail "the Web's only killer app"—Geek-speak for "successful computer application." Most of us would agree. Whether we're journalists, accountants, or experts in process control, millions of us around the world spend part of the day on computers. This takes away E-mail's energy barrier, since the extra effort to send and receive it is negligible once you're already at a keyboard.

If this seems obvious, consider the telephone. There's a big energy barrier to lifting a handset; most people are mildly afraid to pick up a phone. Yet that fear pales beside the malignant aura that oozes from other media. Regular mail embodies the old Army phrase "Hurry up and wait." Find paper, pen, envelope, stamp, mailbox; write the address by hand; then wait for snail mail to live up (or down) to its name. How about a face-to-face meeting? Arranging one is troublesome when you're in the same city. It's difficult from different cities, and absurd when you and your colleague come from separate provinces or countries. It's hardly simpler when the person you want to see works four doors down. Oops! She's at coffee, getting voice-mail, in another meeting . . .

E-mail flattens these barriers into the smallest of speed bumps: you type and send. Messages per hour soar to double digits, more if you mail to a preset list. Contrast this with rough hourly limits of ten phone calls, four face-to-face contacts, and two snail-mail letters. Perhaps the most important of all advantages for E-mail is that distance doesn't count. One of my messages tonight is from an interviewee who's attending an academic colloquium in Leipzig, Germany. Even if snail mail had reached him, it wouldn't have elicited an answer in time. Even if I'd sleuthed out his hotel number and swallowed the cost of phoning, a ten-hour time difference would have made an interview impossible. Short of a real-time downlink via satellite, there was no practical way but E-mail to reach my man. With E-mail, it was simple.

I want to dismiss a charge commonly brought against E-mail: that it alienates users from society. True, E-mail offers a way for the timid and lazy to avoid personal contact, but we're all timid and lazy now and then. It's more important that E-mail lets people communicate when otherwise they might not.

E-mail's popularity extends beyond its unlimited range and ease of use. Like all media it has an irrational component, unconscious and emotional, that explains both its benefits and its pitfalls. I've put a few empirical guidelines for its use at the end of this book.

In the meantime, to bed. A big week starts tomorrow.

———————

This country's climate is crazy. Three days ago on the coast, I froze my tail off running. Today, a thousand klicks inland at the rim of the Prairies, I'm fighting heat prostration.

Calgary is just as I remembered it: sprawling, friendly, bursting its seams with a back-slapping energy that's at odds with the languor of this hot spring day. It's also prone to weather extremes. When my running path dips through hollows by the Bow River, the air feels straight from the Amazon Basin. I call it quits and walk the last kilometre, dripping with sweat. Probably Calgarians don't sweat because they consider this to be *dry* heat. I hate the thought of dressing for a press conference.

Things don't seem so bad when I realize that in Calgary, hardly anyone except oil executives wears a tie. I show up in slacks and turtleneck and feel as if I'm in formal wear. A TV cameraman wears sandals, shorts, and a shirt apparently airlifted from Waikiki. I see why business is vigorous in this city: neckties don't restrict the flow of blood to people's brains.

Lorne Taylor, minister of Science and Innovation for the government of Alberta, steps to the podium and makes an announcement. Tenders for a new provincial communication system have been let and a winning bidder chosen. Over the next three years, BCE will wire ultrafast Internet service into every community in Alberta, no matter how small. The only criterion is that it have a school, a hospital, a library, or a government office.

I shouldn't say *wire*: wires conduct electricity. Alberta's new high-speed network will replace clunky old electrons with visible light piped through fibre optics. This project will provide a high-bandwidth data conduit. Fast fibre optics are like rapid-transit lines: out along them flow the intellectual and economic benefits of knowledge—employment, shops, new housing. Once Alberta's opto-electronic network is complete, knowledge industries such as software engineering will be able to work from Manyberries, AB, as easily as from Calgary or Edmonton.

"This will help our quality of life," Lorne Olsvik says after the government announcements. "It will attract high-paying jobs to small communities. It will disperse professionals and their incomes."

Olsvik is president of the Alberta Urban Municipalities Association, and he's all for the new network. I sip my pop and raise my eyebrows; talk about a leveller! If the knowledge economy can turn the government of Alberta into raving interventionists, there's nothing it can't do. This is a bold move by a province that many liberal thinkers tend to dismiss. Neo-con Alberta may be, but it's begun to see what the knowledge economy can accomplish.

I've come to Calgary by the southern route, through Lethbridge and the Crowsnest Pass. Now I backtrack sixty-five kilometres, to the resort community of Banff, where there's a seminar on something I heard about from Ash Parameswaran.

The Banff Conference Centre has space-age furniture and drop-dead views of the upper Bow Valley, one of the loveliest places in the world. For the next two days I'm going to check out a brand-new field that in ten years may be bigger than biotech. It's called nanotechnology.

Nanotechnology is the study and manufacture of artifacts on the scale of one to ten nanometres. A nanometre is a millionth of a millimetre, the size of an inorganic molecule and only ten times bigger than a hydrogen atom. That's a serious kind of small.

To a chronicler of the knowledge economy, the location of this seminar is as interesting as its content. Alberta has made great strides in using its surplus resource revenues to move its economy away from resources alone. To do this, it has effectively used a strategy of leapfrogging: not merely catching up with Canada's knowledge concentrations but moving to surpass them in strategic fields such as oncology (tumour science) and genomics. Perhaps Alberta is hosting a nanotechnology workshop to explore its next possible leap, passing over the predictable in favour of the extraordinary. No one's said anything definite, but it would make sense.

Besides myself, the audience includes fifty attendees from the upper strata of industry, government, and the universities. They're here by invitation from the president of NRC; I'm here because I can sweet-talk. They listen, I type notes.

Nanotechnology, we hear, is the high frontier of twenty-first-century R&D. Neal Lane, U.S. presidential adviser on science and technology, says, "If I were asked for an area of science and engineering that would produce the breakthroughs of tomorrow, I would point to nanoscale science." Other speakers inform the workshop that nanotechnology captures and applies the amazing properties that materials exhibit at the molecular or atomic scale. At that level, the weird world of the quantum comes into play.

The first nanotech breakthrough may come in molecular computing. Today's CMOS computer chips, based on silicon doped with rare earths such as germanium, will reach their limits of function and assembly in fewer than ten years. To replace them, researchers are experimenting with nanoscale devices that require only a few electrons' difference to "flop." (Flop, or change of state, is a basic action by which machines transmit and process data.) If these elementary nano-devices can be made predictable, reliable, and amenable to mass production, they will routinely attain data-processing speeds that make lightning seem a crawl. In turn, this will open up applications that sound like today's science fiction. Early commercial prototypes of a quantum computer, says Dr. Stan Williams of the PC manufacturer Hewlett-Packard, may be available within five years—just when conventional micro-circuits reach the end of their capacity.

"As we fabricate more sophisticated materials," one scientist announces, "we will create a new generation of lighter, stronger, programmable substances, environmentally less costly to produce but with a longer service life. They will let us make new generations of products."

Already, some researchers have improved the physical properties of polymers by 50 per cent through the addition of nano-sized particles of clay. Worldwide market estimates for these polymeric nanocomposites by 2009 are US$3 billion. A scientist from Ontario describes how he makes invisible wires, using chemical reactions to persuade a nanotech wire to build itself on a silicon substrate. The wire is the thickness of a single atom.

Nanotechnology may also have applications in medicine and health. Biotechnologists could, for example, work upward from single molecules to find, understand, and change the substances of living organisms—from fats and carbohydrates to those master molecules, proteins. Interestingly enough, some of Canada's most advanced work in nanotechnology is being done around the corner from this workshop, in Edmonton. There, scientists from the University of Alberta are developing "laboratory-on-a-chip" sensors so sensitive and so portable that they can be used to detect individual molecules in a patient fluid sample, right at bedside.

Similar nanotechnology-based devices may revolutionize gene sequencing and cancer detection. Soon, medical tests that today require days may take only minutes. One Ottawa company has already established a market for hand-held blood chemistry analyzers using a nanotech approach. Its markets could grow to several billion dollars a year in North America alone.

One of the things this strange new discipline can do is to explain previous explanations. Over the years engineers have derived thousands of formulae that summarize processes from fluid flow to steel plasticity. These formulae describe things well enough to predict broadly how materials behave. But *why* the formulae work has been a mystery. Now, nano-techniques are providing answers.

As in all of today's science, nanotech research involves advanced data processing—*It's All Data* applies to inanimate matter as well as to life. Researchers are making sophisticated computer models of material behaviour at the nanoscale. The gain in understanding, we are told by Dr. Peter Hackett, NRC's VP of research, is "like the difference between photographing planets and mapping cities."

Not all the nanotech news is good, however. While Canada participates in a lot of nanotechnology R&D, Peter tells us, its work falls below critical mass in many fields. "No national strategy has been developed to concentrate the separate pockets of expertise in nanotechnology and nanoscience across Canada. . . . Nor has a federal network of centres of excellence for nanotechnology been created." By contrast, Taiwan and Korea both have centres for nanoelectronics. China has a ten-year nanotech program for materials and probes. The American nanotech budget for 2002 alone exceeds US$0.5 billion.

Peter proposes that Canada take on niche projects that build on our strengths—electronics, aerospace, biomaterials, drug delivery. That strategy, he says, will get Canada to the table with the big guys: Germany, France, Asia, and especially the U.S.

All this is a head stretch, and when we rise for lunch I need to get off by myself and let my brain shrink back to normal size. It's cool but sunny, and while spring is more advanced in Calgary than in Banff, it's a fine day here. Time for some macro-technology. I rent some golf clubs and step onto the first tee of the hilly course that runs along both sides of the ice-green Bow. As I'm preparing to drive, my scratch partner tells me to look at something. Yes, I say—mountains. I've seen lots of 'em. He tugs my jacket, and I look up. Right in the centre of the fairway, a scant hundred metres ahead, stands an elk the size of a Buick. I gape for a while, then walk off the tee. I prefer courses whose hazards aren't hazardous to my health.

The workshop's final session provides a caution: commercially, nanotech is a high-risk venture. Despite its promise, it demands massive up-front investment, and many of its new products may take ten or twenty years to develop. Now, as it did in SYLVER, net present value rears its ugly head. A dime invested for two decades needs to earn a dollar. Few private companies are prepared to invest in such long shots; indeed, these days they have their hands full surviving the current fiscal year. Before firms invest, they need to see a proven market opportunity.

For Canada to profit from nanotechnology, we must slot each commercial opportunity in its proper time frame. Some work must go toward products to be sold in 2005, other work toward products to be marketed in 2025.

The workshop ends in a mood of qualified optimism. Canada may have a big opportunity here, yet success is uncertain. If we give nanotechnology a try and it falls on its prat, we'll have spent billions of dollars for nothing. If we don't invest and nanotech succeeds, we'll miss most of the economic benefits.

On the way out, I walk past Peter Hackett. It's been fascinating, I say, thanks for the information. But realistically, isn't this nano-stuff kind of, well, blue-sky?

Peter stops stuffing paper into his briefcase. "Biotechnology," he says, "is worth billions of dollars today in Canada. Twenty years ago, when its first discoveries were made, few people could even pronounce the word."

He turns back to his briefcase. "You have to look ahead," he says.

––––––––––

I'm on the road again, and the klicks hum by. I cross the Saskatchewan River, then the South Saskatchewan, heading for Saskatoon. "Too big by half," the *New Scientist* once called Canada. I want to see the country and sample its science, I'm trying to hit most major centres, but I still haven't left the populated strip along the U.S. border. At ground level, I actually see about one-half of 1 per cent of Canada. In the meantime, though my car motors on with direction and purpose, my mind roams where it will. Currently it's examining something that's come into focus over the past month: the common nature of the knowledge workers I interview. I am assembling a portrait: the Soul of the Geek.

> At math and science he's a whiz
> Rates an A on every quiz
> But underneath his learned air
> His simple heart is in your care

So runs the doggerel on some Valentine's Day boxer shorts a girlfriend gave me thirty-five years ago. Now as then, the verse fairly describes a certain type of knowledge worker, whether scientist, engineer, or technologist. Both by outsiders and among themselves, the term now applied to this subspecies is *geek*.

The word has a seedy history. Fifty years ago, *geek* meant a penniless addict who travelled with a carnival, a person so degraded that he would do anything for a fix—eating earthworms, biting the heads off live chickens. A geek was the lowest of the low. But from Roundheads and Shakers to Quakers and Copperheads, outcast groups have always co-opted insults and brandished them as banners. Today's geeks rule the knowledge economy.

The geek is like a modern monk. Eight centuries ago Brother Ambrosius was smart, ambitious, and proud of his scholarship. He wrote witty footnotes by lamplight, demolishing the egregious opinions of Brother John in the next cell. The monk lives on; he has merely traded religious studies for secular ones. His bedtime reading is no longer *The Confessions of Augustine* but rather *Suggested Standards for File-Transfer Protocols in Asynchronous Optoelectronic Transmission*. Yet a monk he remains, albeit serving the quirky new god Technology. Herewith some signs by which ye may know him.

First, he is a he. Forty years ago, earnest governmental studies decried the low percentage of women in the knowledge workforce. As if making an original discovery, identical studies continue to appear every few years. Yet the mainstream geek remains male.

Not prototypically male, mind you. Today's geek does not waste time on sports. Nor is he constantly lustful or prone to visit bars or given to violence. Women interest him yet frighten him. Besides, how could a woman compete with work? Where is the lady who will line up for hours to see *X-Men* on opening night? Who plays Dungeons and Dragons for fifteen hours straight? Who buys new computers in preference to new cars?

The second sign of the geek is his lousy dress. The twenty-first-century monk's habit is T-shirt and shorts in summer, sweatshirt and jeans in winter, and sneakers or sandals all year round. While most geek dress is grungy, a hierarchy of grunginess exists within geekdom. As a rule, professional games developers are the best (= least poorly) dressed. They may wear open-necked long-sleeved shirts that are reasonably clean, albeit unironed. Now and then their pants may spend time in a washing machine.

Several strata below, at bedrock, are university biologists, who usually look as if they have been fired by stunt cannons into piles of acid-eaten rags. They may or may not be professors. If they are, and are also CEOs of spinoff companies, their officers and directors may force them to get a make-over.

In terms of nutrition, the geek behaves abominably. K'ung Fu-tsu, c. 450 B.C.: "Describe me as someone who forgets to eat when he is studying." That's partly geekish, but as usual the geek goes one step beyond. Even Confucius didn't break his work-inspired fast by staying on at his desk guzzling Mountain Dew and munching candy.

The truly defining characteristic of the geek is that change holds no terror for him. In this he stands in stark contrast to the rest of humanity. While most humans clutch familiar things in a death grip, the geek is bored by what he already knows. As pants the hart for cooling streams, the geek yearns for the new. He sees change as the convert sees death: as a tiny price to pay for glory. At the drop of a hat he will jettison perfectly functional technology for its replacement or upgrade. The geek never lived who stayed loyal to wringer washers or rotary phones.

In the old economy, employees burrowed into ruts and stayed there. Some of their managers, myself included, were driven crazy by their resistance to the most elementary and necessary new technology. I recall a graphic artist who produced coloured slides as late as the early nineties not on a Mac or with PowerPoint but using a stereoscopic magnifier and a very fine paintbrush. He had to be threatened with dismissal before he would try a computer. (Of course, six weeks after he got it he was a raving convert.)

By contrast, geeks clamour for change. One CIO I interviewed told me that giving his staff new technology was one of the great motivators of his firm. "If you let people keep learning, the results are amazing," he said. But fifteen years ago when I was a manager, employees would rather be vivisected than change. And this was in an R&D institute. Since then, the geeks have taken over.

What finally defines the modern geek is his refusal to grow up. This is true not only in habits such as dress but also in the geek's equivalence of work and play. The geek is the essence of neoteny, which has important consequences. For one thing, the geek enjoys his work the way non-geeks enjoy leisure: it never occurs to him that what earns money can't be fun. Even when a geek toils in a hated corporate job, it's not the work that distresses him as much as oppressive management. On the flip side—now there's a ski-amorph from vinyl days—geeks go at apparently trivial pastimes such as games with an intensity that non-geeks save for courtship or work. *Star Trek* is *real* to geeks. They marvel at Picard's xenoarchaeology; they dream about Deanna Troi.

It's not all bad if the geek is unworldly. Richard Needham, a *Globe and Mail* columnist in the sixties, once told me that no one can be proficient in every evil. The sinner must specialize, he said.

To chase women, you must humble yourself. To be proud, you must forgo worldly pleasures. And if you are oblivious to almost everything but your work, as geeks are, you may preserve a certain innocence. It's not a total loss being Peter Pan. While geeks are socially maladroit, they may also retain a sense of rectitude long since beaten out of the average commerce grad. And while geeks may be emotionally stunted, task obsessed, and immature, they may also nurture a childish purity of heart. They don't accept the old-economy mantra that everyone in business must go for the throat.

"Geeks believe in the Golden Rule," one knowledge-company CEO says. "They actually live their ethics, in the workplace and in their lives. It sounds bizarre, but it's true." This forthrightness has huge consequences, which are just beginning to filter through to a world culture conditioned by a terminally jaded old economy. Though geeks are fascinated with nuts and bolts, it's rarely to the exclusion of what these things are used for. One of the most attractive firms for geeks—the company least likely to have trouble hiring and retaining the best of them—is a firm that makes new technology not an end in itself but a means to a morally laudable goal. Knowledge supports ethics; ethics in turn inspires more knowledge.

One geek put it this way: "My work satisfaction trebles when I work for a good cause. I don't want to sound like Gandhi: money is important; it keeps me going. But in the end, people want to help out. They want to be honest. They want to achieve something good."

It's early days for geekdom, and these summary traits are only a snapshot. Lately I've seen signs that geekdom's great, unwashed, homogeneous mass may soon be fragmenting, because a new type of geek is popping up. He—still a he—calls himself *übergeek* (German *Übermensch*, "superman"). This geek, usually high up in a successful company or otherwise on a career roll, actually has—wait for it—a sense of style. Typically he's director of product development or head of marketing in an IT company. I have one such man in mind as I write this—goatee, earring, hair with highlights, patent-leather shoes, ponytail. Perhaps the knowledge economy's rude mechanicals are at last about to evolve.

———————

As I close in on Saskatoon, the view out my car window catches my attention. Each of the fields I pass is a section in size: about a kilometre and a half each side, 2.6 million square metres in all. And for the past two hours, every section has displayed a single crop that spreads a vast yellow tablecloth over the prairie. It's called canola, and it's made in Canada.

Canola is a recent name change; thirty years ago the crop didn't exist. There was a precursor called rapeseed, which could be pressed for a low-grade oil. The more Canadian scientists analyzed this oil, the richer it proved in fatty acids inimical to the human cardiovascular system. So a federal laboratory in Saskatoon, just up ahead in that pretty treed valley, combined standard plant breeding with the new field of molecular genetics. That let them scrub undesirable elements from the genome of the rapeseed plant. The result was canola.

North American farmers now dedicate about six million hectares to canola every year. That's over fifty thousand square kilometres of this crop, visible in spring and summer by its canary-yellow flowers. Canola has become so ubiquitous that it's visible from planes cruising thirteen kilometres above the ground. The crop's yearly value in North America alone exceeds US$3 billion. Its oil is so low in saturated fats that using it for a lifetime won't do you any harm. And yes, it's a genetically modified food.

———————

I like Saskatoon; it's big enough and small enough, with an intellectual vein as deep as Boston's. Others agree. *The Wall Street Jour-*

nal said, "Here's a recruiting challenge. You need to attract talented professionals to North America's second-coldest city, and it's 650 miles [1046 kilometres] north of Caper, Wyoming . . ."

Guess where? As the *Journal* tells it, talented individuals and entire firms from Bristol, Baltimore, and Bermuda routinely turn down offers from warmer or wealthier climes to live and work in Saskatoon. "A great city is that which has the greatest men and women," wrote Walt Whitman. As Saskatooners see it, their city isn't isolated: it's the centre of the cosmos. It's the rest of reality that is isolated from them.

They may be right. Saskatoon is important to Canada's changing commerce because it contains—or more properly is—a technology cluster. This is defined as a node of firms, institutes, and personnel essential to the knowledge economy. These components strike sparks from one another, exchanging capital not just in money but also in more abstract forms like intellectual property and new, blue-sky ideas.

Governments say that establishing technology clusters is one way for them to kick-start a knowledge economy. If this is true, then Saskatoon is Western Canada's undisputed superhero of the breed. It's why the city, according to *The Wall Street Journal*, "punches well above its weight in the global economy . . . and is home to over 80 companies in the fast-growing sector of biotechnology."

Saskatoon creates and exploits new knowledge in many disciplines. It is, for example, home to the new Canadian Light Source, which produces one of the world's purest, most intense forms of broad-spectrum light. But the city's core technology cluster stresses agricultural biotechnology and its commercial cousin, agricultural business or "AgriBus." Here Saskatoon has attracted such companies as Dow AgroSciences and Monsanto and is steadily spinning off additional start-up firms.

The Saskatoon technology cluster accreted around federal labs in the community. In one of these, about fifty years ago, a Canadian scientist named Art Neish had a brainstorm. At this time the chemistry of carbohydrates—including the sugars and starches found in all food grains—was mostly unknown. Dr. Neish's idea was to remove neutral atoms in some of these important substances and replace them with radioactive variants. Chemically, the atomic siblings behaved just the same. Plants didn't distinguish between "hot" carbon-14 and "cold" carbon-12. But because their nuclei emitted the occasional low-energy particle as they decayed, these harmless, mildly radioactive atoms made perfect tracers. For the first time, scientists could track vital elements such as phosphorus and carbon, following them through every twist and turn they took through the guts of living cells.

Art Neish set up a lab to synthesize and use carbon-14 and other labelling materials in 1952, when few such substances were available. His work transformed plant chemistry, unravelling the mysteries of how plants grow and develop. It also brought the knowledge economy to Saskatoon. A partnership grew up among Dr. Neish's laboratory, Agriculture Canada, and the Universities of Saskatoon and Manitoba. Forty years ago, this nascent cluster took rapeseed and turned it into the low-fatty-acid, heart-friendly canola that is such a valuable crop today.

Today's farm income in the Saskatoon region exceeds $2 billion a year. To a large extent, that's based on Art Neish's work— and just as important, on his *approach* to work. So advanced has Saskatchewan become in the area of technology clusters that a senior official at NRC told me, "The best example for Alberta to emulate is the technology cluster in Saskatoon. That has the most to teach Alberta about what kinds of economic miracles technology clusters can achieve."

A twenty-first-century technology cluster is not an exercise in central planning, my contact adds. "It's not a top-down process by which the federal government, or even a troika of three governments, spends all the money and calls all the shots. Government is an enabler, nothing more. We provide basic knowledge, a geographical locale, start-up management skills, and part of the overall vision. We create a central seed around which a vigorous private sector can coalesce. The private sector then must supply capital, effort, and the most important ingredient of all, an entrepreneurial will to succeed."

Very fine, but very abstract; I need a good example. I find one in a Saskatoon firm called AgrEvo.

———————

AgrEvo Canada was formed as a joint venture between German pharmaceutical giants Hoechst and Schering. The Canadian company has niches in crop protection, environmental health, and seed and crop production, but its main work is in canola—more exactly, in what AgrEvo calls canola systems. These combine a proprietary weed killer with various canola hybrids that possess genetic resistance to it. From the ground up, the new crops are engineered to go with canola-friendly weed control.

Often a new hybrid can be produced by standard plant-breeding techniques and does not require sophisticated science. But now and then AgrEvo's scientists identify a gene from a plant that's too genetically remote from canola for traditional cross-breeding. At that point, biotech takes over and produces what is called a transgenic hybrid. This incorporates into canola one or more genes from another plant species.

AgrEvo has operations centres in several cities in Western Canada. In Saskatoon, seventy-five workers handle research, breeding, seed production, and quality control. The corporate head office in Regina employs 150. In Lethbridge, Alberta, eight full-time employees produce hybrid canola seed.

The manager of biotechnology research for AgrEvo Canada is Dr. Malcolm Devine. He tells me that his Saskatoon-based group "does basic work with DNA—getting it into the right shape and form before it goes into plants. My role is to ensure that every aspect of this runs well."

Plant genes have so many sources and roles that AgrEvo scientists must identify and sift them with great care. Some genes increase resistance to herbicides and plant diseases. Others boost tolerance to heat or cold. Still others help the plant resist drought.

Again, there's more to the knowledge economy than technical data. To catch AgrEvo's interest, a gene must show promise of bringing useful new properties to hybrid canola. It must also add value that farmers will appreciate, acknowledge, and pay good money for. Discovering and assessing such genes, then integrating them into seed, involves rigorous science. It also requires a market analysis that is no less rigorous. Does the problem addressed exist over large areas or is it limited to one corner of one province or state? Does it occur constantly or only every few years? Do farmers consider the problem a minor worry or a gnawing concern?

If a gene meeting these strict requirements turns up within a canola variety and can't be fixed into seed by natural crossing, or if the gene comes from a plant completely unrelated to canola, Malcolm Devine's team is called in. Their work is frustrating and fascinating—exact in technique, unpredictable in final outcome, and with immense potential. "We are trying," Malcolm says, "to modify the canola genome in a way that the plant itself cannot."

Resistance to herbicides, it turns out, may be *oligogenic*, involving one single gene. But some traits, such as resistance to disease and environmental stresses, may be too involved for single genes. These are *polygenic*, involving many genes that work together at different times and in complex, varying ways. Oligogenic mechanisms are shoot-from-the-hip responses that gamble on quick and total victory. Some plants, for example, respond to insect attack by secreting poisons. One tree even releases a hormone mimic. An hour after the bug dines, its gonads shrivel up. Both these plant responses are oligogenic.

By contrast, a polygenic mechanism is slow, subtle, and extremely difficult for a pest to counter, even over time. Interestingly enough, it seems to aim at peaceful coexistence. Oligogenic strategies scream, *Die, invader scum!* Polygenic ones murmur, *Come, let us reason together.* Put another way: say genetic responses were religions. Oligogenic is fundamentalist: certain of its rightness, full of brimstone and fire. Polygenic is bland, suave, worldly, and tolerant. Both strategies can succeed.

Even when a single, simple gene conferring, say, herbicide resistance is isolated and sequenced, Malcolm Devine and his co-workers have no assurance that it can be transgenically imported into canola with all beneficial functions intact. "At present, science has no way of making transgenic inserts at specific sites on a plant genome," he explains. "We can import it, but we cannot say where on the genome it may end up."

This is unfortunate, for genomic location may influence gene function along a gradient that goes from slight to total. It's the lesson of Chromos Molecular, back in B.C.: in the wrong spot, even a good gene can gum up the works.

"It can happen that what at first seems a perfectly straightforward transgenic transplant modifies an existing plant gene," Malcolm says. "The new DNA could land somewhere on the existing genome where it gets in way." The solution: Try the gene out. If it works, great. If it doesn't, back to the drawing board—or rather the lab bench. "We try again," says Malcolm. "On that same gene, or on another one."

A technique called PCR (for polymerase chain reaction, a way of multiplying tiny bits of DNA) lets bioscientists find specific sections of gene. This tells AgrEvo scientists which gene they're working with at all times.

While the scientific requirements for such activity are strict, pressures from legal and political regulation make things far stricter. The fact that canola oil is destined for human consumption adds an even higher level of regulatory scrutiny. "We must be sure what new genetic material is in all varieties we work with," Malcolm tells me. "Nothing else is acceptable."

His team keeps close control over all aspects of this process, from R&D through final seed production. "Our customers must have complete assurance that every seed sold among the billions they purchase has the gene or genes we specify, in the stipulated quantity and place," he says. "The amount and quality of oil derived from the seeds are especially important, since these affect the farmer's return on investment." All these pressures demand meticulous record keeping. Malcolm has a striking term for this work: "Quality control at the DNA level."

Knowledge, knowledge everywhere. Even on the land.

———————

Throughout the world, labs such as Malcolm Devine's have become a hot seat as debate rages about the values and risks of transgenic life. Issues include not only the safety of transgenic species for humans and the environment but also the deep ethical revulsion that many of us feel at the apparent unnaturalness of transgenic research.

In Europe, public antipathy toward GMOs, or genetically modified organisms, has resulted in across-the-board government bans. Canada has stopped short of such drastic action, but pressure from activists and consumers is mounting on federal and provincial governments. Even if legislators continue to accept scientific evidence that GMOs are not only harmless but beneficial, a rising public clamour may force them to give in.

These issues first began to emerge in 1984, when I co-edited a science magazine. We asked two illustrators, Heather Cooper and John Bianchi, to depict the GMO debate in a strong visual image. Both did so in memorable terms. Heather offered a caution. She painted a wonderfully realistic trout, sporting a pair of wonderfully realistic wings—vivid, fascinating, and very scary. John imagined a polar bear in a cold northern landscape, sniffing a big bright sunflower. This view is also vivid, but it's also full of hope. It reflects the promise of knowledge-based GMO crops that can thrive and nourish us anywhere.

Both illustrators were prescient, as good artists are. They neatly caught the two polarized attitudes that continue to dominate debate today. Opponents of transgenic research call GMO for human consumption *Frankenfood*. They view it as an outrage on nature. Even if GMO is harmless, they protest, we don't know that: we're assuming it. The burden of proof is on the biotechnologists to show their work is safe before they sell a grain of GMO seed. At bedrock, the activist attitude is neatly summarized by the last words of the fifties B-movie *I Was a Teenage Werewolf*: "It's not for man to interfere in the ways of God."

On the other side of the GMO debate are most of the scientists—I except David Suzuki, who seems firmly in the Frankenfood camp. We aren't engineering anything loathsome, the scientists protest. We have better ethics than that. We would not undertake this work if it had the slightest possibility of harming anyone. On the contrary, we help people increase crop yields. We grow less food for pests and more for humans. Consider what we've done in turning rapeseed into canola. Our work even cuts pesticide use.

What can we citizens make of this debate? Can we reconcile the irreconcilable? With no qualifications but broad knowledge and nerve, I'm going to try. The first thing I want to do is defuse the rhetoric. I call as my first witness Dr. W. J. Wagner, professor of education at Brock University in St. Catharines, Ontario, and a friend from college days.

Jim tells me about an experiment in which various people were shown an identical photo of an auto accident. Each was asked a slightly different question: "How fast were the cars going when they touched/bumped/smacked/crashed/smashed/totalled?"

As you can guess, the word variable in the question determined the response. The more emphatic the word of collision, the higher a subject's estimate of the autos' speed—on the evidence of one photograph, plus one verb. Conclusion: terms matter. Corollary: those who slag GMO with terms like Frankenfood not only announce their bias but also invite their listeners to share it. They mask the central fact about modern canola: that genetic modification has made an earlier food variety demonstrably, indisputably healthier.

The bio-activists have one good point. It could do no harm to label GMO as such. In the short term, labelling would support Canadians' right to an informed choice. And in a few years, such labelling might grow to be a distinction as coveted as an ISO certification is today. Good bioscience, conscientiously pursued and applied, need not fear the glare of scrutiny. The closer you examine responsible GMO, the better it appears. Bioscientists welcome honesty; it is their métier. They tell whoever asks what they do, how, why, and with what result. This very openness works against them in a public-relations war waged less by brains than by glands.

The trouble is that scientists may use common English words and still speak a different language. You and I see a brown cow. The scientist *detects a brownish quality in this side of that bovine-like animal.*

There are sound reasons for such precision. God is in the details, and those who detect and describe nature's subtlety must do so with high accuracy. And since scientists are trained to exactness, many of them consider simplifications and metaphors misleading. That very precision works against effective mass communication, for many scientists shrink from analogies and explanations. All this makes it hard to reassure Canadians who are uneasy or fearful about GMO. Strict scientific method can seem cold and unfeeling when you're concerned about your family's health.

I don't know who said it, but it's true: to find common ground, take the high ground. If scientists admit the public has real concerns and is not a brainless mob, and if the public listens closely to complex debates and keeps an open mind, we will reach consensus. Call me an optimistic fool, but I'm convinced it can be done. All we need to do is meet at the top.

I have reason for optimism. As this book goes to press, the European Community has announced its willingness to review its blanket ban on GMO. Within months, the EC might license AgriBus to produce and distribute GMO that's clearly labelled as such. A strong argument for this position comes from Canada, where GMO has been in foods such as potato chips for ten years and more, without a single documented case of ill effect. Once again, Canada's knowledge economy shows the way.

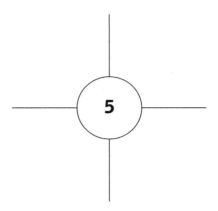

HEARTLAND:

THE REBIRTH OF ONTARIO

Via an informed imagination, the knowledge economy is visible at a distance—from an airplane, say. Still, it's easier to detect at ground level from a car. The drive south down King's Highway 6 to Hamilton, Ontario, provides hard evidence that the knowledge economy is not just a journalistic buzzword: it's real. Furthermore, it came just in time.

Things are happening in the Golden Horseshoe, the Canadian industrial heartland that wraps around the western end of Lake Ontario. This is our most densely populated area, holding more people than the rest of Canada from here to the Pacific.

Until the manufacturing slowdowns of the eighties and nineties, this was Canada's money vault. As late as 1985, the vast manufacturing sites that line Southern Ontario's boulevards and highways had spanking-new machinery parked in rows out front. Then came the hard times, and many of these manufacturing sites grew windswept and deserted.

Driving past them today, I find them renewed but changed. In the past, a typical roadside site had a single huge logo on a company office tower. That's gone, replaced by hundreds of small new companies with synthetic names—Virtek, Lotek, Unis Lumin. These are knowledge firms almost without exception. Some of them are Technology-Intensive Industrial Sector: they create, license, and sell new knowledge, living by their wits alone. Other firms, including a new breed of manufacturer, have transformed themselves into knowledge industries. They license or purchase IP, adapt it, and use it within their own facilities. A third class of firm updates and maintains knowledge-based services, helping its clients to enter the knowledge economy.

The new firms are not like the old ones they replace, or resemble them only superficially. Of course the knowledge economy is a human enterprise, and as human nature is a constant, old and new styles of business share fundamental traits. Greed, envy, pride, rage, malice, and to some extent lust, drive the knowledge economy just as they drove the old. Yet even here there is a critical difference: sloth. The old economy tolerated it, the knowledge economy does not. Most geeks set themselves on MAX and lock down the controls. The knowledge economy has no hidey-hole for the exhausted, the frantic, the fried of brain. The cellphone, rapidly adding the ability to transceive E-mail and facsimile as well as voice, makes the world an office. Even the golf course and fishing lodge, once kept as sanctuaries where ideas could flow and deals shape up, are on fast forward. New golf links forbid players to walk; they must take motorized carts, which double or triple the speed of play—the throughput, in accountants' terms. In ten years, people may ride rockets between tees. I'd rather deal with Alberta elk.

The remaining similarities are quickly listed. Old-style or new, companies still spring from an idea, start small, and grow. For initial financing, the founders remortgage their houses, cash in savings, and put other personal assets on the line. Fledgling firms lurch from one crisis to another, often changing their raison d'être several times. StressGen, for example, a Vancouver company incorporated to develop drugs based on a newly discovered family of cell proteins, stayed alive for its first ten years by selling run-of-the-mill laboratory reagents to other drug firms. Only after a decade did it get the money to pursue its original vision.

After several years of hand-to-mouth existence, surviving start-ups usually (not always) become publicly traded corporations listed on a recognized stock exchange. Initial floats are closely held by a handful of institutions and individuals, so that little stock changes hands: the firm is public in name, private in fact. At the end of its youth, the new company becomes a mature firm employing hundreds or thousands. Its stock is intensely traded and may swing wildly in value. The company hires or subcontracts procurement, product development, and sales. Ten years later, it is a grand old dowager among knowledge firms.

Here, however, similarities between old and new firms end. One cynic in a government ministry told me he could recognize a successful Canadian company because it was for sale. Indeed, many of Canada's new firms are devoured by bigger companies who lust for proprietary knowledge or, more crudely, for less competition. Yet nothing shows the vast gap between new and old firms so much as what happens post-buyout. Old-firm owners tend to acquire land and settle down as gentry. Their motto always has been "Get Rich and Get Out." A knowledge firm's founder views a buyout as a new beginning. Rich in cash, richer still in the more valuable coin of experience, he or she launches another start-up within months, sometimes within days. To the knowledge-economy addict, the cut and thrust of high-tech business is an amphetamine. This single fact will ensure Canada's robust economic performance well into the new century.

Despite the surface similarities, then, today's high-technology company is a thing apart. Are you over forty? All those business notions you have in your head, laboriously acquired over decades of work experience, are largely dross. Things aren't like that any more. Standard pyramidal organization charts are as dead as dodos.

Few employers or employees risk making lasting loyalties. Young people don't necessarily defer to old ones. Owners of high-tech firms are often younger than those they hire. People take turns reporting to one another, based on the project in hand. Team managers must often justify themselves to their own teams, like defendants before a jury. Employers hunt and woo employees, as well as the other way around.

One unforeseen benefit of the knowledge economy has been its impact on the old economy. Although mining, logging, manufacturing, and banking employ fewer people every year, and though investors dazzled by the knowledge sector consider long-standing stocks passé, some older firms have become almost indistinguishable from their upstart high-tech cousins. The influence extends to that traditional litmus test, knowledge creation. Ten years ago, new firms originated technology; old firms consumed it. This has changed. Increasingly, old-economy firms develop proprietary technology in-house. When they do, they may find their solutions to specific problems have applications so wide that they overshadow the user company's original purpose. In such ways as this, the knowledge economy remakes society in its own image. Economically and technologically, it is an exercise in self-reinvention: the child is father to the man.

Here comes Hamilton, whose mills the sportswriter Dick Beddoes once called "as lovely as acne." When I grew up here, the city had a standing joke. Whenever a visitor wrinkled his nose and asked what that sulphurous stink was, a local would tell him, "Money." And so it was. When my Grandfather Illsey was an executive of the Bank of Hamilton, his city was kid brother to Sandburg's Chicago. "Tool maker, stacker of wheat . . . Stormy, husky, brawling, City of the big shoulders." From the forties through the seventies, Hamilton embodied all the classic theories of economic geography. It was sixty kilometres from Toronto, a hundred from Buffalo, and three seconds' transmission time from the unlimited clean megawattage of Niagara Falls. It was an equidistant 560 kilometres from Montreal, Windsor, and Detroit. It had a fabulous harbour; it was a railway nexus. Two-hundred-fifty-metre lakers, made rapier-thin to slide through freshwater locks, brought in iron ore; kilometre-long trains unloaded coal. Hamilton put these raw materials together in its huge steel mills. Plates, bolts, and I-beams for the skyscrapers; nails for houses; galvanized eight-gauge sheet for metal roofs and kitchenware. Not for nothing did Hamilton style herself the Ambitious City. She wore her mill-stink like *L'Air du Temps.*

And then the deluge. Not since the Great Depression did a city suffer a downturn like Hamilton's in the 1980s. For every new business that opened, two others closed. The economy—the old economy—went into meltdown.

But this is twenty years later. Notice something? Hamilton Harbour isn't chemical green or sewage grey or runoff brown: it's bright clear blue. The steel mills are still there, and have even ramped up output, but their discharge is cleaner than before. Sulphur scrubbers, electrostatic precipitators, and other antipollution devices are doing their work, process-monitored by digital computer. For the first time in decades, Hamiltonians and their visitors can freely breathe their air and swim in their water again.

Now take a close look at the land along the harbour: it's cleaner too. Oil-soaked storage yards and sooty factories have given way to cycle paths and parks. A new kind of ecologist, the urban activist, has grown up here in the past two decades. These people don't favour flashy West Coast acts like chaining themselves to tree trunks; after all, this is sober, decorous Ontario. Instead, quietly and unobtrusively—and very effectively—they collect funds by public subscription, leverage them with grants from governments and private institutions, and snap up industrial land whose owners consider it almost worthless. It *is* worthless, to the old economy.

For offices and shops that trade in knowledge rather than in coal or steel, the land is a gold mine. It has been resurrected into parkland that lets knowledge workers run, walk, cycle, and sail.

The Hamilton Bay lands symbolize a triumph of faith that no area on Earth is totally irredeemable. Old-economy Hamilton was ambitious, yes, but in a blinkered way. Its civic boosterism, my city right or wrong, made parts of Hamilton as polluted as the Love Canal. The well-dressed urban activists in the Hamilton Region Conservation Association—guerrillas of the knowledge economy —restored many of these properties to graceful waterside parkland. They made the whole city more livable, and thus more valuable too. For paradoxically, it was precisely in its own sacred criterion of property value that boosterism failed. *Conservation* best generates wealth, material as well as spiritual. The get-rich-quick approach of generations of Hamilton governments had trashed property values and suppressed knowledge businesses and skilled immigration throughout the city. Now Hamilton is working again, but for the knowledge economy. The economy is dead; long live the economy.

Hamilton's enforced transformation to a knowledge economy has a close parallel. About the time the late-eighties depression hit Hamilton, the State of Oregon took a body blow to its forest industry, at that time the economic mainspring of the state. A U.S. appeal court upheld a ruling by the U.S. Environmental Protection Agency that further logging in federal forests would compromise the habitat of an endangered species, the spotted owl. Oregon's old economy reacted with astonishment and rage, but when all appeals failed and the decision proved final, the state turned to the knowledge economy to replace the old one. It had no choice. Twenty-five years later, Portland and Eugene are world centres for advanced IT. The knowledge economy employs more people, at higher salaries, than the forest industry did when it boomed.

So Hamilton. The city, it turned out, had more than manufacturing plants and steel mills. It had affordable housing, gracious and historic suburbs, and a fine small university. One young knowledge entrepreneur from Hamilton, fresh from school, started a company in his basement. He thought the future lay in open-source operating software rather than in the expensive proprietary systems sold by Microsoft, Apple, and IBM. He called his firm Red Hat. At last report it had paid-up capital of US$11 billion.

———————

One of my interviews in the Ambitious City takes place in the park-like campus of McMaster University. In its enormous Health Sciences Centre, Dr. Patricia Chang meets me and, over cafeteria coffee, tells me about her work.

Patricia and her team are investigating a novel form of therapy for a whole family of hereditary afflictions. These are called lysoso-mal storage diseases, or LSDs. Three dozen have been identified; together they affect three thousand people across Canada. LSDs include Tay-Sachs disease, which affects so many Israelis that tests for Tay-Sachs in Israel are routine for parents-to-be. Victims of other LSDs, if untreated, develop cloudy corneas and bone problems.

Chang *et al.* have found a way to deliver new, healthy genes into bodies afflicted by LSDs. The therapy is free of viral vectors—disembowelled natural viruses used by some gene therapists as gene-delivery trucks. Such vectors are not only troublesome to use; if they decide to act like viruses again they can be harmful or even lethal. To replace them, Patricia and her colleagues use MIIDs, or micro-immuno-isolation devices. These are synthetic containers, too tiny to be seen without a microscope, that are hypodermically injected into an LSD patient. Each MIID contains a single genetically engineered cell, designed to produce sub-stances that the patient's body cannot. The micro-capsules have tiny holes, allowing the life-giving molecules they produce to es-cape. But the exit holes are too small to admit the killer cells that the host's immune system dispatches against all invaders. Think of an MIID as a shark cage. In this way, enzymes and human growth hormone have successfully been produced in patients who cannot synthesize the compounds by themselves. Technically, the disease continues; symptomatically, it disappears. It's all thanks to synthetic factories hardly bigger than a single cell. It is through advanced knowledge such as Patricia Chang's that Hamilton has established a vigorous and growing diversity.

───────────

Hamilton to Toronto, along the Queen Elizabeth Way. I've driven this route so often I could do it blindfolded, with a seeing-eye dog to bark when I'm about to hit another car. Factories, service roads, concrete walls to screen the suburbs, the occasional tree. Here's a firm that makes shutters for windows. Of course these shutters aren't meant to shut; builders bolt them to a house as decorations. Modern glass can withstand rain, snow, frost, and hail. But up go the shutters in every new subdivision, as useless (in my father's phrase) as teats on a bull.

We respect earlier technology because it's beautiful, because it represents great achievement, because it defined and shaped us. Another, hidden reason is that lots of old things still exist. A surprising percentage of what we assume to be modern is in fact a remnant of the past.

A few years ago I was talking to my editor at the *Globe and Mail* when my eye fell on her Rolodex. Two things about this name-filing device struck me in quick succession. First, it was no longer based on file cards but on microchip electronics. Second, the new version needlessly featured the hand-turned cylinder that characterized the old form. "You have a skiamorph," I said.

Skiamorph: there's a word to win a Scrabble game. I got it from *The New Science of Materials*, a book I lent and sadly lost. Its author was an English engineer, eccentric in his opinions but flawless in his prose, and skiamorph (alt. *skeuomorph*) is Greek for "shadow form." My long-lost author used it to describe the unnecessary holdovers that show up when old knowledge gives way to new.

Twenty-six hundred years ago, when classical Greece began to build its temples from stone instead of wood, its masons continued to reproduce—in stone—architectural details from wooden structures. Today's tourist may spot the square heads of what look like wooden pegs and wedges protruding from the tops of marble columns.

Or consider a bridge that has little bumps at each end of its span. These are skiamorphic guardhouses. They are holdovers from the time when streams were territorial borders, and bridges over them needed houses for customs officials and soldiers. While the guardhouse shadows on modern bridges can be mere suggestions, a more exuberant architect may detail something out of eleventh-century Burgundy, down to its crenellations and arrow slits.

Since rediscovering the skiamorph, I have looked for other examples and found dozens. Take the item that triggered my memory, my *Globe* editor's Rolodex. The cylindrical silhouette of the original address file was an icon: countless yuppies came to link its knobs with wealth and power. When silicon-based IT permitted systems that were far more convenient and capacious than cardboard-based systems, the Rolodex designers responded with a skiamorph. Even their electronic models use hand-turned cylinders to scroll through names. This is not an engineering requirement: it is a marketing decision. In technical terms, a rocker switch would be better, or a PC with a search function. But that would eliminate the Success Cylinder. I'd bet a bottle of Scotch that nobody at Rolodex knows the word skiamorph; the company used it brilliantly, nonetheless.

To deserve its name, a skiamorph cannot be an operable, if old-fashioned, way of doing things. A fountain pen is not a skiamorph. The true skiamorph is as exuberantly needless as those bull teats.

Even the computer on which I write these words has a skiamorph or two. An L-shaped arrow on its ENTER key points left and down. This traces (in mirror image) the return movement of a manual typewriter platen, long since gone with the wind. (In fact, the ENTER key was once labelled RETURN.) And my keyboard does more than give me a stroke-confirming aural feedback when I hit a key: it goes *click-clack* like a 1925 Underwood. Who benefits from these things? Me, I suppose. I accept both skiamorphs subconsciously; they pitch to buried myths. Tackatacka-*ding! Rrrrip!* Get me Rewrite, honey!

Skiamorphs are born of human insecurity—a truth that the marketing department remembers, even as the engineering department is enraged by it. When new knowledge emerges, even when it is safe and useful, it remains mysterious to all but a handful of acolytes. Since the unknown is fearsome, users are reassured if new ways of doing things take on the trappings of the old. Think of the London taxi, the British phone booth, the cast-iron post box. Consider the nostalgic adulation showered on noisy, high-maintenance, high-pollution, low-efficiency steam trains. The root of the skiamorph is not mind but emotion. Any day now, someone's going to start a club called Friends of Linoleum.

Since snobbery fosters skiamorphs, fashion is a hotbed of the things, and long after technology loses function, it survives as ornament. The hole patterns on men's brogue shoes once drained water from gentlemen's boots when they went shooting on boggy ground. Wing chairs once deflected drafts in gloomy men's clubs. Today, few of us blast away at quail, and central heating has banished anything so ungentlemanly as a cold draft from our living rooms. But holes in shoes and wings on chairs remain.

Housing, another area where emotion triumphs over reason, is a rich source of skiamorphs. Excellent new materials such as aluminum, prefinished steel, and self-adhesive vinyl are too self-conscious to appear in their own guise and tart themselves up as wood grain. In Elizabethan England, the windows of great houses were big, labour-intensive to produce, and costly. To make them, bits of hand-blown glass were painstakingly stapled together with lead strips. These leaded panes, early examples of conspicuous consumption, became identified with the gentry. This preserved leading even when new knowledge gave us large, distortion-free picture windows. Plain float glass simply could not speak to people's gland-based concept of the House on the Hill. Hence the skiamorph of modern leaded glass—a web of expanded metal, glued to a seamless and optically perfect pane. It's technically stupid but emotionally understandable.

On automobiles, an S-shaped landau mark is visible in chrome on the roof pillars of upscale American cars. Now it's decoration; a hundred years ago it was a hinge that let the top fold back on carriages that originated in Landau, Germany. Yesterday's functional hinge is today's skiamorph, thanks to the marketing quirks of Detroit.

Finally, consider how cars and housing interact. The carriage-trade homes creeping into my own area have detached garages. This makes no sense in a wet climate like North Vancouver's: the sprint from garage to house gets you drenched. But real-estate agents have found that many customers harbour the unspoken notion that the toffs keep their horseless carriages in outbuildings. Indeed they do, but only because the structures used a century ago for the newly invented auto were usually converted stables. And stables were isolated from living quarters because of the noise, odour, and proximity of undesirables—not the horses, noble beasts that they were, but those lower-class grooms. In 1902, function; in 2002, skiamorph.

Skiamorphs form a fascinating back door to the knowledge economy. Spotting them in their subtler forms delights the mind and sharpens the eye. Like architecture, they are essays penned in material, edifying all who look.

Toronto. Too much to see or summarize in a single visit; no spe-
cialties; in the knowledge economy, lots of everything. Biotechnology, biopharmaceuticals, software, telecommunications software
and hardware, numerically controlled manufacturing. Three universities and probably more on the way. A firm that began as a
recycler and developed the world's most advanced inventory system; another firm that saves clients millions of dollars by shaving
seconds from TV production lines; still another that makes its
living from applied ethics. Each reveals a defining aspect of the
knowledge economy; unlike old-economy firms, knowledge companies constantly reinvent themselves.

Still, the heavy stuff can wait until tomorrow. As I've found I
must do continually throughout my voyage, I start my research
into this big new knowledge concentration by goofing off. I park
my car at the southern terminus of Yonge Street and join the Sunday crowds that stream toward the Island Ferry.

What a contrast to B.C.! No megatonne ships and onboard
transport trucks here; this ferry's just for people. It's built to human
scale, and I'm glad of it. So much of Canada seems designed to
make people feel like ants. Around me are laughing children, cry-
ing babies, spicy smells from picnic baskets, a babble of languages.
I asked a friend who'd worked in Japan for five years what he
missed most when he was away, and his answer surprised me. It's
the different hair colours, he said. In Asia, nearly everyone in every
crowd has black hair. Canadian heads make a rainbow. He saw this
in our school playgrounds; I see it on this little ship. A sudden
pride, no less fierce for being unexpected, wells in me as I think
what this country has created.

Toronto Island is as I left it, tranquil and relaxing. It's what
commercial theme parks try to be and never are: serene and real.
Compared with it, all the Fun Lands and Amusement Worlds are
a gimcrack pretence, like sad outdoor malls with tacky rides. I buy
ice cream, rent a bicycle, watch the boats race on the lake. A little

rhyme from Archibald MacLeish's play *J.B.* catches the mood perfectly: "Take the even with the odd, I would not stay here if I could: Except for the little green leaves in the wood, And the wind on the water . . ."

———————

Most of us treat corporations as things that do not change. Though individual workers may quit, the firm is immortal—at least in theory. But as the Canadian historian Michael Bliss shows us, corporations like species evolve or die. Look what happened to shipping companies when steam replaced sail, he says. Firms that saw themselves as owner-operators of sailing ships went under. Other firms, viewing their business not as sailing but as transportation, flourished. Rather than resisting new technical data, they embraced it—furthering what a modern analyst would call their core knowledge competency.

Though the Bliss Principle still holds true, the time frame over which it operates has vastly shortened. Some sailing companies took decades to atrophy; today's knowledge firms may have to perform and recover from radical surgery in less than a year. Sometimes a company perceives altering conditions in advance and moves smoothly to meet them. More often the change falls with no warning, and then and it's run or die.

Beyond a doubt, the knowledge economy's perfect instance of the self-transforming company is Mitel Corporation. Twenty years ago Mitel became a high-tech powerhouse. Though it has flagged since then, its founders having moved to other firms (Cowpland to Corel), Mitel is still a global force in high-speed switching for local-area telephone networks, or LANs.

Oddly enough, the firm was not high-tech at all when two transplanted Englishmen, Michael Cowpland and Terry Matthews, first created it. Its name betrays their first intent: Mitel stands for

Mike and Terry's Lawnmowers. The idea of servicing something more advanced than crabgrass came after the company's principals spent some time together at Bell-Northern Research, a precursor of today's Nortel Networks.

> If any newer firm stands comparison with Mitel's changeover, it's Games Traders of Brampton, Ontario. Again, the firm's name reveals its owners' initial plans: Games Traders began as a recycler for the low end of the games industry.

Computer gamers, like all addicts, continually crave new sensations, and their lust for the new creates enormous sales. In 2000 the total economic activity for TV and computer games exceeded that of all motion picture sales worldwide. Behind this staggering fact lies a related statistic. Each new game creates a mound of not-quite-new apparatus: consoles, joysticks, hand-held controller pads, steering wheels, and software cartridges. Games Traders emerged when some Canadian entrepreneurs saw an opportunity in this.

At its start-up in 1993, GT did nothing more than collect and re-sell cast-off gaming items at low, low prices. It cleaned, tested, and refurbished its remaindered items, repackaged them with short-term guarantees, and sold them to downscale retailers. The items then moved to the all-but-cashless addicts who infest the bottom rung of gaming. It wasn't much, but for Games Traders, it was a living.

Then the change began. In 1997 senior staff at Games Traders led a management buyout of the firm. They raised $12 million, paid the vendor $8 million, and obtained $1 million in inventory. More important, they also got a customer list.

Why an MBO? "The firm had a good idea but was suffering," says Peter Kozicz, Games Traders' CEO and one of the buyout group. Peter doesn't say what the firm suffered from; I suspect it was a case of timid management. Within a year, GT had reworked its relationships with retailers and transformed itself.

Peter's team visualized GT in a new way. No longer need it be only a junk man. Instead it could be part of the "interactive enter-tainment industry," as gaming now calls itself. Rags and bones was about to become riches.

In May 1998, funded by Yorkton Securities, GT effected a re-verse takeover of a shell company on the Toronto Stock Exchange. This gave GT what it needed most: shareholders, a TSE listing, and $10 million in cash to fuel its expansion plans. Eleven months later—things often move quickly in the knowledge economy, for good or ill—GT raised an additional $14.5 million; five months after that, another $21 million. At the second tranche the stock listed at 90 cents. At the third, share price had more than quintu-pled to $4.52. It has now subsided somewhat, partly through profit taking, but at the time of my interview still hovered around $3. GT now has its sights on NASDAQ, the U.S. automated quotation system that's the Holy Grail for the knowledge economy. NASDAQ specializes in knowledge firms that are small cap, i.e., with little business capital, defined as the number of outstanding shares times the price per share. A typical cap range for NASDAQ is US$200 mil-lion to US$2 billion.

Games Traders is a widely held stock. In addition to its own management and 2500 private individuals (whom GT calls "retail shareholders"), small-cap mutual funds and other institutions hold 25 to 30 per cent of the total issue. Why the interest? I be-lieve it's because GT differs from many dot-com floats. Its share activity stems from real plans, decisions, and accomplishments: its stock reflects its product, and its product is not its stock. GT knows what a fly-by-night dot-com doesn't: an IPO is not a business plan.

GT plans to diversify through acquisition, a strategy adopted by giants such as Nortel as well as by many successful small-cap firms. One of GT's first acquisitions was a U.S. company called Mad-Catz, which designs game hardware such as joysticks and consoles. Under the umbrella of GTR Group, MadCatz became a wholly owned subsidiary of GT.

Now, step back from the details, and see what's happened. In thirty months GT moved from salvaging old components (which were knowledge-intensive, but in yesterday's technology) and began creating new ones. The firm left a re-world—repackaging, reselling, refurbishing, remaindering—to design and make what experts call the best race-wheel console in E-games today. The MC2 wheel console opened as OEM for two big names in gaming: Sony PlayStation and Sega Dreamcast. (OEM, or original equipment manufacture, refers to a subcontractor who supplies part or all of a new product sold under a better-known name. Cummins supplies OEM diesel engines for GM and Dodge; Magna's OEM car parts go to all the Big Three.) Even after Sega's decision in mid-2001 to shut down game-hardware sales, the MC2 remained on Sony's OEM list.

GT designed the MC2 in consultation with engineers from Sega and its own MadCatz division. In 2000 *Gaming* magazine rated GT's new hardware "the best wheel console ever developed for home consumption." The wheel retails for US$40, and has been endorsed by the famous race driver Mario Andretti. GT's initial production run was twenty thousand units.

GT's self-transformation has widened its assets from material inventory to intellectual property. It has the same corporate name and many of the same personnel, but the firm is a bit like a kid's pyjama bag—zip, invert, and one animal turns into another. This is an extraordinarily difficult thing to bring about, but Peter Kozicz and colleagues proved they could do it.

Next in GT's pipeline is a wireless console, operating on 900 MHZ radio frequency, or RF. It will eliminate connecting wires and permit play from anywhere within the room. "Wireless has been around for ages," Peter Kozicz says. "But it's based on infrared, which requires an unbroken line of sight. With RF, your game won't crash if your little brother runs in front of the screen."

The challenges to GT in moving from a rags-and-bones reseller to OEM production are enormous. With each piece of new equipment, GT must adapt to the engineering design protocols that its games-company partner has established for compatible hardware. This is no small matter, for modern games consoles are so complex that they are really little supercomputers. Some new consoles can support simultaneous play by up to eight separate controllers. In 2000 Japan briefly held up export of its Sony PlayStation II because it suspected the console had the computational power to control a guided missile.

To preserve corporate security, GT and its big-name clients work separately. Each produces a module that talks to other modules through a standard interface.

"It's like having two people to launch a nuclear strike," Peter says. "Each holds a separate key, and both must use the keys together." Via MadCatz, GT develops its new hardware to the 85 per cent level. The remaining 15 per cent of development, and all manufacture, take place in Hong Kong. Ensuring all the modules function when they finally hook up involves great gouts of the most expensive thing in the knowledge economy: the time of expert personnel. But GT gladly pays its prima donnas their astronomical hourly rates; it knows they're worth it.

"MadCatz has some of the grand old men of gaming," Peter says. "They're not really *old*, but they've been around for years. They're critical to our future."

Given its sector's speed and complexity, how does Games Traders advertise? "We don't have to," Peter says. "We sell nine million units a year by word of mouth alone. If you make great hardware, games publishers will seek you out." When they do, GT eases the process by generating "middleware," which meshes its own hardware and software with those of any games publisher.

Seventy per cent of GT's sales are to the U.S. Thirty per cent go to Australia, New Zealand, Europe, and South America. For Canada that leaves, let's see . . .

"Nothing," Peter admits. "We have negligible sales in our own backyard." Though GT has proven strong in funding, technical acumen, and business savvy, it lacks what its main competitor has: a Canadian distribution network. Any plans to address that? Enigmatic smile: "Let's say it's an option."

Like its poor siblings the dot-coms, GT pins its strategy to the Internet. But with substantial material achievement behind it, GT is not one more dot-com dangling hope and greed instead of ideas, or stock instead of product.

"We think direct on-line retail will be very big in interactive," Peter tells me. "We see that being followed by widespread downloading of software via the Net and ultimately by game playing over the Net in real time. We've positioned ourselves to benefit from all of that." While on-line gaming is now "limited to a cult," he says, GT is banking that the approach will steadily broaden. "People will get used to the idea of instant upgrades, or of going head-to-head with the best games players in the world."

GT has boosted its retail sales by piggybacking on its customers' Web sites. The firm often sets up what's called a portal, an icon on a big-name client site that instantly transfers someone to GT's server farm—an air-conditioned room outside Toronto, near Highway 407. Portal operation, Peter tells me, is "as smooth as silk. Our add-ons are completely invisible." He adds: "What makes the red ink in most E-firms is their cost of customer acquisition, and our CCA is rock bottom. Piggybacking on a client Web site gives us the added benefit of not competing head-to-head with our own customers. They get a percentage of all our portal sales." Has this worked? "Put it this way. If we listed our portal network as a separate Web site, it would be the twenty-fifth busiest home page on the planet."

Now comes what is, for me at any rate, the most fascinating part of GT's self-reinvention. To support its retail portals, GT needed an efficient system for sales and inventory control. None existed, so GT developed its own. In this it was so successful that it may have blundered into something ten times bigger than everything it's handled to date. As always in the knowledge economy, serendipity rules: the tail wags the dog.

"The consumer at the customer Web site gets real-time data," Peter explains. "The instant he uses his mouse to drag an item over to his shopping-cart icon, that item is removed from our inventory. There's no possibility of what he wants being back-ordered: an actual item is immediately reserved for him. The system then prints a shipping label, assuring the customer of immediate delivery. Every time GT makes a sale in this way, it also improves customer loyalty and achieves instant low-cost inventory control.

"It's almost scary," Peter says, loosening his tie and sipping black coffee. "We've barked our shins on the commercial possibilities of this thing. It works like a charm, it saves vast amounts, it pleases the customers, and there's nothing like it anywhere. Do we go with it in a big way? I mean, do we become software engineers and flog it everywhere? We've already changed this firm six ways from Sunday. But the worldwide market for this inventory-management product may be billions of dollars yearly."

Pause; sip. "We have to make some decisions, and fast."

The picture element of a standard TV is a CRT, or cathode-ray tube. Inside it, a jet of high-voltage electrons hits phosphors on the inside of a glass screen, making them glow. If the jet is strong, the screen glows brightly where it hits. If the jet weakens, the phosphors fade to black. Magnets move the electron jet hither and yon, so that it tirelessly sweeps every pixel (picture element) on the screen one after another. The jet repeats its journey twenty-five times a second—the frequency of the conscious scan by which the human brain samples reality. TV's swift succession of still pictures shows us a slightly different view each time we look, thereby fooling us into thinking we see smooth motion.

So total a fib demands vast technical support. In hardware, microchips and larger-scale electronics must work together seamlessly. Phosphor layers must be deposited within thickness constraints of a few microns; the optical-quality lead glass that fronts the picture tube must be without flaw. TV may be a cultural Neanderthal, but its technology is as elegant as ballet.

A Canadian firm that benefits from the planetary TV obsession is IPS of Markham, Ontario (the letters stand for Image Processing Systems). IPS is on Fast Fifty, a list of rapidly expanding knowledge firms compiled by the management consultants Deloitte & Touche. They have good reason to highlight IPS.

IPS markets several applications of its core competency: the fast, precise, automatic inspection of video display systems. IPS saves its customers large amounts of money by letting them test glass-based components ranging from TV and computer screens to auto glass. It's a niche in which IPS leads the world, so that 95 per cent of its production is exported. This small firm from Markham is an indispensable ally of giant hardware manufacturers such as Philips and Hitachi.

IPS president Ken Wawrew says that electronic vision technology, his firm's knowledge expertise, "is a tough, complex business. Optics, illumination, hardware, software—we need them all." Though technology usually applies what science discovers, IPS can't wait for academe to find out what it needs to know. The firm pushes the envelope of science through its own R&D program.

IPS stands to make major gains with the imminent pan-industry switch to high-definition television, or HDTV. For the consumer, HDTV means bigger screens, with an aspect ratio—the proportion of width to height—changing from today's 4:3 (almost square) to 16:9 (rectangular or landscape format). This will mean a convergence in film and TV images. No disclaimers that motion pictures have been modified to fit, no black-stripe sandwiches. Nearly every image will be letterbox.

The changeover to HDTV means millions of new TV picture tubes, all requiring custom-configured inspection systems. That creates a big opportunity for IPS. "HDTV has given the entire display sector a big shot in the arm," Ken tells me as we walk around the IPS factory floor. "HDTV could dominate the video industry for the next twenty years. It could be as significant as the recent shift in audio from vinyl to CD." IPS, he says, is already gearing up for the change: in lockstep with its customers, the "little supplier that could" is reinventing itself.

An IPS inspection system, Wawrew explains, analyzes every TV display tube that comes off a production line. The analysis must be done in real time: bottlenecks are not an option. The word *bottleneck*, in fact, reminds him of another part of his company's self-reinvention. In 1995 IPS adapted its image-analysis technology to inspect empty beer bottles. This IPS system examines every item on a brewery line whose bottles rush by at speeds up to fifty kilometres an hour. The IPS system has forty milliseconds, literally an eye-blink, to scan each bottle. In this time it must determine if, after fifteen to twenty fillings, washings, and shippings, any glass threads are starting to splinter or crack.

"Not only do the bottles move fast," says Ken, "but they also vibrate like crazy. This was a real challenge." In meeting it, IPS has gone beyond inspection systems to achieve something like machine intelligence.

For the phosphor component of CRTs, a typical IPS test system generates and analyzes images that reveal a tube's hidden quality. Does its electron beam hit every phosphor dead centre, a quality known in the trade as purity? Are there red shadows behind the straight lines, a defect called misconvergence? Both for IPS and its clients, there's a lot of money in answering such questions. Reducing inspection time for a completed CRT unit by one second may save a big plant US$2 million a year. In 1998–99, IPS sold eighty purity and convergence test units. New equipment is normally approved by a customer's accountants if it achieves payback within two years. An IPS unit may repay its installed cost in less than a year.

Interestingly, IPS's strongest customers are the big Asian electronics firms that ten years ago defined the state of the art in R&D—Hitachi, Panasonic, Samsung, Sony, Toshiba. A decade of recession cut these firms' R&D budgets so deeply that they now line up to buy state-of-the-art knowledge from Canada.

What's in the works? IPS wants to grow, Ken says, but not through acquisition. The firm will add clients as it has to date, by diversifying within existing markets. It will extend its core competencies into related areas—automated inspection of auto glass and unpolished CRT faceplates, for example—only if this is possible with relative ease. Ken explains what this might involve. "The auto-glass industry generates US$10–15 billion a year. Addressing even a small part of its total inspection requirements would increase our revenues significantly."

Finding otherwise invisible defects in glass is best done early, he says. Otherwise, the defective units undergo additional processes such as etching, cutting, and polishing. These are meant to add value, but if they are performed on a defective blank they are wasted effort. IPS systems cull rejects early on.

Other options for IPS diversification include rapid inspection of the new flat-panel and HDTV displays. Here the company may go beyond its chosen niche of parts inspection and OEM the new-generation display systems that its customers are currently designing. "Clients come back to us for their new products," Ken tells me. "That pares our marketing costs."

When I talked to him, Ken Wawrew had been at IPS's helm two years and was optimistic, even euphoric. "IPS is sitting on a key technology, an 'enabling technology,'" he told me. "You can't automate most industrial processes without the kind of sophisticated vision system that IPS provides. We're shooting for 30 per cent annual growth for the next few years. But growth may not be something we can restrain."

Thirty kilometres southwest of IPS, across the smoke and pavement of Greater Toronto, a third young knowledge company is reinventing itself. Unis Lumin occupies a small one-storey building in Oakville, Ontario.

At the time of our interview Mauro Lollo, Unis Lumin's chief technology officer and partner, had just turned thirty-six. Yet this personable, good-humoured youngster is Canada's elder statesman of the Internet's commercial infrastructure. When few people owned computers, and those who had them did little else but bash out text and crunch financials, Marco visualized a future highly interconnected world of E-commerce. He then spent the next twelve years working to realize his goal.

In 1990 Mauro was a survivor of a failed firm that had specialized in data communications. When mismanagement put his employer under, Marco sat at his basement desk and wondered, What do I need to be successful? How can I do better than before? He drafted "the most rudimentary business plan you've ever seen." Then he and his partner, John Breakey, began calling their previous company's customers for work.

Since 1990 Unis Lumin has grown steadily at 50 per cent yearly and today bills in the $20 million range. Even this breakneck pace, Mauro says, is sustainable only because he stomps hard on the brakes. "We have deliberately limited ourselves to baby steps," he says. Without serious anti-growth measures, Unis Lumin would take off like a ballistic missile, landing God knows where.

Unis Lumin's niche is creating and managing data-communications systems. In 2000 the firm added a division that provides software solutions for E-business. Core clientele includes schools and hospitals that have been merged by governments eager to cut costs. Unis Lumin prides itself on having cushioned the blow of many of these forced mergers, making its clients more efficient and economical and giving them closer integration and higher morale. Ideally, this fuses dispersed nodes into single entities, giving the *clients'* clients better service. As Mauro puts it, "We don't really work for the hospitals. We work for the patients."

The company's growth strategy was, first, to "meet the numbers," achieving target billings, net revenues, and return on investment. If the numbers were met—and they were, except when Unis Lumin surpassed them—Marco then did something that would have horrified every old-economy executive: he treated his employees like gold. At a time when many CEO's reified workers into "workforce" and regarded them as necessary evils, Mauro saw that his company *was* its people and managed accordingly. He trusted people but held them accountable for performance. The result: very low employee turnover.

Headhunters sometimes ask Mauro what he does to retain his staff. "They've told me it's difficult if not impossible to hire our people away," he says. "They can't poach, tempt, or dislodge anybody. But I have no magic formula. I use only respect and common sense." No magic, true, but far from universal—even in the knowledge economy, even now.

"We used employee-management tactics that were different but effective," Mauro says. Until his firm grew too large, for example, the partners recognized extraordinary work by chartering a plane, keeping a skeleton staff (including the partners) at home to mind the office, and sending all available employees away for a week to the Bahamas. Today everyone at Unis Lumin, from CEO to receptionist, is eligible for performance-based bonuses.

"There's no way you can control a firm from the front end, by making rules and penalties," Mauro explains. "You have to do it from the opposite end, by gaining people's enthusiasm. We try to hold turnover to the absolute minimum required to import fresh blood. That creates and sustains an atmosphere where people really want to stay."

Share price doesn't matter in Mauro's managerial calculations: Unis Lumin is privately held. "We're doing due diligence now, but we're not rushing into an IPO," he explains. "We won't go public until we know how to avoid being controlled by people who look not at the long-term qualities of our company but only at the quarterly numbers."

Parasites, Henry Ford called such shareholders, as he bought back his stock and returned Ford Motor Company to private status. "There's a lesson here for many dot-coms," Mauro comments, smiling. "At least those that have survived."

Because of its stringent approach to growth and financing, after ten years of operation Unis Lumin doesn't owe anyone a cent. At a time when the number-one activity of many companies is scoring the next hit of external capital, Unis Lumin pays its own way—and always has. Isn't a debt-free firm a rarity in today's deficit economy? Yes, Mauro says: and so is good old-fashioned service.

"A lot of new dot-coms and knowledge companies don't show much concern for filling needs and satisfying customers," he says. "To them that's old-fashioned. They'd rather run up their share price and F off." Marco mouths the F-word, too homeboy polite to speak it out loud.

One of the ways Marco and his colleague, CEO John Breakey, have kept their growth manageable is through partnerships. Where an old-economy firm prides itself on its expansion, acquiring new buildings and filling them with new hires, Unis Lumin has rolled out its products coast to coast by networking with local firms. In this way Lollo and Breakey have conquered geography, that bane of Canadian business, while avoiding the high fixed overhead of a central HQ.

"We can expand our reach without being overly greedy in capital, personnel, or client fees," Mauro explains. "We look for firms with strengths and skill sets that are complementary to ours. We rely on their expertise in technology and their familiarity with local clients. That puts the necessary knowledge right next to the customer."

Mauro sees big corporations typically restrict their best people to head office or at most a few core locations. But partnering, the way Unis Lumin does it, "delivers services and skills everywhere.

There are no 'edges' or 'frontiers' in the sense of outlying areas far from expertise."

Does this work? Mauro shrugs when I ask him, as if the answer is obvious. "It's easier to keep an existing customer than to find another one. That's elementary marketing. If you remain in touch with your clients, they will stay loyal. If you're not in touch with your clients and their needs, you'll get into trouble fast." The proof comes in one key fact: Unis Lumin still has its first client.

At the same time, Mauro cautions, "It's easy to keep your head too far down"—that is, to focus on your customers to the exclusion of all else. "You have to pay attention to your own people and to the bottom line. Otherwise, there are problems in morale or in financial health. Whether you're in IT, biotech, or something else, there must be a balance between internal and external issues."

Any final comments on his success?

Mauro gazes out the window at the traffic buzzing by. "Not too many companies are nimble and enormous," he says. "We're nimble and small; we try to use our size to our advantage. From the start, we went head-to-head with large firms and took work away from them.

"A while back, I heard a rumour that IBM had formed a review committee to examine why they lost bids to us. The committee had more members than Unis Lumin's total workforce at the time."

The Prototype: Fifth Attribute

Think big, act small
Avoid debt—stay lean
Control growth—grow via partnerships
TREAT YOUR PEOPLE WELL

I used to go fishing with a friend whose middle initial was E. Whenever anyone asked him what it stood for, he would look solemn and say, "Ediot." A similar explanation lies behind some modern terms, particularly in E-business. Here, the prefix stands for Ediot Claims and Ediot Expectations.

E-bus is not the groundbreaking departure that its converts claim it is. Don't be fooled when millennialists say E-bus will revolutionize all transactions, leaving other methods in the dust. It hasn't happened yet and may not happen at all. Besides, at least for retail, E-bus isn't revolutionary at all. It's merely the latest example of a historical process that's been around for decades.

Electronic fund transfer? People have been wiring cash by telegraph for a century and a half. Retail E-shopping, then: surely that's novel? Not at all. Fifty years ago, my grandmother could lift her rotary-dial phone and call in orders to a grocery store five kilometres away. Nor are cash and service incentives to loyal customers very new. Grandma's store delivered free of charge and often threw in an extra loaf of bread or pound of bananas. How about leveraging operating capital via consumer debt purchasing? Mrmph, old hat. Stores in the 1940s routinely gave credit and sent monthly invoices. Records were kept by hand, using file cards and pencils, but overall the system worked like a charm.

Today's E-systems for goods purchase and delivery are seldom more advanced. More often they're attempts to reintroduce what existed widely throughout North America decades ago. From 1955 through 1959, for example, I did my Christmas shopping by phoning in COD orders to department stores. The stores delivered via truck within five days, and I paid the delivery man by personal cheque. This antiquated process got goods out faster than amazon.com. Its human phone operators guided a nine-year-old through the process of ordering, without any of the security risks associated with tossing credit-card data into the void. Best of all, this ancient variety of E-retail had constant cross-checking. Operators confirmed each item number, code number, and page number and correlated these with the catalogue's extensive qualitative descriptions. This guaranteed accurate ordering. Purchasers also had a bulletproof backstop from the vendor: Goods Satisfactory or Money Refunded.

Hence what's happening now is not Miranda's brave new world, but a concerted effort to recapture what we once had. Today's E-bus uses digital systems to replace high-priced labour that made functions such as order taking no longer cost-effective for humans. Nor is retail the only sector to suffer such retrenchment. Over the same period and for the same reasons, the traffic cop gave way to that first example of industrial robotics, the stoplight.

But while the innovation represented by E-retail is minimal, E-bus has another area whose potential impact is far greater: B2B, or computer-mediated business-to-business commerce. Here, for once in IT, reality exceeds hype. E-retail boasts a high number of start-ups, but deduct subsequent failures and the continued operation of loss-leader Web sites, and its stats are less impressive. By contrast, B2B is surging ahead to embrace entire sectors such as auto parts and government contracting. So great is the rush that federal regulators worry about B2B's possibilities for price-fixing, collusion, and other trust-like activity. Not to worry: since B2B is the tool of choice for a monopolist trying to curtail fair trade, it operates beneath a governmental magnifying glass.

In late 2000 the American Department of Commerce estimated that with present rates of growth, B2B in the continental U.S. will move goods of greater value by 2010 than all retail trade, electronic or traditional. A fair appraisal of so surprising a prediction requires an expert, preferably a cautious one. John Breakey, Unis Lumin's CEO and head of its new E-business division, says his initial aim is to help clients interact better with their own customers and partners. But, he emphasizes, "We're about business, not electronics. The electronic technology is just another tool of business—a means to an end."

Unis Lumin's product is to help its customers leverage their businesses onto the Internet. "These are existing businesses, not things specifically created for the Net," John says. Adds Mauro Lollo, "We're targeting real companies—ones that have revenue, customers, and a viable future. The rest of the B2B marketplace, and by that I mean the smaller dot-coms, can't defy the laws of good business practice forever."

It seems a sound enough strategy, for established businesses are no longer transfixed by the dot-com phenomenon like birds before a snake. When pundits said the dot-coms would devour old-economy retail, they coined the contemptuous phrase *bricks and mortar*. That dismissed established retailers as mere takeover prey. Bricks and mortar evoked images of a sector chained to its physical plant, musclebound by its own huge inventories. But in the past eighteen months, even the most rabid of the dot-com E-men have had to admit that the materials they sell still originate in factories that are not virtual, but made of—guess what—bricks and mortar. At the same time, the older firms reawoke to their own neglected clout. Some unknown genius then coined a term for an established firm that neither stands mesmerized before E-business nor disdains it, but profits from it as it would from any business option. The savvy old firms with the new attitude call themselves—I love this—*clicks and bricks*.

While E-retail's trend is toward clicks and bricks, Mauro says, B2B will rule in bulk and wholesale. And of the two subsectors, B2B is fast becoming the more important by far.

Unis Lumin develops B2B clients in a surprising way: they minimize or even eliminate all talk of technology. "The best technology in the world won't help you if your business fundamentals are suspect," John tells me. "The clients don't need to concern themselves with technology. In fact, they shouldn't. That's our job."

John and Mauro are convinced that from now on, key B2B Web sites within certain sectors will be encrypted, restricted, and accessible only to a privileged audience. Auto manufacturers, for example, might save billions of dollars yearly by exchanging information on parts designs, specifications, and uses within secure B2B environments. A pre-screened group of suppliers could also bid on job lots using a standard format. Farewell forever the sealed envelope.

Not surprisingly, one aim of B2B is perfect functional transparency—like the Web site portals devised by Games Traders. A subcontractor who uses one of the new B2B sites need know nothing of the technology behind it. At this point, B2B technology will have exceeded a complexity threshold and, paradoxically, become far simpler to use and exploit.

Perhaps a fifth of Canadian businesses, Mauro says, have the money to buy state-of-the-art technological solutions outright. Some firms from whom they acquire their technology are similarly rich. "That still leaves the vast majority of companies, and that's our market," says Mauro. "These firms want a reliable, low-cost solution that works the first time. As we see it, successful B2B requires clarity, dependability, and real benefits to the client."

Unis Lumin's main difficulty, say its partners, is in convincing the small to medium size businesses who are its principal targets that advanced B2B knowledge can work.

"Often these people are fearful, uninformed, and suspicious of new technology," John Breakey says. "Strangely enough, this can happen even if our clients are in knowledge businesses themselves."

———

Newmarket, Ontario, is a pretty little town that's fast becoming a city. My early-morning run goes past Fairy Lake, where sleepy ducks float on glassy water. Downstream is Holland Marsh, twenty-five square kilometres of rich black bottomland that feeds half of Southern Ontario. But farmland isn't the main source of Newmarket's recent prosperity: that comes from the area's crop of new knowledge industries.

Games Traders, IPS, and Unis Lumin all belong to a type of knowledge company that has transformed itself. This morning I interview a company that's gone one step further—transforming an entire academic discipline and creating a lucrative business niche for itself in the process.

Lotek Engineering makes wireless telemetry systems for wildlife biologists. This sophisticated technology, called state-of-the-art RF data transponsion, replaces binoculars as a field observer's main professional tool. Lotek's new knowledge is part of a discipline called biotelemetry—gathering information on animal movement, behaviour, and physiology so non-invasively, and at such great distances, that the animals behave exactly as they would if unobserved. Now scientists can track their quarry automatically, day and night. Even better, what they find will be honest-to-God behaviour, not desperate flight from bothersome guys with binoculars.

Take elephants. You can't believe the reality of elephants until you've seen them for yourself—or more accurately, not seen them. In 1985 my wife visited her father, a road engineer, in West Africa. On a road trip four hundred kilometres north of Accra, their driver flushed a herd of elephants in the dry savannah. The elephants, aware of approaching humans, entered a small copse of deciduous trees. Then, amazingly, they disappeared.

It was spooky, my wife said. Twelve or fifteen enormous mammals, with a total weight of fifty tonnes or so, vanished. Not only were they invisible the instant they entered the copse, but they were inaudible as well. The herd remained as silent as spectres.

My wife endured a lot of ridicule for her report. Years afterwards, my daughter would hold a thin pencil in front of a large wooden elephant sculpture and ask her brother, "What do you see?" Whereupon my son would say, "Why, the elephant . . . has . . . *vanished!*"

Family kidding aside, my wife's report was dead accurate. Elephants are masters of concealment: they can shimmer out of existence like P. G. Wodehouse's mythical butler Jeeves. It explains the kids' joke, How do you know an elephant's been in your fridge? Answer: tracks in the butter. When they want to be, elephants are dancers. They have an incredible delicacy of movement.

For millions of years, elephants' ability to hide protected them; now things are reversed. Science needs to know exactly where elephants are, all the time, in order to preserve them. It's all due to Earth's too-successful species—*H. sapiens*, us. Human settlement is increasingly denying elephants a place to forage, mate, or hide. A hundred fifty years ago, wrote one explorer, Africa was a few islands of people in a sea of elephants. Today the continent is a few elephant islands in a human sea. It's not merely the resident humans that are the problem; it's the tourists who come from all over the world to see something that, paradoxically, their very numbers then disturb. The population squeeze on elephants—pressure not from their own numbers but ours—is steadily worsening.

Here's an example. Within the Dzanga-Sangha National Park in the Central African Republic, halfway between Cameroon and the Democratic Republic of Congo, field scientists of the Wildlife Conservation Society are studying African forest elephants. This is a distinct subspecies. Males have shorter tusks, adapted to restricted forest pathways; females are smaller than their savannah-dwelling cousins. But other than this, little is known about forest elephants. What do they eat? What are their mating habits? Exactly where within their huge, poorly mapped territory do they live? It's all unknown. Yet if the forest elephant is to be protected and reestablished, scientists must get answers while there is still time.

The WCS team examining forest elephants includes the animal biologist Dr. William Karesh, an internationally renowned ethologist and wildlife veterinarian. Bill Karesh wants to unearth the movement patterns of forest elephants. If he can discover the animals' habitat and map their movements through it, he believes, all else will fall into place—how to protect from poachers, how to safeguard breeding.

Fine in theory, but in practice, how? Elephants, even en masse, blend into their environment so well that the most acute human trackers may detect them only sporadically. Though Bill Karesh has stalked elephants for more than fifteen years, he is still astonished at how silently and quickly elephants move when they want to. Bill often learns after the fact that he came within metres of an elephant herd without seeing or hearing anything but forest. Whichever elephant detects him first alerts its fellows using a medium that humans used to think was our invention: ULF, or ultra-low-frequency sound. Since 1982 the U.S. Navy has spent billions of dollars establishing a global network of ULF audio stations to let its nuclear submarines communicate with one another and with the shore. But elephants constantly talk to one another below humans' threshold of hearing; they were ULF experts before our ancestors walked on two legs. No wonder elephants could avoid us whenever they wanted: technologically, they were more advanced.

Lotek's new knowledge gives humans the advantage in the ancient game of hide-and-seek. Despite its name, Lotek is the highest of high tech. The company takes its title from Jim Lotimer, who established the firm in 1984. Lotek leads the world in biotelemetry. It equips wild animals with custom-designed radio transmitters, then monitors their movement via remote sensing.

From a biologist's viewpoint, an elephant's size has drawbacks and advantages. On the minus side, it's amazingly hard to track, find, and immobilize. Once this is done, however, the elephant will hardly be bothered by a five-kilogram RF device that's large enough to have powerful batteries and long-range antennae. To it, the telemetry equipment is lighter than a feather.

The Lotek elephant system is a tough collar that holds batteries and a transmitter. It also has an aerial that senses global positioning data, broadcast by a planetary network of GPS satellites. Although the elephant collar is loose enough to rotate around the elephant's neck, the aerial stays atop the elephant's neck, counterbalanced by the battery-circuitry pack beneath; otherwise, the elephant's vast bulk would interpose and cut off the satellite signals.

But how do you make a biotelemetry unit so rugged that a full-grown forest elephant won't scrape it off on the first tree he comes to? A unit whose electronics work reliably in brutal droughts and tropical downpours? Lotek found its answers by a combination of careful initial design and empirical refinement based on field performance. Factory machine-belting, for instance, proved a perfect material for elephant collars. It's a heavy-duty synthetic fabric, reinforced with steel mesh like a car tire. Elephants find it hard to remove, then get used to it.

Of course there's the issue of who will bell the elephant, so to speak. *Someone* has to find a likely subject without himself being detected, creep within forty metres of it, and tranquilize it with an opiate-laden hypodermic dart from a compressed-air gun. That someone is Bill Karesh. As the collar for a big bull is up to three metres long, fitting the transmitter can be a hard job even on tranquilized animals. But once that's done, all Bill has to do is inject the collared elephant with an opiate antagonist that breaks down the remaining drug inside the elephant's bloodstream. In three minutes, the beast gets up and ambles off. This time, however, it is no longer able to disappear: the Lotek unit continually samples and records the animal's position to within a few metres.

Position data can be 2-D only (longitude and latitude), or 3-D, which adds an altitude co-ordinate. Conveniently, the information can be remotely downloaded to a receiving module in a light airplane. The elephant collar is designed with a link that corrodes over a preset time: at the end of its service life, the collar detaches itself and falls off.

Before approving its GPS biotelemetry system for elephants, Lotek tried it out on moose in Northern Ontario. Though smaller than elephants, moose aren't lapdogs: they can grow to about a tonne. The system traced their movement through fifty-seven hundred downloaded position records, sampled at three-hour intervals over ten months. That adds up to a more detailed movement record than anything previously obtained for moose.

As biotelemetry data pour in for various large species, surprises are shaping up for field ethologists who study animal behaviour. Forest elephants, for example, seem to know when they're in a protected environment. Position plots for collared animals show a consistent pattern of slow foraging in areas where hunting is forbidden. But when the elephant has culled available forage and wants to find better dining, it moves through unsafe areas quickly and nocturnally in a movement that Bill Karesh calls *streaking*.

"When they leave their haven and traverse unprotected corridors, elephants rush from cover to cover," Bill notes. "Like human soldiers, they minimize exposure to enemy fire by running as fast as they can."

GPS data also shed light on elephants' sex lives. Like men together at a bar, male elephants often form gentlemen's clubs and forage by themselves, away from calves and females. And like men, elephants have no fixed mating season. Cows come into estrus unpredictably, so that bulls must be ready to respond at zero notice. What's that, darling? *Now?!*

When a bull detects a receptive female—probably by a combination of airborne sex pheromones and that mysterious, elephantine ULF—movement patterns of both bull and cow abruptly change. A courting pair may do a slow, intricate dance of parallel movement long before they catch sight of each other.

Older technology, in the form of weapons and farming, has threatened the elephant. New technology, in the form of RF transponsion, is helping to save it. It's all there on the maps.

I go from Newmarket to Kitchener-Waterloo through a series of blinding thunderstorms. This isn't driving, it's surfing. Good thing my car's so heavily loaded or I'd be hanging ten in the wave curl. It's mid-May now, and the landscape—what I can see of it through a smeared windshield—is turning green. It's traditionally the season for hope, renewal, and rebirth, and I find myself thinking about something I remarked on before: the knowledge worker's odd affinity for ethics.

For hundreds of years, the fount of principled behaviour in the workplace was the university. Faculty were called *professors* because they were entitled to profess the truth as they saw it, without fear or favour. Millwrights and farmhands might get sacked for slagging the boss or noting his errors. But the "universal community" of scholars fought for and obtained freedom of speech centuries before it was enshrined in secular charters and constitutions. The right to retain academic position despite your stated opinions was called *tenure* from the Latin verb *tenere*, "to hold."

But even as freedom of speech percolated from the universities into the secular world, inside the universities it started to decline. Tenure became not the champion of truth and protector of liberty but a waterproof door behind which stupidity, sloth, and outright incompetence could flourish untouched. A cartoon I once saw showed a mad scientist, rubbing his hands before a chained prisoner. "Mad?" cackles the scientist. "Perhaps I am mad! But I have tenure."

Then, when universities discovered that knowledge pays not just in mental satisfaction but also in material wealth, some odd fellowships sprang up. These were not always bad; in fact, they led to some amazing technical and economic gains. But at times they could be ethically troubling. The University of Waterloo, where I'm going this morning, yields two perfect examples: one bad, one good.

UWaterloo is a kind of field marshal in the knowledge economy. Forty years ago, it was a small school with a few dozen professors and a purely regional base. Then a new president, Dr. Douglas Wright, implemented four sweeping changes. First, he promoted applied mathematics from its traditional obscurity and made it a cornerstone of his school. A second cornerstone was a radical new science, automated computation, or cybernetics. Wright's third innovation was a co-operative work program. His engineering and computer science students alternated four months of school with four months of work. Wright's final change fully welcomed industry—its problems, personnel, and profit motive—to a Canadian university for the first time.

The Wright Revolution broke down Canadian universities' entrenched bias against "trade." This wasn't indigenous so much as it was imported holus-bolus from Britain. In the U.S., universities such as MIT and Stanford had long-standing industry alliances. But whatever its origin, the bias against industry took firm root here. A professor with key knowledge—how to make synthetic rubber, say—might be seconded to industry during crises such as war. But the peacetime norm was for the eggheads to stay within their ivy-covered walls and leave industry to the industrialists.

Wright punched a hole in that comfortable assumption. In so doing, he dragged Canada's universities into the knowledge age. The eggheads dumped on him, but he didn't care: he knew he was Wright. (Sorry.)

So did his students. Suddenly, the country's brightest kids were clamouring to get into UWaterloo. Once there, they didn't just learn from labs and textbooks; they tried out their theoretical knowledge in the real world. They also made more money than students at any other school. My philosophy tutor at McMaster, a grad student in Indian religion, told us he lived on spaghetti and mint jelly for the week before his grant cheque came. Undergrads in UWaterloo Co-op had savings accounts and drove their own cars.

My best friend went to UWaterloo after high school. Our high school's motto was *Scientia Est Libertas*, Knowledge Is Freedom. I met him at Thanksgiving; he showed me the motto of his computer-science co-op program, embroidered onto his school jacket. *Concordia cum Pecunia*, it said—Comfortable with Money.

Forty years later, the UWaterloo model has become the norm for many top Canadian schools. Co-op programs, and their underlying assumption that industry makes a better friend than enemy, have transformed not only education but industry as well. The profs know an IPO from a blackboard; industry realizes that success depends on what you know. The knowledge economy is upon us, and everyone's rich.

———————

Enter ethics, the ghost at the table. Don't nature's truths belong to everyone? Shouldn't learning be shared? Has academic freedom debased itself to sheltering professorial incompetence on the one hand, and on the other, handing private companies new knowledge obtained at public expense?

A recent case at UWaterloo sheds disturbing light on these questions. Eight years ago, the university hired a distinguished European professor of chemistry. With the school's blessing, her academic superior then incorporated a firm to "transfer and apply" (i.e., sell) new knowledge from his department to private industry. When the European professor published some of her important new findings in a learned journal, putting them into the public domain, she thereby made it impossible for her boss to patent-protect them as commercial secrets. UWaterloo did not renew the lady's contract. Her suit for unjust dismissal is now before the Supreme Court of Canada.

Does the knowledge economy have too high a price tag? Are we becoming prosperous at the cost of our principles? Or is it possible for a university to transfer its new knowledge to industry without bending ethics? If so, can I find an example of knowledge transfer that's been done right? Troubling thoughts, reflecting the blurred view through my windows. I find answers at a company spun off from academic research at UWaterloo: Virtek Vision Corporation.

———————

Scientific instrumentation involves amplifying tiny effects until they're visible—importing them to the macroworld, as the instrument makers say. An example is the galvanometer, which moves a needle in response to a slight electric current. The instrument's most common form is the VU meter on a reel-to-reel tape recorder.

Eight years ago, two professors at the University of Waterloo wondered what would happen if the free end of a galvanometer needle held a mirror. Could a computer precisely direct light shone onto such a device? If so, could such precise control be extended from a single dimension to a plane?

In a word, yes. Drs. Mohamed Kamel and Andrew Wong are colleagues in the UWaterloo Pattern Analysis and Machine Intelligence Group. They devised and perfected new software that lets a computer drive a "galvo" to very precise locations, very quickly. The two professors obtained patents on their work and formed a new firm, Virtek, to commercialize their ideas.

The new firm immediately messed things up. The snafu wasn't intentional: just university-trained academics thinking they were still on a lab bench at school. Profs. Kamel and Wong had imposed on their new company the task of commercializing not just the new laser-control system but everything else that their college lab was working on, from intelligent robotics to vision systems. Every time another item appeared on the list, off ran Virtek in a new direction. "They were certainly having fun when I arrived," says James Crocker. He does not mean it as a compliment.

A businessman, marketer, and turnaround consultant with no previous experience in knowledge corporations, Jim Crocker was hired as Virtek's CEO in 1996. That was eighteen months after Virtek went public—and just as it was about to burn through the last of its start-up capital.

"There was a business plan, but it didn't drive the company's efforts," Jim tells me in his sunny office. "The firm needed to define a core competency, then focus on it. It had to let go of all the other stuff, no matter how scientifically interesting."

Jim Crocker showed them how. The year after he arrived, Virtek's balance sheet went from red to black and stayed there. The firm makes well over $1 million of profit each year; gross margins consistently hit 65 to 75 per cent and are rising steadily. In the past five years, Virtek has had only two unprofitable quarters.

The core competency that Jim helped his new firm find was this: Virtek would be the best in the world at driving a laser beam quickly and accurately. From this one sentence flowed all subsequent success. Far from limiting imagination or achievement, Virtek's mission statement has brought the knowledge economy to sectors previously dominated by rule of thumb.

Roof trusses, for example. Most single-family houses, as well as low-rise multiple units and low-rise commercial structures, are stick-built—assembled on site from commodity components. If the building is framed in wood, "sticks" include two-by-fours for studs and headers, and two-by-eights for joists. Stick-built carpentry goes up quickly: wood is easy to cut, shape, and join with simple tools. Labour, however, is increasingly expensive. A while ago, some savvy engineers looked at the complex woodwork that underpins a pitched roof and realized its labour component could be cut in half if it were done under factory conditions. Thus was born the prefabricated roof truss. Since then, this simple technology has saved millions of person-hours in North America alone.

Today's trusses are pre-made in a variety of standard sizes, with provision by the truss manufacturer for custom sizes on request. The most popular trusses take the form of a shallow isosceles triangle with a base of three to five metres and a rise, or height, of two metres or less. Chords within the outer triangle subdivide it into smaller triangles, increasing truss rigidity and distributing and supporting dead loads (structure, sheathing, shingles) and live loads (wind, earthquake, snow).

In the factory, a wooden truss is put together from many short chords, each pre-cut like a puzzle piece. Factory workers fit the chord-pieces into place using working patterns called templates.

When the pieces are aligned, the workers put down spiked steel plates over each truss joint and hammer them in. Presto! Several hours' less work for on-site carpenters.

But while this procedure is an improvement over what went before, it is by no means perfect. The trouble lies in the truss pattern, or template. It can't be a rigid metal jig: truss configurations vary too often for workers to manhandle several hundred kilograms of steel all the time. Paper templates are in widespread use; but they tear frequently, and so are frustrating and time-consuming.

Or they were. Throughout the North American truss industry, Virtek laser patterning systems are quickly replacing paper.

This is how the system works. Driven by microcomputers, a ruby-red laser beam traces out a pre-set truss pattern on a table. Even if assembly workers look directly into the beam, it is too low-power to endanger human eyes. The Virtek system is so accurate that it subdivides a right angle into sixty thousand equal parts. And it drives its laser beam so fast—forty kilometres per hour on a work table five metres from beam source—that workers see a complete pattern at all times. It flickers slightly, but the entire outline is always there. No muss, no fuss, no paper: drop each chord in its proper spot, hammer down the truss plates, and you're done. The workers see a dead-accurate pattern at all times.

Until recently the truss industry, like the on-site carpentry it supplements, used plumb line, level, driven fastener and saw—much the same technology as in ancient Carthage. Virtek makes no-tech into high-tech. One-fifth of all North American truss companies now use a Virtek system. It's obvious why market penetration is growing: the system saves 50 to 90 per cent in set-up time.

———————

As Virtek's CEO, Jim Crocker is supervising a controlled, organic growth, via market expansion and acquisitions. In June 2000 Virtek raised $22 million to help fund this plan. Crocker's goals are audacious. He wants Virtek revenues to grow sixfold in the next five years, to $100 million. He is positive the company can do it, even though such sustained growth will involve continual self-reinvention throughout that time. "We're going to build the business quickly," he says. "And we're going to have a blast doing it."

Jim's optimism rests on a three-pronged approach:

1. Put existing knowledge into new industrial markets;
2. Develop new knowledge;
3. Ensure all knowledge exploits your core competency.

Take the first case. Laser patterning, it turns out, is as useful for ultra-high-tech jet aircraft as it is for house trusses. Airplane manufacturers have tried Mylar and other synthetic-polymer templates instead of paper. But even for advanced aircraft, workers who use 2-D patterns still must trace them onto a sheet matrix—composite materials and duralumin—and then snip them out using hand-held shears.

All over the world, Virtek is changing that cottage-industry approach. Its customers include Boeing, with whom Virtek co-developed a new template system; British Aerospace, whose production costs Virtek systems have cut by 25 per cent; Airbus-Industrie; and Canada's own Bombardier.

If it's fascinating to see the truss template flicker into life, watching the aircraft patterning system in action is nothing short of eerie. As a demonstration, technologists on Virtek's new operations floor push in a low wheeled dolly. It holds a sheet of composite aircraft material, pre-bent to the proper curvature. One of the technologists sticks a translucent plastic ruler into a line of symbols that the laser projects. The ruler is studded with corner reflectors, like those on a car's taillights, geometrically designed to reflect light back to its source. Sensors mounted beside the projector pick up the wand's reflected signal and treat it like a mouse click on a screen icon. This lets workers control Virtek systems directly.

As I watch, a technologist trips an icon that starts template projection. The red laser beam leaps into life, racing faster than my eye can follow. First it locates special dots in the work dolly. In seconds it deduces where things are and throws a clear parts outline right in the centre of the matrix.

I raise an objection. The dolly's not fixed; if it moves during a cut, won't that spoil the pattern? "Watch this," says a technologist. He kicks off the dolly's brakes and slides the table away. The pattern projection *follows the table*, shifting as the table does, keeping the pattern centred. How? The technologists explain that even as the system projects the part template, it continually consults the positioning dots to verify the table's location. To me it's spooky, like the first glimmer of artificial intelligence.

I think of another objection. Surely the template won't follow the dolly to the horizon? The laser is coherent light: it would stay together in a tight, unspreading beam even over fifty kilometres. But as the dolly recedes, the laser beam sweeps across it more obliquely. Won't this distort the pattern?

The technologists smile again, but this time they say nothing. They move the dolly again. When it's five metres from source, the racing laser dot abruptly snaps off. An accuracy threshold has been crossed. Any farther from light source and the projection on the dolly would exceed a pre-set dimension tolerance of fifteen thou—a third of a millimetre. It's a kind of mother reflex. *When you come back and sit down with me, dear, I'll know you're ready for a serious discussion.* Did I say artificial intelligence? This is more like artificial guilt.

Virtek is doubling the considerable revenue it derives from templating, by building and selling systems that do the reverse. Instead of projecting a flawless pattern for a 2-D part, the system scans existing parts and calculates if they're up to snuff. It's a big, tedious job to do this by traditional means. A master mechanic has to sample random parts, taking measurement after measurement with a hand-held micrometer or a roller-rule, then comparing each value to a master outline. This process is hit and miss.

Note I said *sample*. The time required for old-fashioned part verification means that only fifty parts may be thoroughly checked in a run of five thousand—the first ten, the last one, and thirty-nine parts dispersed randomly between. The supposition is that if these parts check out, so will everything else. Yet this is like an economist opening a can by assuming a can opener.

Billions of flat parts—stamped, drilled, forged, sheared, and laser cut—are produced in North America every year. They go into things from fender flanges and brake disks for the auto industry to support sheets that underpin the circuit boards of medical instruments. Dimensional tolerances are critical: if one hole in a hundred is too small in diameter, or if one tab is thirty microns off-centre, the part is a reject. Worse, the parts manufacturer, Virtek's customer, must then deal with clients whose high-speed assembly lines have come to a screeching halt.

Virtek's verification system is called LaserQC, for quality control. The system can take every measurement, in every item, in every flat-part run as fast as the parts are churned out—even when a part falls anywhere on the inspection table. LaserQC can also reverse-engineer parts, tracing their external and internal outlines and using the data to create a CAD file (CAD stands for computer-aided design). That instructs a numerically controlled machine, which then churns out the reverse-engineered part in any quantity.

Virtek is now nearing the Holy Grail of CAD: fast, precise verification of parts that are 3-D rather than 2-D. It's a process of mind-boggling complexity, but Virtek believes it's almost there. After that, the company may even scale down its precision laser drive to the molecular level, scan-reading DNA sequences faster than any system yet developed: mechanical engineering meets biotechnology. In the third quarter of 2000, Virtek's biotech instrumentation division became its largest business unit. It's also creating the most investor interest.

All Virtek's achievements involve business as much as they do new technology. Throughout the knowledge economy, these two elements tolerate each other with the corporate equivalent of clenched teeth: yet business and technology are mutually indispensable. The best ideas in the world, and the most creative people wither without business direction; and the most astute bean-counters, lawyers and CEOs will go bankrupt if they fail to protect, inspire, motivate, understand, and learn from their geeks. But while each camp holds a shotgun to the other's head, there are ways the two can reach a living arrangement. One is for each subculture to appreciate the other's domain—to walk awhile in its neighbour's moccasins. Another is for a knowledge company to find a CEO who's a kind of modern philosopher king. Both avenues may break down. As we'll hear from an ex–telephone company employee in Montreal, a lifetime geek with an MBA makes the worst manager in the world. And as I'll shortly testify from my own experience, the businessman who learns a few words of high-tech jargon may delude himself into thinking he's Bill Gates.

But these are cavils, like reminding acrobats of heights. When circus performers are really cooking, they neither ignore gravity nor defy it: they make it work for them. The result is beautiful to watch, and even more beautiful to do. Jim Lotimer of Lotek puts it this way: "Business in high-tech is one type of technology in support of another. You have to respect both types. If you ignore either, you'll fail."

Virtek's approach has been to find a philosopher king in its CEO, Jim Crocker. Jim is emphatic that he is a businessman first, last and middle. "My background is marketing, not engineering or science. I happen to be in a knowledge business, but I approach it as another business. The old rules still apply. Hire first-rate people, make first-rate products, take care of your customers, don't avoid tough decisions. And set down strong, clear, simple core values that everyone understands, accepts, and practices."

Virtek has four core values. First is *Initiative*. Don't wait to be ordered: if you see an opportunity, act. Second is *Sense of Urgency*. "Lose not an hour," Horatio Nelson said; Virtek beats his lordship by fifty-nine minutes or so. Virtek's third core value is *Teamwork*. No prima donnas here: all hang together, lest all hang separately. This is *true* teamwork, not one old-economy manager's breathtakingly cynical definition: "a lot of people doing what I say."

Virtek's fourth and final value is *Honesty*. This must flow in all possible directions—up, down, and sideways. Honesty should be blended with respect, but it must be applied unsparingly. The greatest mark of respect one can give colleagues, employees, or bosses at Virtek is to level with them. It's not surprising that Value Four is Jim's own favourite.

"Brutal honesty eliminates politics and gamesmanship," he tells me. "It promotes urgency; it doesn't leave you anywhere to hide."

————

At last, good weather for driving. High cloud, warm weather, no wind, a sweet day. I'm on my way to Ottawa, driving east to the 416 interchange along Highway 401. At Gananoque I turn on to the St. Lawrence Parkway and cruise beside a cold ink-blue river as big as an inland sea. Time after time, what I think is the far shore proves to be another of the Thousand Islands. Like the Ottawa, the St. Lawrence could swallow every river, creek, and lake in Great Britain and hardly rise a centimetre. It carries the fresh water of half a continent as an aorta carries blood.

I'm midway in my journey—both to Ottawa and in my cross-country research tour. Time to consider the knowledge firms I've seen, to extract some lessons from them if I can. One issue particularly interests me. Technology is a human enterprise, and so is the knowledge economy it spawns. That's good in many ways, for people can be hard-working and imaginative. But people also have a darker side. What if they aren't up to the challenge of the knowledge economy? What happens if, say, the founder of a knowledge firm one day proves to be a company-sinking liability?

Chief executive officers are odd critters. I think that's particularly true in the knowledge economy. It's more than length of association that makes a CEO feel and act like the father of a family: he really does function like the sire of a brood. The role of the knowledge-company CEO is even gender independent. Like the female warriors in the kung-fu movie *Crouching Tiger, Hidden Dragon*, female CEOs are usually treated like honorary males.

A CEO's strengths, flaws, moods, and quirks profoundly affect a knowledge company. Sometimes this happens immediately; sometimes it takes time. But sooner or later the CEO sets his whole firm's tone. His confidence, or lack of it, saturates a company's walls. If he's irresolute or paranoid, his employees will be too. If he's confident and in control, firm or flexible as occasion demands—in short, perfect—the firm grows and prospers; employees are relaxed but full of energy; and people get rich. "My most important role," one knowledge-company CEO told me, "is to keep people calm."

And happy, too, for fun pervades good business. Evolution created fun as it did the orgasm, as a payoff for doing well. *Good boy, perpetuating the species! Here's a cookie!*

Of course it's possible to take fun out of context: fiddling while Rome burns, or shooting dice on the deck of the *Titanic*. But every knowledge company executive I've seen oppose fun on principle, as having no place in a well-run shop, has proven a stunted, dysfunctional, unimaginative jerk who was not only ineffective but justly hated by those forced to report to him—"people under me," he'd say. Workers know when they're hot and when they're not; they won't stay hot for a tight-assed, stone-faced martinet.

A second area where the family-marriage analogy works is in the relationship's evolution. In both company and family, senior members play several roles over time: what seems a single thing to external observers is in truth a sequence of relationships. These have different emphases and sometimes different demands, but note the similarities.

#	STAGE	NECESSARY ATTRIBUTES (HUSBAND)
H0	Meeting	Good background, right personality
H1	Honeymoon	Attentive, purposeful without obsession
H2	W/toddlers	Energetic, clear, fair, firm as needed
H3	W/teens	Accessible, visionary, relaxed
H4	Empty nest	Discerns and adapts to new course

#	STAGE	NECESSARY ATTRIBUTES (CEO)
C0	Hiring	Good background, right personality
C1	First Year	Attentive, purposeful without obsession
C2	Turnaround	Energetic, clear, fair, firm as needed
C3	Steady-State	Accessible, visionary, relaxed
C4	Growth	Discerns and adapts to new course

This list of attributes is not exhaustive: it merely summarizes some important skills a CEO or spouse should exhibit at a given stage. It is always important to determine a course, for example, but indispensable during fast growth. As for clarity, employees must always know what the CEO expects them to do. But in times of redirection this lack of second-guessing becomes vital.

Some readers will be puzzled at my omissions. A knowledge-company CEO hired without demonstrated success in the technology he is to lead? Yes, that's a surprising discovery from my field research. One of the most successful CEOs I interviewed—energetic, skilled, good-humoured, leading his firm from excellence to excellence—was Jim Crocker. When he first signed on as CEO for Virtek, Jim didn't know anything about its technology. He was a turnaround expert who came to Virtek from a paper manufacturer in Northern Ontario. Since then, Virtek has done a reverse takeover on Jim's mind: he's been subverted and brainwashed until one may fairly call him a laser freak. That re-education is a major factor in Virtek's success. But at the outset, Jim was hired, he says, to run "just another business."

That attitude didn't hurt him as a hire. On the contrary, he convinced Virtek's directors, including the two professors whose knowledge investment he would safeguard, that business skills were as important to their company as technical abilities in optics, electronics, or engineering physics. And Jim was right. Knowing a technology too well at the outset can compromise the effectiveness of a new CEO. He loses objectivity.

This was confirmed for me by a source at IBM Canada. He said that the last thing a salesman needs is to treat his product line religiously: unswerving faith reduces sales performance. The Salesman Who Believes reacts to the scepticism of a potential client not with the genial persuasion that's most effective in reaching a close but with pity and disbelief. "Surely it's obvious," he says, shaking his head. A similar thing may happen when a CEO with vast knowledge about his new firm's subject area takes the helm. He doesn't have to learn, he thinks: he knows it all.

That's fatal. A knowledge-economy CEO must see with open eyes. He must understand the uses, perils, and promises of his firm's technology, yet stop short of falling in love with it—at least at the beginning. His passion must stop with imagination and involvement. If it becomes blind adoration, if his eyes mist over with the discipline's romance and glamour, he may balk at making hard decisions. He will then imperil both his company and his position in it. By contrast, effective CEOs like Jim Crocker begin a new post free of preconceptions. Only later may they fall in love with their métier.

Then there's the attribute I call right personality. This need not mean smiles and handshakes: it may involve a ruthless willingness to shed blood. I merely mean the CEO has a style that fits him for the position.

Fit for the position: if only it were that simple to know in advance. How do you tell? Individuals, even committees, make mistakes. Besides, my tabled attributes are for the ideal *new* hire, someone brought to a company that's up and running. What happens when a company grows up around someone who lacks a vital attribute? Someone who, though an expert in another profession —a brilliant scientist, say—is no captain of industry, not even a competent line manager? Worse—someone bizarre enough to be locked up but who somehow succeeds in launching a firm? How do you get rid of the guy to whom you owe it all—the insight, the vision, the imminent corporate collapse? I'm glad you asked that question, because I don't know. Let's say that in the knowledge economy, the winning CEO needs to be half geek, half business-man. He may start off as one or the other, but in very short order he must fuse the disciplines; otherwise, chaos ensues.

To make his necessary conversion, the knowledge-company CEO must jettison some established prejudices. The worst of these is the mutual incomprehension, nay, the ongoing warfare, that occurs whenever the business and technical mindsets collide. It's a very old war, going back two or three thousand years. Hephaestos, the god of the forge in classical Greek mythology and the Hellenistic symbol of technical skill, had a good heart, a keen mind, and consummate artistry. But whoever said that knowledge is power forgot about Hephaestos. He was bullied by Ares, who was loud-mouthed, brutal, vain, and thick as two short planks. The reason? The war god was well formed and handsome; the forge god was ugly and lame. Hephaestos lacked image.

These characteristics were not accidental. Theology comes from reality, not the other way round: Olympus mimics Earth. The ancients would deliberately lame a smith by severing his leg tendons. So crippled, he could not escape and produce tools and weapons for a rival town.

Once brute practice became solemnized by myth, the concept of the misshapen artificer grew deep roots in classical culture. From there it was transmitted to every society that considered itself the heir of Greece. From Augustan Rome to C. P. Snow's London, the elite saw engineering as a seamy trade, unfit for gentlemen and best left to "rude mechanicals." It's the attitude that Doug Wright had to defeat before he could transform UWaterloo and, through it, Canada's knowledge economy.

This multi-thousand-year prejudice lives on today not only among arts groups and financial professionals but even in some knowledge companies. Boards of directors seem irresistibly drawn to wrench control from the geeks and give it to overhead people, especially lawyers and accountants. The geek nickname for these people is *suits*. It's a perfect case of metonymy, since it's the aim of many suits to divest themselves of any aspect of humanity except formal clothes. A distressing proportion of suits achieve that aim.

In a successful knowledge company, geeks and suits relate as equals, or else the suits are the ones treated as interchangeable commodities, mere hired help. This is anathema to a dyed-in-the-wool suit, who hates all competence but his own. *Its* own, rather: the suit is the prototype of reification. Paradoxically, this has the effect of compromising the suit's own effectiveness. It's as if he wanted a spotless house but despised his cleaning staff.

Case in point. Ten years ago I helped a high-tech start-up in Vancouver demystify its technological consumer and investor com-munications. This required a lot of on-site work. Although a con-tractor and not an employee, I had a perfect seat at the drawn-out wrestling match between geek and suit. To this day it blows my mind to remember what I saw.

The three head suits top my list of the most unattractive human beings I have ever met. The chairman bought his chairmanship, just as he bought his $200,000 sports car and a post in his com-pany for his eldest child. He was prone to flashy generosities that, later regretting their expense, he would then retract. But at least the chairman had a pleasant manner. Much higher on the Offensi-Meter was the CEO, described by one of his technical managers as "a classic charlatan." The CEO was a European American who found frequent ways to remind us that back home he had a large personal fortune and a family crest.

The company's investment-relations officer told me the CEO had arrived in Vancouver several years ago "with a suitcase"—in other words, with no capital but the clothes on his back. Two things led him to Canada. One was a pool of competent geeks, trained at public expense and willing to work for what in U.S. terms were unshelled peanuts. Canada's second big attraction was an endless source of public funds in the form of grants, loan guarantees, and assistance for hiring and training personnel. All this assistance was "soft"—that is, forgivable.

The CEO did have some technical credentials, including several hardware patents in the manufacturing industry. He also had a list of contacts that stretched from heads of corporations and U.S. senators to Harvard professors. But his core competency lay elsewhere: he was without doubt the most effective motivator I have ever encountered. He was the prototypical con.

I still have no idea how he did it. He never thumped a table or raised his voice. He hardly even gave orders, only offered suggestions. But in seconds he could make you feel absolutely vital, as if you were the linchpin to the firm's—*your* firm's—success. Your ideas, your work, could alone avert failure. The CEO didn't make you work stupid hours. He made you *want* to, then got out of your way.

Yet while he made you feel like a hero, you were never out of his grasp. He could call from Finland or Boston or downtown, at midnight or at 5:30 a.m. For some reason I accepted this, at least initially. Perhaps it was because he didn't spare himself. He was a grandfather, he had an implanted pacemaker, yet he never seemed to sleep or even slow. One day I told him I wouldn't be in because my wife was having an operation, and I was going with her to the hospital. The CEO asked me the name of the hospital so he could contact me. I didn't comply; I drew the line at that. But I did—I find this hard to believe even as I write it—find myself calling him from the hospital. Just a quick chat, dear, and I'll get right back to the recovery room. . . .

That was my wake-up call. I blinked, shook my head, and realized no money was enough to let myself and my family be treated this way. And I began to make my own inquiries on this man, to find out whom I was working for.

I soon hit paydirt. The talk on the street was that when the CEO reached Vancouver, suitcase in hand, the first place he went was a public agency that financed promising knowledge start-ups. He showed them an IP portfolio, painted a grandiose plan of a firm that in five years would (he said) employ more people than Microsoft and earn more revenue than Boeing, and asked for $1 million. The agency scrutinized his material and threw him out on his ear. At this point, the CEO went directly to the provincial minister responsible for the agency that had "insulted" him. He complained about his treatment and renewed his demands; the minister caved in and released some funds.

The CEO used his public funding to print letterhead, open a storefront, and make himself seem respectable. He hired recent geek graduates at rock-bottom salaries and acquired additional IP, much of it local. By the time I came on the scene, the CEO had twenty employees and three product lines. Since public funds had grown inadequate, he made a devil's deal with the chairman, selling some of his shares and much control in return for operating capital. The chairman redelegated much of his power to his chief financial officer.

If the CEO was a horror, the CFO knocks my Offensi-Meter off its bolts. The chairman used the CFO as a junkyard Doberman not merely to control costs—that was legitimate enough—but to keep the geeks in line. I grope for words to describe this man; all I can do is repeat the old definition of an accountant as a computer without the personality. His lack of any human touch was profoundly disconcerting, almost pathological. I saw him enthusiastic on only two occasions: being cruel and being conned.

First, the cruelty. At a dinner with the CEO and chairman after the company's IPO, the CFO described how he had eaten sushi in Japan. It was lobster, and the meat was not only raw, it wasn't dead. Thin slices were cut from the living creature before his eyes and fed to him. As he told this tale, his spectacles (in Stephen Leacock's phrase) "glittered with excitement."

Second, the con. Like most tyrants, the CFO was only too glad to lick the boots of greater tyrants; like all con men, he was forever being conned. Suit that he was, he never understood the knowledge that his own company sold. His attitude toward it, and toward all geeks, was contemptuous. But every month or so, some geek would get the CFO's ear and sell him a line. Why, this process is *revolutionary!* It will make *billions!* If we do an M&A we can *dominate the world market* and *charge what we want!*

At these times the CFO's face would develop a sheen of greed-sweat. His attitude toward technology was the same he showed to human resources, public relations, or anything else unconnected with money: scorn alternating with pathetic hope. Then the CFO would realize he needed his geeks and bestow smiles on them for half an hour.

Since these times coincided with visits from prospective investors, I diagnosed the CFO as a self-con. You can't lie well to others till you've lied to yourself; and in whipping himself into a froth of enthusiasm, the CFO prepared himself to bilk his bankers. It still amazes me that he got a dime. Yet he did, and his success reveals the frenzy of a financial establishment playing catch-up with a knowledge economy it had so long ignored. The money men were trying to offset their lack of vision by hurling money at anything that called itself IP.

If so, they got what they deserved. The firm of Wiley, Sharp, and Base has now bled investment money for forty-two quarters straight. I almost—*almost*—pity the poor damned banks.

Such cases, while not isolated, may soon be the exception rather than the rule. The geeks in the knowledge economy have engineered a counter-revolution and are everywhere striking off the chains into which the suits have locked them. My loathsome CFO must gaze back wistfully to the time when the boys in the shop could be kept around by a little leg surgery. Now it is he and his kind that are being pushed inexorably away from the main action, suffered by the geeks to hang around as long as they mind their manners and haul slop to the computers on command. They can even wear their suits if they want to. While geeks consider such frippery a laughable anachronism in one another, they tolerate it in a corporate drudge.

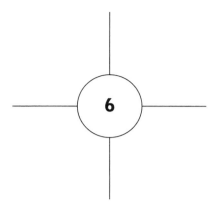

DINOSAURS

AND MARKETERS

Though Ontario remains the nation's industrial core, its late-century recessions forced the province to reinvent itself. It did so in two key ways. First, it shifted to a knowledge-dominated economy; then it began to roll that brand-new economy out across Canada.

Knowledge companies can exist anywhere. New knowledge, especially IT, is like a medieval theologian's concept of an angel: dimensionless and immaterial. There's no reason why most ideas, and the start-up companies that exploit them, can't work as well in Antigonish or Corner Brook as in Vancouver or Montreal.

This is apparent when you drive up the 416 parkway that approaches the National Capital Region through its southern and western satellites. I lived in Ottawa from 1974 to 1988, both in central neighbourhoods and in suburbia. When I left them, the new burbs to the west and east were sterile. Their trees were small, their parks and playing fields were scrubland; they baked in summer and in winter they froze. The city core, by contrast, was gracious, treed, and habitable. More to the point, it also held most of the jobs.

Fourteen years and one economic revolution later, the situation stands on its head. Trees and all, the burbs have grown up: they are prosperous, well groomed, and growing. Downtown Ottawa is filled with blowing trash and boarded-up storefronts. Its vaunted core renewal, the Rideau Centre, is a crumbling eyesore anchored by derelict stores. Only millions of dollars of tax revenue flooding in from outside the city, and lavished on parks and monuments by the National Capital Commission, keep central Ottawa from displaying the subtle charm of Inner Cleveland. The new, heavily fortified U.S. Embassy—paranoia manifest in steel and concrete—completes the portrait of a garrison under siege.

What devastated Ottawa's core was the death of the old economy. Trees, wheat, and ore could no longer sustain the Capital Region's First World lifestyle. When the world rebuilt from the Second World War, it churned out commodities and manufactured items at bargain-basement prices, undercutting Canada. Suddenly we no longer had the only businesses on the block, and throughout the eighties, Canada's biggest export was old-economy jobs.

Official Ottawa, which is to say the inner city, has yet to learn this lesson. The suburbs learned it immediately and made themselves the motors of a clean and vigorous knowledge economy. The process of geographical wealth redistribution began with them: the high-technology road-roller squeezed wealth from the core to the suburbs, on its way out across the land. The process continues to enrich suburbia at centretown's expense. What's being spread out here is the new wealth, knowledge.

All that being said, the human element continues to intervene, slowing down the knowledge economy's flat distribution across the land. Some geeks get lonely in windowless rooms with only a keyboard for company; clients still inhabit cities. So once past a kitchen-table start-up and into rapid growth, many knowledge firms indulge an atavistic wish to concentrate. Single or childless employees want bars and theatres; families need daycares and schools. So for now, and for whatever reason—habit, fear, perceived efficiency—knowledge-economy firms will huddle almost as much as their old-economy counterparts. For a while, the rationale for technology clusters will remain.

This is changing, as more of us see that intellectually or physically, nothing hinders us from evenly spreading the contents of our cities across the Earth. The geographical economy will probably wither away in a couple of decades. For the commonest misapprehension about the Internet is that it isn't revolutionary—and it is. It has already transformed work, letting teams operate intimately and effectively while continents apart.

Still, it will take time for us as a society to recognize and acknowledge that we can work at least as well in E-teams as we can in a scrum of bodies. Thus, although technology clusters and other high-tech concentrations exist on borrowed time that is steadily ticking away, in the short term they may flourish.

Don't get me wrong: I don't think *meat*—as radical geeks call the bodies that support both human minds and machine cyberspace—is a mere annoyance. Yet the RadGeeks have a point: even in Canada, geography's apotheosis, geography is steadily losing its power. Virtual teams may still meet physically at the outset of work, to put names and faces to E-colleagues. As the Arab proverb says, Don't do a deal with anyone you're not close enough to smell. Yet after one face-to-face encounter, most teams can complete their work in cyberspace. That's the thought behind Alberta's new fibre-optic network. The province realizes that 'meat' can live and work anywhere, as long as it has a high-bandwidth data link. In the knowledge economy, knowledge is almost all that needs to move.

Ottawa jogs a lot of memories. Twenty years ago when I was media officer for the NRC here, I showed a bright young *Financial Post* reporter named Robert Steklasa around NRC's Montreal Road campus. We saw the towing tank in which boat designers studied the performance of advanced ship hulls; the vertical wind tunnel that solved the most intractable aeronautical problem of the 1950s, the dive that decayed to a tailspin; the alternative-energy program that investigated hydrogen storage years before fuel cells existed outside spacecraft. At the end of our tour I spread my arms and said with apostolic enthusiasm, "*This* is where history is made. What happens here eclipses Parliament. Years from now, when nobody remembers the name of anyone in Cabinet, what I've shown you will reshape the country."

Bob Steklasa was one of the best reporters I ever dealt with, whether in science or in finance, but at heart he was a political animal. When I finished my aria, he turned politely and looked out the window so I wouldn't see his disbelieving smile. Then I was nettled; now I can smile myself, because my predictions were bang-on correct. Today the knowledge economy employs more people in the National Capital Region than all levels of public service combined. Given that a lot of civil servants don't look out the window in the morning so they'll have something to do in the afternoon, this finally gives official Ottawa something it can crow about. As one government VP told me, "Even mandarins must now admit that shift happens."

I pulled into my former hometown late on Easter Day, and stopped outside the condo of my friend Will Williams. At first glance, Will is a most unlikely geek. He's tall and rugged, and the smartest, sweetest-tempered man I've ever met. Ask him a question, and he'll gaze into space. Those who don't know him think he's slow-witted; then he answers. His pauses betray high-speed mental scrolls through a thousand different responses, each cross-referenced to a massive database. This guy is *bright*.

Will is a keen student of the knowledge economy—and its ideal observer, because he's unobserved. His quiet, unassuming exterior lets him blend in anywhere, like wallpaper, and everything he sees, he remembers. He's the proverbial fly on the wall.

This is very good for my research, because Will's personal history over the past two decades encapsulates some key trends of the knowledge economy—boom, bust, job changes, mergers and acquisitions, and some breathtaking corporate tomfoolery.

Will, a bachelor, lives in Kanata, a western suburb of Ottawa. Along with Nepean, the burb beside it, Kanata has been dubbed Silicon Valley North because of its intense concentration of knowledge corporations. When commentators say Ottawa has a lot of high tech, they mean Nepean and Kanata have a lot of IT. For a researcher eager to show how IT powers the knowledge economy, this is the place to go. For a writer who hungers for the human element of the knowledge economy, Will is the perfect interview.

When I arrive, Will is on his living-room couch making chain mail. Like many IT geeks, he's a fantasy fan who hosts role-playing games, sometimes computer mediated but just as often played on paper pads around his battered dining-room table.

"I wanted to see what was involved in making a mail shirt," Will tells me as I walk in. "See here? You take the wire, bend it until it forms a circle, snip it, then crimp it closed." The medieval artisans would rivet or weld a closed loop, Will tells me. He's content to forgo this extra step. I ask how long this takes him per link, without the welding.

"Six minutes or so. I average ten an hour." How many links in a full-sleeved shirt? "Six thousand, maybe." Fifteen forty-hour weeks for *one shirt*? "Oh no, far more. I can't do this more than an hour at a time. I have to stop every so often and figure out where I'm going." When will he be finished? "Five years or so." Why is he *doing* this? "To get a sense of what a tenth-century warrior had to put up with. To see how much a mail shirt weighs." Big grin. "Because it's nearly as much fun as writing software."

I'm here to see Will Williams because of economic geography. Kanata, I suspect, became a hotbed of IT because the presence over many years of various laboratories run by the government of

Canada. While that long-term process advanced all sorts of sciences and technologies, for informatics it produced that governmental Holy Grail, a technology cluster.

I have a love-hate affair with government. Two-thirds of it is unnecessary; two-thirds of the remaining third behaves like Larry, Curly, and Moe trying to wash floors. But the remaining one-ninth does what nothing else could do: it funds and undertakes the leaps that make Canada great—in the 1880s, the cross-country railway; in the 1950s, the Auto Pact and the Avro Arrow; in the 1960s, universal medicare; in the 1980s, the Canadarm space manipulator and the basis of biotechnology. Government was the source of all these. To the list can now be added the IT nexus around Ottawa.

Will Williams and I saw the process take shape from different viewpoints, he in industry, I in government. What he did, I wrote about—a duality that still goes on. Here's his story.

Will graduated university in 1977 with a bachelor's degree in computer science, magna cum laude. It was a boom year in IT, and Will was snapped up by Bell-Northern Research. BNR, later absorbed into the colossus Nortel Networks, was at that time a placid, respectable R&D consortium developing new IT knowledge, mostly mainframe software. It had been established, and was jointly owned, by Bell Canada and Northern Telecom. Bell ran one of North America's biggest telephone systems. NorTel was a corporate offshoot that made telephonic hardware for Bell. BNR did original research and development for the two linked firms.

For Canadian IT, then, Will Williams was in at the creation. From bright-eyed grad to good-humoured fortysomething, he has soldiered through the whole six-reel epic. I offer his biography not merely as fascinating in itself but as general, almost mythical. If you're his age and you work in high-tech, you've walked the walk: *de te fabula narratur*—the tale is told of you.

"I've never been much into hardware," Will says, crimping chain mail. "Where I work now, they call me a technical architect.

I design B2B for financial transactions—product sales, mostly. One of our recent clients, a big manufacturer, wanted a site on the World Wide Web where wholesale customers could call in, examine his products and inventory, and place orders. Previous to this, the client had an on-line system—a toll-free phone number that businesses used to place fast orders."

Except the orders were fast only in theory, not in practice. The call centre was unwieldy and expensive. It required two hundred full-time people to handle the huge quantity of small orders that came in via phone lines, both voice and fax. And it was far too complex and cumbersome for users to deal with, especially the Mom and Pop retailers with small orders—a case of this, ten packs of that.

"Orders coming along the old 800-number line used to need ten or twelve re-edits before they could be processed," Will tells me. "The philosophy at the client's head office was 'That's our system. If they can't handle it, fuck 'em.'"

Will helped his client develop a new Web site, which he calls "a poor man's EDI." EDI? "Electronic data input. We figured that these days, even a Mom and Pop store would have a PC and an ISP —Internet service provider, sorry—to give it Net access. I was in charge of designing the new Web site, testing it, and doing proof of concept."

To what result? "It went on-line and saved gazillions," Will says. "Two or three US dollars a product case." Product? Will smiles; he can't be specific, he tells me, or he'd give away his client's identity. At any rate, his new B2B site "walks Mom and Pop through the order process. It does this so well that every order is right the first time." What volume are we talking about here? "Hundreds of millions of cases a year," Will says. "This is a very, very large producer."

The new site, Will tells me, is multinational and multilingual. And it's so effective that his unnamed client is rolling out Will's knowledge innovations throughout the world. Two new countries are added to the roster every six weeks.

What's it like to work on something this new and different? "Fun," Will says. "There's no other word for it. It's a lot of fun."

Though there was only one fly in this ointment, it was a big one. Will's project, his team, his company, and he himself were so competent and successful that the company that employed them kept getting bought. Each new buyer challenged the most recent victor for Will's chain-mail-scarred hand, requiring his team to do IT miracles in the midst of a raging corporate battle zone.

"Every time we got close to signing a contract with our client, we'd have another merger," Will says, shaking his head in disbelief. "Every merger meant a brand-new set of lawyers. And every new legal team insisted on examining all documents and procedures back to Day One. I calculate that every penny of profit on this project went to legal fees."

What did this do to the contract? By now, Will is wiping tears of laughter from his eyes. "What contract? We never had one. Our team did $3 million worth of work on a handshake. Luckily the client was trustworthy, and everyone got paid." Yet surely the lawyers had a point, I say. What if Will and his team had been stiffed in some legal no-man's land? What if all the clauses and whereupons weren't perfect, and the client refused to pay?

Will's smile becomes seraphic. "At that point, the client might have found his new site did not work too efficiently."

In the course of his work, and purely by accident, Will ran a security check for his client. "I accessed the client's original site, requested some information, and discovered I had inadvertently hacked into his whole internal system," he says. "There was his entire product pipeline laid out, clear as a bell. God help him if I'd been his competitor: anyone could have seen what he had up his sleeve for the next six years. If they'd really been malicious, they could have reconfigured his Web server, using his extranet [the public Web site] to get at his intranet [the site for corporate, internal-only use]. That could have put him out of business."

Will dug deeper and discovered why something so critical had had to wait for chance discovery. Although the client firm took pride in doing all its own computer work, it had kept what Will calls a mainframe mentality. "Our new owners were as hidebound as the client. They were suspicious of the PC-driven Net, suspicious of all distributed processing." But aren't the current owners an enormous IT firm? "Yes, but you have to look at their roots. They sprang up forty years ago when a big multinational outsourced its IT functions. The firm (Will's owners) went out of its way to reassure their huge client that doing business with them was just like working with its own internal staff." It was the IT equivalent of biological mimicry, Will explains: "They acted like GrossCorp, dressed like GrossCorp, thought like GrossCorp. They *became* GrossCorp." Oh, my God: the Reifiers? Snip, crimp. "Yep."

Over the years, Will's most recent employer became mired in its symbiotic relationship with its enormous client. It was imprisoned in an old-economy mindset—pyramidal org charts, top-down instructions, no bottom-up data flow at all. *If the underlings had anything to say they'd be VPs like us, right?*

Then the Internet appeared, and the world changed. The first thing that altered, Will tells me, was the size of the B2B deals.

"They shrank drastically," he says. "Though the Net is already taking over B2B applications, there haven't been any $1 billion Internet deals that I know of. Today's mid-size Internet B2B project grosses $1.5 million, spread over a year or two. Most projects are a lot smaller and take only a few months. There are no six-year mega-projects in today's B2B."

Will then fits his new owners with a brilliant epitaph. "They evolved to eat bison," he says. "They don't realize there's no longer anything around but mice."

When Will's current employers made their takeover bid, they moved quickly to impose their old-economy mindset. That instantly began to erode the culture that had made Will's company such a tempting takeover target in the first place. The takeover occurred in early December. Will summarizes the first corporate memo this way:

> Hi! Welcome to xyz Inc., a People Company! The Christmas party is hereby cancelled! So are all bonuses, because that's not our policy! Here's a list of top performers for last year, whom we salute and applaud! They're the people who would have got bonuses if we hadn't cancelled 'em! Reward vacations are cancelled too! Have a nice day!

"The owners have yet to get with the 1990s, let alone the new century," Will says mildly. "They're saying the right words, but they're not walking the walk. People have been leaving in droves. That has to send a message." It's a fascinating contradiction, a company dealing in advanced IT but exhibiting the mindset of an insurance firm in an old Jack Lemmon movie.

Will is so easygoing that he's willing to forgive and forget; besides, he "wants to see some projects through." So he's staying. And, he says, for all their blunders and stupidities and bureaucratic stodginess, the new owners may finally be learning something. "Recently they re-established some bonuses. They even recognized that what we're doing up in Canada is better than anything being done at HQ. They used to think, If it's not happening down here in the U.S.A., it's not happening. They'd never been properly briefed on what we've accomplished in Kanata.

"And of course all our salaries are cheaper than heck, compared with U.S. salaries. Up here, a hundred grand a year is a good rate for a senior software engineer. That's $67K U.S. They're getting cutting-edge technology for chicken feed."

Will finishes crimping a row of chain mail. "Who knows?" he muses. "Maybe the dinosaur will evolve."

———

Will has raised a bigger issue, what a Toronto CEO calls "the Canadian discount." Wages are low here, which helps our exports. But the Canadian discount also works to Canada's disadvantage: it makes our companies so undervalued that they're sitting ducks for foreign takeovers. Another CEO, this time in Montreal, tells me that if he could magically transport his firm a few kilometres south into Vermont, he would instantly double its value. Same people, same work, same clients, same bricks and mortar, and twice the asking price.

In early 2000 I attended a Vancouver Enterprise Forum at which a third CEO, this one based in Richmond B.C., fielded questions from the floor. Most of these were technical or financial; then I put up my hand. "William Atkinson, *Globe and Mail*. Why is your company still in Canada?" The room got very quiet; the CEO cleared his throat.

"I don't know," he said. "Seattle or Bellingham make better sense. All I know is that I want to stay in Canada as long as I can."

———————

I meet Peter Hackett again in his offices at NRC's headquarters on Sussex Drive. Like me, he's criss-crossing the country; unlike me, he never stops. He's just as he seemed in Banff last month: a large, loose, baggy man with an engaging grin. His scientific credentials are impeccable and include a quarter century of pure research in chemical physics. Many of his publications are cited by other scientists, which is a strong sign of a researcher's originality and importance. But despite this, and his recent receipt of the Royal Society of Canada Rutherford Medal in Physics, Peter spends little time in the lab. As VP research, he spends his time these days helping a generation of younger scientists make discoveries of their own.

Despite having to curtail his own research, Peter considers himself fortunate. On this mild day in May, I cannot disagree. The office we sit in is larger than most apartments and flooded at the moment with birdsong and sun. Modern architects have conspired to make us forget that at its best, their profession is one of the humanities, able to lift the soul. This room, this whole building, do that. Mackenzie King built the laboratory in 1932 to consolidate NRC operations. Chiselled in stone over its main-entrance lintel are words from the Apocrypha chosen by King himself: "Great is truth and mighty above all things. The more thou searchest the more thou shalt marvel." The building is so lovely in plan, proportions and detailing—three-metre ceilings, wainscoting of fossiliferous Manitoba limestone—that Foreign Affairs, headquartered directly across Sussex Drive, has lusted after it for years. Fat chance. Federal cabinets have learned that while Foreign Affairs eats money, NRC coins it.

It wasn't always that way. When senior people like Peter Hackett survey NRC's past, they can't like everything they see. For years, large parts of NRC used to live in an ivory tower; its scientists studied a topic only because they found it interesting. Not that there's anything wrong with that: the whole world rests on work done from curiosity. When Michael Faraday showed George III around his electrical laboratory, the king asked what use it was. Faraday said: "Your Majesty, what use is a baby?"

But as recently as twenty years ago, NRC had gone too far into science for its own sake. Even when it barked its shins on something with commercial potential, it would publish a paper and then stick the paper on the shelf. Instead of technology transfer, the organization had something that Peter Hackett calls "throwing it over the wall." This meant that when the NRC had done its curiosity-based research, it considered that its work was over. Its results might sit in a library for decades, until someone happened to discover them and turn them into a product. As often as not, that entrepreneur wasn't Canadian. But although NRC's current appreciation of business and industry is long overdue, Peter assures me it has now taken place: the NRC has learned its lesson.

Examples? Peter scratches his head, as if uncertain where to begin, then case histories come tumbling out. BioBrite, an enzyme for pulp bleaching, which cuts toxic chlorine emissions by a hundred tonnes a mill a year and can save a Canadian pulp mill $0.5 million annually. Food from algae harvested on the East Coast, which earns $10 million a year in Japan and whose markets grow 20 per cent annually.

And then there's 'optoelectronics.' One aim of this new technology, Peter explains, is a single microchip that accepts data transmitted by visible light and processes this data either by light or by electricity. Pure-light processing has so far eluded researchers, but Peter is convinced it can be done.

While an optoelectronic chip is a tall order, Canada may be perfectly positioned to achieve it. Largely because of NRC's efforts, the National Capital Region is as important to Canadian IT as IT is to high tech in general. This is true today, when IT makes use of charged particles called electrons. It will be truer tomorrow, when IT uses photons, the tiny particles of light.

Electrons are unspeakably small compared to our everyday world, but next to photons they are clumsy, heavy, and huge. About 1850 electrons equal the mass of a proton, the main constituent of atoms. Roughly three quintillion photons are needed to equal one proton's mass. And while electrons have negative charge, a photon (though it interacts with electrical fields) is electrically neutral. The photon transmits electromagnetic radiation and also mediates the electromagnetic bond.

In a grand pun, photons—the indivisible quanta of light—are as light as can be. The total weight of sunlight falling on the whole Earth every day is only thirteen kilograms. Photons cannot exist at rest, for then even their negligible weight would fall to zero. Their only mass comes from their staggering velocity: three hundred million metres per second in vacuum, the fastest speed known. Photonic velocity is so fixed that Einstein took it as his ultimate constant. All the flabbergasting conclusions of relativity stem from this one premise: photons rule.

Although IT owes its past and present achievements to electricity, its future is with photons. Electrons may soon be passé in IT: computers will operate not with lightning but with light.

"When we began our optoelectronic initiative in 1987," Peter Hackett tells me, "it was so far beyond the most advanced current research that critics sneered at it as science fiction. Now look what's happening. In first quarter of 2000, Mitel announced a new microchip developed in collaboration with us, a forty-channel multiplexing device that doubles IT bandwidth. That led to Mitel's best stock gain in eight years, and it came directly from collaborative optoelectronics. Nortel and JDS Uniphase may also benefit from this work."

In the past half decade, Peter tells me, NRC has spun off sixty new companies in the Ottawa region alone. "One of them, Trillium Photonics, received US$6.5 million in financial support the week it was born. Another, SiGe Microsystems, already employs seventy people and has landed $34 million in venture capital to finance growth."

Peter springs from his chair and paces around the room. "European investors are flocking here: Marconi from the U.K., Nokia from Finland, Dow from the U.S., Alcatel of Paris just paid $7 billion for Newbridge Networks, a company that was 100 per cent made in Ottawa." While governments throughout the world are static or contracting, Peter tells me, private investment in Canada's technology clusters shows an annual employment growth rate of 15 per cent. In Ottawa, the knowledge economy includes more than a thousand companies and employs 6.3 per cent of the region's 1.3 million inhabitants; in Canada overall, knowledge firms produce $20 billion a year in export goods and employ half a million Canadians. In both value added and people employed, this significantly surpasses Canada's mighty forest industry.

Peter stops pacing and looks out the window. "Not bad for a single decade, is it? I'd say that NRC has learned her lesson."

She must have, I remark acidly. When I worked for the old girl, she'd have taken poison if a business, even a business she herself had started, eclipsed her.

My barb doesn't faze Peter Hackett. He grins like a kid who's thrown a brick through a window and got clean away.

Away from grim and grungy Rideau Street, May in Ottawa can be a magic time. The tulips are out, a gift from the Netherlands to thank Canada for harbouring Queen Juliana in the Second World War. Every year bulbs arrive by the planeload and are planted in enormous beds all over the city. For my money, the best way to see the tulips is how I'm doing it now: flying past them on a rented twelve-speed bicycle till the colours blur as if they're melting. Gold, deep purple, red-and-white like peppermint candy; I'd be a happy man if I didn't have to wear a helmet. The cycle paths along the canal are dead flat, and I can reach forty klicks an hour, but with my head covered, I'm roasting. I suppose it's worth some discomfort to protect my brain.

Where I live in North Vancouver, winter visits briefly and departs by March. If you want snow, you drive up into the mountains. At home I'd have started cutting the lawn sixty days ago; here winter hangs on like grim disaster. Even today, with the thermometer well into the twenties, I see the odd bit of snow in the shadows of north-facing walls.

Still, a long winter simply makes it all the sweeter when spring finally arrives. The waiting's over; it's time for growth. And with that thought, I'm off on another meditation.

In the knowledge economy, growth is like Godzilla—irresistible, yet wildly dangerous. Those who incorporate a knowledge company find this out the minute they're no longer able to run things off the tailgate of a truck. If you grow too slowly, you atrophy; if too quickly, you explode. In both cases the firm dies. CEO after CEO tells me how vital it is to hit your perfect growth rate— and also how hard.

Growth causes dozens of specific headaches. For one, high-tech start-ups are top heavy with knowledge experts, i.e., geeks. But companies that grow beyond three people develop needs in non-geek areas: tax, finance, office management, marketing. As pay-roll mounts, non-geek functions—recruiting, training, pension planning, inventory control—get progressively more important.

One thing is continuous through all the change: everyone in the knowledge economy wants to be in its elite. It's part of the equality myth. When firms call their receptionists *customer liaison managers*, no one accepts the notion that they don't make the company run by themselves. Everyone wants to be head body styl-ist; nobody wants to change the tires.

Unfortunately, everyone can't be an expert—a software engi-neer, a specialist in advanced materials, a games designer. This state of affairs, the Revenge of Democracy if you will, can immo-bilize a knowledge company. A CEO may go on record denying that creating product has a higher value than answering phones.

The CEO's temptation is especially true if he pretends to be first among equals. If he does this to maximize his power while mini-mizing protests about it; then his own myth ties his hands. Yet any knowledge company so configured is in handcuffs. One of the worst results comes on payday, when the janitor wants a cheque that's not radically different from that of vice-president R&D. Knowledge firms in the grip of their own equality myth have been known to pay Og the custodian far more than he's worth and Dr. Cranium of R&D far less.

The effect is magnified if there's a union. CEOs may find it expe-dient to "front-end load" a contract settlement by offering lower-paid employees a higher percentage increase than specialists receive, thus reducing total salary outlay. Dr. Cranium may even agree with Albert Einstein, who found it fair to earn less than a plumber be-cause plumbers don't enjoy their work as much. Still, the firm ends by paying higher-level salaries for lower-level activity. That makes it difficult to find and keep good people in key areas.

And yet there exists a back door for companies that have trussed themselves in this way: outsourcing their grunt work. Who changes the tires? Why, another firm! This keeps almost everyone in the company demonstrably within its elite. It would all seem like self-delusion, except that now and then it works.

High tech's best example of divesting low-grade work is the fabless semiconductor firm. It's a company that does everything involved in making silicon microchips except actually *making* them. Hence *fabless*, which is Geekspeak for "without fabrication facilities."

An FSF conducts careful marketing analyses and keeps close technical liaison with existing and potential customers to determine what its client industries want, need, and are willing to pay for in a new microchip design. If the numbers work out, the FSF creates and tests a new design. Its work ends when it makes "masks," or a series of photo-templates, for the new chip. The masks, along with a list of technical specifications the thickness of a pulpit Bible, are sent to a subcontractor's manufacturing facility, which actually produces the chip.

The sub's factory may be next door or in the next continent: no matter. The FSF does retain some support staff—the CEO's executive assistant or the head of PR—but the firm approaches that mythical ideal, a company comprising no one but designers and other high-level personnel. The FSF is all cream and no milk. To alter the analogy, someone else changes the tires.

It's late morning on a grey day when I arrive at an FSF west of Ottawa. Tundra Semiconductor is in Kanata, directly across from Newbridge Networks. Ten years ago, Tundra started out within Newbridge as a small, incubated sub-unit: what the industry calls a *Skunk Works*.

I love the vivid terms the knowledge economy constantly thinks up, tosses off, and throws away. I've traced Skunk Works back to the Al Capp comic *Li'l Abner*. The Dogpatch Skonk Works was a factory whose interior the reader was never shown and had to imagine: in it, the antisocial character Big Barnsmell worked all alone doing mysterious, smelly things. *Skunk Works* entered the lexicon of the knowledge economy when 3M, the Minnesota Mining and Manufacturing Company, studied the birth of its most successful products. To senior management's astonishment, most of its biggest money-makers had never been planned and implemented from the top down. Instead, some geek on a lab bench had a brainstorm and began pursuing it by himself out of curiosity. Often the employee-cum-inventor would have to hide his wealth-producing work from his own bosses, lest they shut him down. Dow-Corning's heat-resistant glass Corelle and 3M's ubiquitous Post-it notes both emerged from a Skunk Works process.

By the late 1980s, the Skunk Works approach was firmly established in the more forward-looking knowledge companies. Someone with what appears to be a good idea is given a small budget (usually a few hours a week and little or no capital budget) and turned loose. A more recent word for a Skunk Works operator is *intrapreneur*, a coinage from *intra*-corporate entre*preneur*.

The Prototype: Sixth Attribute

Skunk Works work.

Dr. Adam Chowaniec, Tundra's CEO, led a management buyout of his Skunk Works unit in 1995 from his then employer, Newbridge Networks. Ever since, conditions within the knowledge economy have put Tundra into explosive growth. In 1996 its market capitalization was $18 million; five years later it had grown by sixty times.

Though his parent firm, Newbridge, was begun by Terry Matthews, Michael's Cowpland's original partner in Mitel, Adam is light-years away from Mike Cowpland's cowboy mould. He's typical of what I found was a new breed of high-tech entrepreneur: eloquent, thoughtful, knowledgeable, good-humoured, and even (gasp) well-dressed—Übergeek writ large.

Adam is in his early fifties; most of his employees are in their twenties and thirties. While not at all what one would call controlling, he is thoroughly in control. Adam's personality is to be found wherever that of any knowledge-company CEO appears: in hallways, workstations, test labs. In Tundra, these areas resonate with excitement, anticipation, and laughter. The atmosphere blends Hallowe'en with Christmas Eve.

The knowledge firms in the Ottawa area do more than generate growth and ideas or attract venture capital: they have sparked a communications revolution, of which Adam's FSF is a leader. In knowledge-economy Ottawa, Tundra sits atop the food chain.

"JDS Uniphase is here, and so is Nortel," Adam tells me as we sit together in his quiet boardroom. "They and the other big telecommunication firms are changing rapidly, paring down to their core competencies. As they become less vertically integrated, they acquire new abilities not by building new divisions but by acquisition. More to the point for our company, our clients are outsourcing more instead of trying to do everything by themselves. It's a worldwide trend, which creates a huge opportunity for component providers like ourselves."

Adam Chowaniec has impeccable credentials for understanding and exploiting rapidly changing conditions in the knowledge economy. After spending his early career at BNR he moved to Commodore Amiga, which in the mid-eighties was a sizable computer manufacturer. He came to Newbridge when that company purchased his division from Commodore.

Tundra's products are staggeringly complex: its typical chip (I can't bring myself to call it "average") has six million to ten million

separate transistors. As Adam and I talk, I notice an optical pho-
tomicrograph of a late-model Tundra chip hanging on a wall behind him. The photo is one metre to a side, ten thousand times the
area of the actual chip, yet its finest details are too small to be seen.
The whole thing looks like nothing so much as a living cell, and
illustrates the coming convergence between tissue and machine.
As life becomes data, data systems are becoming as intricate as life.

Like most knowledge firms, Tundra occupies a paper-thin
niche. It must make chips that are useful in a number of generic
applications, yet it cannot start work until it is intimately familiar
with the chips' end use. How does Tundra reconcile such conflict-
ing pressures? Simple, says Adam with a grin: "We must be prescient. We must anticipate what the customer wants before he
himself knows." A fabless semiconductor firm succeeds not by
reading its customers' minds but by *becoming* their minds.

While it costs Tundra $9 million over two years to design a
new chip, the unit sells for $50—two pizzas and a twelve pack. All
that knowledge goes for a ridiculously low unit cost. Tundra makes
its money by sheer volume.

Tundra's latest chip is an "intelligent" communications device
for routing Internet data. The chip functions like a smart, error-
free, and incredibly fast traffic cop, simultaneously directing many
information streams and deciding which data go where. The speed,
volume, and number of connections (interconnectivity) of these
modern data streams make them comparable to full-scale metro-
politan freeway networks. Just like vehicular highways, in fact,
these "dataways" reduce their number of intersections as they
handle more traffic at higher speeds.

The new Tundra chip is an intersection for these data paths. Its
architecture lets it make a large number of decisions at dizzying
speeds. Like the living cell it resembles in Adam's micrograph, or
like rooms in a vast mansion, the chip is subdivided into many
sub-areas. Many of these blocks are so highly innovative that
Adam will not tell me precisely what they do. The chip is, he says,

"part hard-wired and part reprogrammable. Data flows into the chip matrix, then software inside the chip decides how and where to dispatch the data."

The most critical business aspect of designing a new chip, Adam tells me, is the elapsed time from first design work to first sale. This "time to market" must be minimized, even though the chip's final uses are not even known as it is being designed. Tundra cannot design its chip around settled customer needs; customers must design their systems around the chip. Thus the chip must be in nearly final form before the customers can complete their own design work. This creates enormous pressure on Tundra to make something that is fast, reliable, quick to market, and state-of-the-art innovative, and that operates perfectly the first time it's plugged in. So far Tundra has consistently done this, explaining part of its pre-eminence among the world's limited number of FSFs.

Another factor in Tundra's success involves its design approach. The firm builds a large-scale model of a chip before it makes its final masks, or phototemplates. This early-stage model looks nothing like the final chip: it's a brightly coloured metal container about the size of a small kitchen trash can, crammed with solid-state hardware. Adam calls it the Purple Box. Since the Purple Box is reprogrammable, Tundra engineers can configure it in endless ways to test their designs in advance. Only when a design works out is it shrunk to the scale of the final microchip.

Although the Purple Box operates fifty times more slowly than the chips it models, it functions just like them. The finished chip hums along at 50 MHZ, or fifty million cycles per second; the Purple Box dawdles along at a snail's pace of 1 MHZ. It is programmed from a computer database that is Tundra's first step in new-chip design.

The Purple Box has proven so effective that it has given Tundra and its clients an added, unexpected benefit: it is adept at finding flaws in other chips used by the clients—chips made by Tundra's competitors. "If our customer's systems develop a bottleneck,"

Adam says, "we want to ensure it isn't caused by anything we make."

Tundra has designed its new gating chip for universal use in state-of-the-art telecom hardware. Think of it as the parliamentary speaker: everyone who talks to anyone else must talk through him. Since the hardware the chip supports is built around it, sales should be brisk from the get-go. As the equivalent in IT of a limited edition, the chip is in effect pre-subscribed.

Tundra's subsector is evolving so fast that chip complexity doubles every two years. Put another way, every two years the price for a chip of given complexity is halved. All this is *electronic* data processing, which according to Peter Hackett is about to be overtaken by optoelectronics, then photonics, and finally by quantum nanotechnology. Already data are transferred over thousands of kilometres via fibre optics. The day is coming when information will be processed, as well as sent, by light.

What the "light chip" will look like is anyone's guess. It will almost certainly not be like today's chip, a semiconductor sandwich. It might not even be a chip at all. It could be grown in tanks like a crystal. It could be made from organic materials. It might be excreted by living organisms from plans artificially encoded onto DNA. The light chip itself might be alive. But that's all for the future. In the meantime, chips are silicon, and Tundra's design work must go on as before.

Some final questions for Dr. Chowaniec. Does Tundra use the full capacity of its offshore fabrication plants?

"Oh, no. Those things are huge."

So Tundra's subcontractors also work for competing firms?

"Of course."

What keeps a rogue employee in the overseas fab plant from reverse-engineering one of Tundra's designs and selling it to the highest bidder?

"We put our faith in complexity," Adam says, shrugging. "Our chips are so detailed that it would take the best team in the world several years to reverse-engineer them. That's twice the time it takes us to finish a new design. We certainly don't make life easy for potential pirates. For example, our chips randomize the component locations. Visual inspection won't tell anyone what a chip element does."

Aha! You put in booby traps, Dr. Chowaniec? You make resistors that look like transistors, and transistors that look like data buses, to drive would-be pirates crazy with frustration?

The subtle smile returns. "I'm afraid I can't comment on that," Adam says.

By the time I reach Montreal Vieille-Ville, my head hurts. Maybe it's navigating the *autoroute-expresse* Décarie at rush hour, which is like flying a low-level bomb run under ack-ack fire. But my headache has another cause: an anomaly that's been nagging me since my first day in Ottawa. There's a woman in Montreal I want to talk to: a survivor of the big, old knowledge firms. I'm hoping she can answer two questions. Why are the smaller knowledge firms so helpful? And: Why don't big firms return my calls?

The whole situation seems impossible. When I started my research, I thought new technical ideas didn't come out of a garage; they demanded huge investments in workers and equipment. No small firm, however good its ideas or people, could do this. Only big firms, or at least mid-size companies with a minimum of five hundred employees, would develop knowledge to the point that it could be transferred. And herein lay the headache. If the big guys were the knowledge economy's engines, and if I were writing a book that extolled this, why weren't they co-operating?

I couldn't figure it. Whenever I tried to set up field interviews, every one of the big firms was suspicious. CEOs did not return calls; fine, they were busy. But neither did their assistants or *their* assistants. I got tired of explaining myself to receptionists, but even their cool, snotty tones were better than endless voice mail.

Now and then I got a response from the larger firms' flak catchers but these dripped arrogance. *Globe and Mail? That's the* press, *isn't it? I'm sorry, we're posting our quarterly results and no one's available. You want to reach an* engineer? *You're joking. All our engineers know that media contact must go through this office. If they talk to you they'll be fired. What are you doing? A book? You'll let us review your drafts, of course . . . No? Well, well. Leave your number, and we'll try to get back to you.* When through bloody-minded persistence I did bulldoze my way into one or two big firms, their representatives handed me the corporate line verbatim from the corporate Web site or company brochure.

The contrast with small firms was amazing. *Of course we've read your columns. Would you prefer the* CEO, CTO, CFO, *or all three? No need to sign a non-disclosure agreement: just write what you uncover. See you soon.*

Now in Montreal, I find my hotel room, hang up my clothes, glance at the view—smog, clouds, honking traffic—call room service for a pot of coffee, and fall into a chair to think things through. What was going on here? Why did big firms want a chokehold on how they're portrayed? Why did they parcel out information like a miser paying gold? Why this slit-eyed mistrust, the view that everything beyond their borders was as threatening as a pack of wolves? Why were all the energetic, fast-moving, self-confident, good-humoured firms also small?

It didn't make sense. Big knowledge companies behaved like some jaded fop, venturing out in public only after hours of fussy grooming. The young firms were like healthy, handsome twenty-year-olds. They looked good in tattered jeans and had nothing to hide.

At this point, I got the buzz that every writer knows and lives for: the sense that he's on to something. But where to go from here? I was still ignorant of what I most wanted to know: the precise nature of work in larger high-tech firm. What's it like to be in one? What are its triumphs and tragedies? What's the *feel* of it? I needed someone on the inside to tell me.

Poor corporate flak catchers—they have no idea how many detours there are around their stonewalling. Denied entry to big firms, unwilling to compromise their workers with midnight rendezvous, I turned to an equally good source: a big firm's recent employee. She lived right here in Montreal.

———

Rue St-Denis, Tuesday, early June. Sunshine and few tourists; air sweet as sugar; the *Plateau* as bright, loud and colourful as a family reunion. The best-looking women in the world float by on the arms of intense, chain-smoking men. Here comes my contact, walking briskly toward me, smiling, with her hand outstretched: Ms. Ellie Grey. She's the interview I need: an energetic professional who spent twelve years at a large telecommunications firm and recently left them to work at a small start-up.

Big companies issue press releases pretending that absent sales or plummeting market share were foreseen by clever management, but Ellie spares me that transparently silly company line. Instead, she dishes the dirt on her former employers. The big firms that she knows best, she tells me, are telcos—*telco* being Geekspeak for a telephone service provider. As our interview proceeds, my eyes are opened to another world. The telcos, I discover, share many traits with other big knowledge firms.

"Telcos are dinosaurs," says Ellie. "They're regulation driven, staid, and cautious to the point of paranoia." In fairness, she adds, telcos have to be conservative to some extent. "Phone systems must be bulletproof [Geekspeak for "absolutely reliable"] because society depends on them. That's the legitimate reason the telcos are so stolid."

Are there any illegitimate reasons? "Sheer size and inertia. Most telcos are fat, cumbersome Goliaths with pyramidal, hierarchical structures that wouldn't be out of place in the 1880s. Even steel mills aren't run like that any more, not that anyone's told the telcos. Telcos also have no competition. As monopolies, they move only when they're goaded."

But didn't federal deregulation open things up? "A little. Telcos have to accommodate hardware other than their own, and they have to let other companies offer long-distance service over their lines. But they still consider local areas their private fiefdoms. That's because most phone use occurs in local areas. They're the largest source of revenue for the big telcos."

And then the revelation. "You can tell a lot about the telcos' corporate culture," Ellie says, "by the technology they use."

I don't understand, I say. The structure of a knowledge company reflects its own technology? I thought it was the other way around. That too, Ellie says: it's a circular, repetitive process, what geeks call iterative. A firm adopts a type of knowledge, which slowly conditions the thought of everyone in the firm. Let me see if I have this straight, I say: technology springs from an approach, then reinforces that approach. Exactly, Ellie says: Mindset Maketh Man. Hm! I say. Give me an example.

"A telco connects people by opening and sustaining a two-way circuit," she says. "That must occur for speech or data to flow over a standard phone line." Lily Tomlin doesn't plug copper jacks into chrome receptacles any more, Ellie says; switching is now done electronically. "But the principle hasn't changed since the invention of the phone. You need to sustain a dedicated circuit over the full time that people talk."

Imagine a big telco as a nest of wires, says Ellie, carrying the telco's beloved dedicated circuits. Each wire may be removed or reconnected, but no wire exchanges any information with any adjacent wire. Facts go from source to end without horizontal interaction—what geeks call crosstalk. And since technology subtly determines thought patterns, the mindset of the big telcos is as linear as wire.

At this point, I'm quivering like a spaniel on a scent. Does this, I ask Ellie Grey, also explain the configuration and behaviour of the smaller, newer firms?

"Oh, absolutely. Like the big telcos, the small firms think like the technology that spawned them. But unlike the big telcos, the newer firms use a non-linear technology that requires non-linear thought." And that technology is. . . ? "The Internet," Ellie says. "The World Wide Web."

The 1980s cliché *information superhighway* never caught on, she tells me, because the metaphor was obsolete before it was coined. "*Highway* is a telco image: it implies a dedicated path, a two-way circuit. Twelve lanes in each direction, sure: but nonetheless a permanent, physical, paved road. The Internet is radically different."

Over the next two hours, a fascinating story emerges. To visualize the Net, says Ellie, picture rush hour in Shanghai—a mass of cars, cycles, rickshaws, peasants with live chickens over their shoulders. Everyone's in constant motion, jostling one another, crossing paths; no one slows down. It seems ridiculously chaotic. But everyone gets through; there are no collisions. The chaos is apparent, not real.

That's how the Net works. No superhighways, no dedicated circuits. At source, computers knock data into signal bundles called packets. Love letters, travelogues, business proposals, porn— content doesn't matter to this motionless, dimensionless, global machine. Not only is content unimportant, but so is the medium. Voice, text, drawings, sound effects, broadband colour video with twelve-channel surround sound—the Net doesn't care.

The dispatching minicomputer, called a router, tags each packet with an address that encodes source and goal, then dumps the mulched-up message into cyberspace. At that point each packet, like a newly released homing pigeon, wings off on its own. It may take any route whatsoever to its destination. A thirty-millisecond chunk of message, about the time it takes to purse your lips to make a *W* sound, may go from Saint John to Hawaii via servers in Los Angeles and Buenos Aires. The chunk that comes right after it starts and finishes in the same places but may go through Nunavut, Terre Haute, and Tokyo. At destination, the receiving computer fields the packets as they tumble in and splices them together in their proper order. Neither sender nor receiver knows their crisp, clear conversation has been through the equivalent of a *Star Trek* transporter: knocked into atoms, flung all over hell, and stitched back together at point of receipt. Routing doesn't matter: that's the lesson of the Net. That distant bell you're hearing is the death knell of the dedicated circuit—and maybe of the whole big-telco mindset as well.

The big firms haven't realized this yet, probably because the Net is in baby days and still evolving. Today only dedicated geeks use the Net for more than written text and the odd still photo, both of which can go via standard E-mail protocols. Yet in theory, nothing hinders the Net from carrying radio, telephony, or even real-time video. The Net distinguishes these media only by the volume of data they encode. A line drawing takes more bytes to describe than a page of text; a black-and-white photo, more bytes; a colour photo, still more. Video is the most data-rich medium of all. A full-colour TV picture, in the form sent over standard home cable, may break down into twenty-five full-screen stills per second, plus stereo sound and closed captioning. That gobbles up more digital description than an evening of Mahler at the symphony.

It is this richness of video that is currently the stumbling block to its wider use on the Net. While the Net itself is lightning fast, most people connect to it via existing phone lines, which have very low limits in transmitting data. Geeks call this narrowband, the image being of a bottleneck. (After Waterloo, Blucher cut the *grande armée* to ribbons as thirty thousand French soldiers tried to cross a bridge two metres wide. That bridge is like a telco link.)

Narrowband limits video to one or two frames per second, so that today's Internet TV or Netcast has a jumpy, *cinéma-vérité* look. Now, however, some companies are addressing this with a technology they call *video streaming*. And guess what? Every one of these innovative new companies is small.

Video streaming replaces the two-shots-a-second jump-cuts that currently lurch down telco lines. In their place is true video with silk-smooth motion. Ellie says the approach is called compression, and she explains how it works. In today's brute-force video broadcasting, cable TV or the Net dispatch one still frame after another. Every pixel in every frame is fully specified for variables such as position, brightness, and hue. Compression is more elegant. Its algorithms, or software procedures, assume each frame is like the previous one and specify only *changes* between successive stills. Since stills are no longer transmitted in excess detail, the system frees up data capacity, or bandwidth, to carry more stills per second. Result: a smoothly moving Netcast. This new technology will soon revolutionize Internet communications. God help us home workers: the day of face-to-face E-mail is at hand. *Hi, Bill! Unshaven in your skivvies at 2:00 p.m., I see!*

Compression technology can also convey phone conversations; this is called *Netelephony*. Advanced Net users already use this feature to phone around the world free.

Consider the mindset that different types of technical knowledge both require and confirm. A telco's corporate thought begins and ends with the dedicated circuit, a technology that's mirrored in its corporate structure. The big telco is linear, plodding. A small firm is also like the knowledge it uses, but that knowledge is based a new thing—the Internet.

And what an innovation that is. The Net is like a honeycomb of individual cells; its pattern is infinitely extensible. Data flow freely: no fact is constrained to a fixed route. If stymied somewhere, a datum instantly takes another path. This configuration makes the Net "robust"—powerful, self-healing, and nearly impossible to shut down. It was to attain this bulletproof robustness that the U.S. Department of Defense first created the Net. DOD wanted to retain U.S. computing power even if atomic attack destroyed computing cells (buildings) or nodes (whole cities).

Now, extend your analysis from knowledge set to mindset. In a prototypical new firm, each worker acts like a cell in the Net's honeycomb. A torrent of facts constantly rushes by each cell's periphery. Workers take what they need from this data flow at any time. From budgets to project proposals, most workers have continuous access to whatever data they require. In a sense, the model is still need-to-know, but the determination of need is entrusted to the individual worker. It is no longer dictated from above.

––––––––––

After leaving her final big-telco job, Ellie Grey went to work for a new, small firm, a kind of anti-telco. Her new company has no hardware fixation, because its raison d'être is to help start up alternative "mini-telcos" to attack the dinosaurs' stranglehold on local-area phone service. In mid-2001 there were over eighteen hundred of these mini-telcos in the U.S., with more appearing daily. Look for the mini-telcos to start appearing in Canada soon: the saurians are about to get some mammalian competition.

Today, Ellie Grey is in charge of a team that builds control and supervisory software for these upstart firms, most of whom, she says, "admit they know nothing about telephony." And small blame to them: a telephone system, she tells me, is unbelievably intricate. "It's like a nuclear reactor. It's too complex for any one human, even a genius, to understand."

That's where Ellie's present firm comes in. With elegant software, it lets a mini-telco provide the service of a giant firm. Even better, in fact: for like Unis Lumin, another pint-sized upstart, these little knowledge-economy firms are closer to their customers. This is true geographically—head office is a dozen kilometres away, not two thousand—and, more important, true philosophically as well. Humungous Telco (HTI) Inc. may soon be the exception, not the rule.

Ellie says her company is bursting at the seams. "We can't build software or get it out to customers fast enough to fill demand. Our client base has more than doubled in the past six months."

Which introduces a classic problem. How is her new firm going to avoid growing so precipitately that it re-creates all the woes, worries, and problems of the dinosaurs it is working to replace? Ellie admits the difficulty. "Size and efficiency are trade-offs," she says. "Small companies are more adaptable, but they also have less capital and infrastructural support. When the firm is nobody but Jim and Fred, you can call a meeting by running down the hall and snagging people. Try doing that when you're a senior VP with a staff of fifteen hundred."

Other growth-based issues seem like the corporate equivalent of senility. As a company grows, says Ellie, "risk takers are replaced by the risk averse. Hunches and intuitions give way to plans, projections, and policies. Engineers are pushed aside by lawyers, accountants, and human-resources types. Informal becomes formal." More significantly, the governing question changes from Why Not to Why; the burden of proof is on the innovator, not on those who resist innovation. And another mainstream telco is born.

Big companies can't be blamed for all their unsavoury characteristics, says Ellie: some of these come wrapped up with greater size. "At the telco where I worked, a security guard told me it's as hard to police a company that size as it is a small town. You're statistically as likely to have a murderer, a wife abuser, a pederast, or an alcoholic."

And yet some big-company errors do seem to be wilful, especially close-mindedness. As Ellie explains, the true bane of the big telco lurks in its lowest tier of technical managers. At that stratum, the Curse of the Dedicated Circuit starts to show.

"These are the guys—they're almost always guys—who think they know all there is to know technically because of an engineering degree," Ellie says with a grimace. "Plus they also know all there is to know about business because they've managed to get an MBA." An E-MBA, moreover, acquired via tele-learning: pure knowledge, certified free of all human interaction whatsoever.

Mercifully for the shareholders if not their own department's employees, such draft animals usually toil at mid-level treadmills till they're put out to pasture. Yet sometimes, if they are adept at company politics and get a break, they may rise high. Ellie remembers one example, an opinionated bully whose mind was shut tighter than a vault door. Seeing his quality—or rather lack of it— his superiors sidelined him into what they thought was an out-of-the-way technology. Unfortunately, Dr. Deadwood's predecessor had been a man of action, imagination, and energy. When his plans became realities, Dr. Deadwood rode them up—and up. The "marginal technology" was wireless, one of the hottest things in the knowledge economy. Today Dr. Deadwood is CEO.

"We certainly didn't revere him for his wild leaps of imagination," Ellie remembers drily. "He was the company's equivalent of a party hack. But he also had a rat's cunning and lots of corporate connections." How could the commissars who sent him to Siberia know that his place of exile sat on solid gold? Now he's in the corner office, thanks to the exceptional man (now retired) who laid the groundwork for Dr. D's undeserved success.

(Late note at presstime: Dr. D. has just presided over a tenfold drop in share price and is stepping down. There's justice after all.)

––––––––

Despite everything she's experienced, Ellie Grey retains "an unjustified optimism that a company doesn't have to be a dinosaur just because it's grown large. A company's highest levels can actually foster innovation, instead of killing it." She cites Bell Laboratories, which in the 1950s and '60s made many major breakthroughs, including the laser. "They had no idea what these things might do, they just thought they were nifty. Or Xerox, which derived the graphical user interface decades ago."

To a telco executive, free data flow is as appalling as communism: it turns nice linear traffic into an ant's nest. To the small-firm geek, free flow is the only way to work and think. This old-new, big-little split explains why, in Ellie Grey's words, "telco people are obsessed by hardware" while "the new people, the Net people, are not." In the Net part of the knowledge economy, hardware is something you acquire, use, jettison as necessary, and forget about. Net geeks aren't in love with fibre optics and neat connectors, blinking lights and whirring drives. Their goal is to make all hardware as invisibly efficient—in Geekspeak, *transparent*—as an athlete's sense of balance. As for data, they may be as vital as air; but like the air, they're always and everywhere available.

The big telcos formed, grew, and ossified before the World Wide Web existed. They understand the Web as well as *Giganotosaurus* understood mammals. Data inside the telcos are squeezed through narrow conduits that rarely intersect. Send reports up; take orders from above; and eyes front, Corporal. Don't look at what's happening in the next department or the adjacent desk: it's none of your concern.

"Telcos guard information jealously," says Ellie as we amble down Rue Ste-Catherine. "Their entire structure exists to mete it out as sparingly as possible; to safeguard information, as if it were a precious and irreplaceable commodity. To a telco, facts are a nonrenewable resource."

As she says this, a light goes on in my head. I see why I couldn't squeeze anything but flak-catcher's drivel out of big firms: they run on a "need-to-know basis"—telcospeak for *We'll tell you as little as we can, because knowledge is power*. Meanwhile, the little firms have a good time, chat with the neighbours while hanging out washing, wave at passersby, and prosper. Too bad the dinosaurs can't see the connection. But then they wouldn't be dinosaurs, would they? They'd be small, nimble, and smart: in a word, mammals. Big, old, linear, hardware based, secretive: moribund. Small, new, nonlinear, software based, open: vigorously alive. The saurians haven't seen this yet and never may.

Big and Small Firms in Information Technology (IT)

Firm	*Age*	*Size*	*Focus*	*Mindset*	*Data Flow*
Telco	Old	Big	Hardware	Linear	Restricted
Internet	New	Small	Software	Non-Linear	Free Flow

While the biggest knowledge firms are also the best known, they are often morons at thinking up the very ideas that make them money. The knowledge economy's true powerhouses are the ad hoc gangs of geeks that infest small companies; the movers and shakers really *are* the guys in the garage. The big firms' role is self-limited to invention's poor cousin, technology transfer.

Whatever their faults, the juggernauts do have the muscle to get ideas—okay, other people's ideas—to market. One way they do this is by bullying, the ruthless application of brute force. A kinder, gentler way to transfer technology uses marketing, a peculiarly modern form of black magic. Marketing is vague but vital, expensive but indeterminate. Though all companies need it, big firms are the likeliest to afford it. And while my field research has turned up several fault lines in the knowledge economy—geek/suit, little/big, linear/non-linear—geek/marketer may represent the deepest rift of all.

As I walk down avenue Président-Kennedy, ducking my head to keep my hat on in the strong breeze off the river, I congratulate myself on my luck. Someone I've been trying to reach for weeks has at last responded to my E-mails and has agreed to an interview. Even better, he's here in Montreal, and we're having dinner tonight. I'm hoping he can tell me about the gap—canyon might be a better word—between two types of knowledge, technical and marketing. Once again, two camps in the knowledge economy have different mindsets. Both are necessary to a company's success, but nobody in one camp seems to understand the other. I'd like to find out why.

———————

In the past two centuries, novelists and opera librettists have explored a strange phenomenon. An intelligent person, caught in a crisis unsolvable by his expertise, turns in desperation to a source of information he once held in contempt. The student fails and reads Tarot. The impotent writer visits a Gypsy. The geek creates a perfect product that does not sell and turns, half in superstition and half in desperation, to the witch doctors in marketing.

In good times, geeks scorn marketing; in a crunch, they demand miracles of it. Will my modules interface? What will sales be? Madam Zomfre, can you see a pattern in the cards?

Even if the marketers understand geek questions, there's no certainty the geeks will understand the marketers' answers. As in all the knowledge economy's fissures, between geek and marketer is a great gulf fixed. To a marketer, geeks are troglodytes; to a geek, marketing is the sister of sorcery. A geek shows himself *pure laine* by mocking marketers as loudmouthed jerks in checkered suits. Marketers pride themselves on their ignorance of engineering— Ares mocking Hephaestos. Yet marketing and engineering are more alike than either admits: marketing has its logic and geekdom has its blind faith. Here's how this works in the knowledge economy, as related by one who knows.

———————

➤ "I have a problem with engineers," Brian Leeners tells me as he pours his beer. "In fact I have a problem with anyone who has an engineering mindset. They're trained to believe in themselves totally, to think that no problem is insoluble to analytic logic. And not just by analytic logic, but by *them*. In my experience most geeks have a rock-solid belief that given inclination and time, they could do anything better than you, me or anyone. They're completely delusional."

Harsh words; harsh weather. Beyond the window, fat raindrops smack the sidewalk. Here in the *auberge* it's dim and cozy, the only sounds the chime of glassware and my tape recorder's hiss.

Until 1999 Brian Leeners was CEO of Totally Hip Software of Gastown, a funky waterfront area in Vancouver. He recently retired from the firm to set up as a venture capitalist. Brian displays two things in our interview: a knowledge of law (he has an LL.B.) and a bias toward marketing. His mindset is not innate, he says: he acquired it through many years of knocking heads with geeks.

"I don't deny that the technical aspect of high technology is demanding," Brian concedes. "But that's not the issue. Technology is only part of the knowledge that high-tech companies need for success. A company neglects any of these non-technical activities at its peril."

Such neglect, Brian tells me, is often a form of swaggering. The knowledge economy, which marries technology and business, requires of its entrepreneurs an intense self-confidence whose side effect is arrogance. Everyone slips into arrogance from time to time, Brian says. But geeks are to the manner born.

"Engineers who are under-supervised will wander off and develop something because they think it's nifty," Brian says. "After a year they dump it on marketing's desk and say, 'Here it is! Stuff it in a package and sell a million units!' As if marketing were a gift-wrap service."

Brian has a point. Properly undertaken, marketing is far more than packaging: it embraces every aspect of a company. It monitors competitors. It performs basic research to find out what potential customers will pay for. The colour of the wrap is the last thing on a long, long list.

"If a company isn't market driven *and* marketing driven," Brian says, "it may as well go off and join a university."

One of marketing's tools is advertising—notifying target audiences that a product exists and is worth its cost. Good technology may fail if no one knows about it; second-rate technology may succeed if an advertising campaign is precise. According to Brian, however, sometimes even flawless advertising cannot move good technology. There are too many imponderables.

"Advertising has a concept called *mindshare*," Brian says. "It's a good description. You won't sell anything unless you get that critical share of a customer's mind. He won't buy until he knows about you, and can't know about you until you attract his attention.

"But, my God! the difficulty. Your target works fifty or sixty hours a week. His deadlines are ugly, his authority's a joke, he's stressed beyond belief. Now he's eating lunch at his desk, flipping through a magazine, and he sees your ad. You have *one second* to create enough mindshare to make him check you out. Good luck! It's not impossible, just harder than hell."

Such sound arguments, whether by geek or marketer, often go unheard by the other side. Take intuition, perfectly defined by one old newspaperman as "your mind's unconscious memory of past mistakes." Marketers take pride in their intuition. Geeks tend to see it as unquantifiable, which it is, and as worthless, which it is not. Effective people, even geeks, use intuition daily. To a good engineer, a bad design *feels* wrong.

But if engineering has its intuitive side, marketing also has its science. Perhaps marketing's most important intellectual concept is *positioning*. Dr. Dan Monison, a professor of marketing at Queen's University in Kingston, Ontario, and widely regarded as a guru of his discipline, used to define a product to his M.B.A. classes as the sum of its attributes. To Danny Monison, *attributes* are those product traits that a consumer understands and acknowledges. Traits become attributes if, and only if, a consumer concedes the traits are specifically useful to him. Only then will money change hands.

Marketing considerations work for computers as well as for soda pop; effectively used, they operate equally well on post-docs as on teens. Many geeks don't see this. Partly from arrogance and partly from that innocent altruism of theirs; they think marketing is the last refuge of a scoundrel.

Indisputably, marketing can be perverted. Whether it's flogging a lousy product or telling voters that a war is noble, marketing can further sordid aims. But despite its misuse in high tech or anywhere else, marketing—like sex and writing—is innately neutral, or even good. It can serve masters who are decent, and others who are vile. A product both excellent and successful— a notebook computer, or a running shoe that keeps its owner fit for pennies a kilometre—blends engineering with marketing in a positive way and benefits designers, consumers, and everyone in between.

As Brian Leeners says, effective marketing pervades all aspects of a business. A geek cabal that makes things without reference to the outside world, that has no idea of what people want and no interest in finding out, may design things that are technical marvels but impossible to sell. Almost by definition, the successful firm is market driven. Its products have genuine attributes, and its sales will keep geeks employed. The geeks may bitch about those ignorant marketers, but they'll still get paid.

The knowledge economy creates strange bedfellows. Given their wildly different mindsets, marketers and geeks may never totally understand each other. But in any successful company, they're forced to sleep in the same bed. And while that marriage is one of total inconvenience, it's amazingly fecund. Its partners may say, with Walt Kelly's character Molester Mole: *Our mutual dislike will never interfere with our true friendship.*

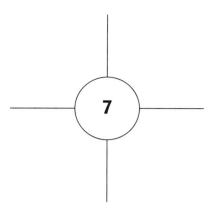

ATLANTIS

Out of Montreal's downtown. As usual, there's little knowledge industry in *centre-ville*: the action is out in the suburbs, on its way across the country. Twenty-three-hundred-block Cohen Street, the headquarters of Phoenix International; Christopher Columbus Street; Parc la fontaine. I swoop across the Jacques Cartier Bridge, and the vast St. Lawrence opens out below me as if I'd taken off in a light plane. There's the old site of Expo 67. It's crumbled almost past recognition, but Montreal can't let go of the last time it felt like a world city. Relax, folks, you're there again; you just don't realize it yet. There's no more need to clutch at old-economy leftovers. The knowledge economy awaits.

The South Shore now, and beyond it the grey-green hills of Vermont. There's Boucherville, where the NRC has its Industrial Materials Institute and one of Canada's strongest programs in nano-technology research. And here's the head office of one of Quebec's major knowledge successes, Softimage.

Softimage is an entirely home-grown company. Almost uniquely in Canada's knowledge economy, the name is pronounced *à la française*: sof-tee-*mazh*. In less than five years, it grew from a hand-ful of young Québécois software engineers to gross yearly revenues approaching US$100 million. Softimage products let artists depict real or imaginary objects convincingly, by producing 3-D stills and animation on a VDT screen. The company's early products were so good that they quickly became the standard for many, if not most, graphic production houses in North America. But in 1998 the Canadian discount raised its ugly head, and Softimage was 100 per cent acquired by Microsoft.

The rest of the story closely parallels Will Williams's experi-ence of constant buyouts and the turmoil they cause. Microsoft began by trying to wean Softimage's wildly successful products from a non-MS operating system, porting them instead to the less effective, less expensive Windows NT. On this rather wobbly foundation, Microsoft then began developing new graphic soft-ware called XSI. This finally reached the marketplace in early 2000—two years late. In the same time Maya, Softimage's princi-pal competing software, released three full iterations, or upgrades, and for the first time permanently exceeded Softimage's market share. At that point Microsoft unloaded Softimage, a firm it had acquired and then nearly derailed, to Avid Corporation of Tewks-bury, Massachusetts.

Softimage XSI Version 1.5 is still an astoundingly good product, according to a Montreal graphic artist I know. But, he adds, Soft-image as a corporation appears to have lost something of its funky edge—almost as if it's no longer willing to take risks. *Quelle sur-prise!*

So much can hurt new knowledge, and one of the worst is product delay. There's a story I got from an IT geek about three women who meet over coffee. One boasts that after they've made love, she gets roses from her florist husband. The second woman says her husband, a jeweller, sends her diamonds. The third woman, married to a Microsoft executive, says he never makes love to her.

Instead he sits on the edge of her bed and tells her how wonderful it's going to be when it finally happens.

———————

Important as information technology is, it's not at the core of Quebec's knowledge economy. That distinction lies with the biotechnology and biopharmaceutical industries. In the past ten years, this is the sector that has given Montreal the most astonishing turnaround in Canada. From Montreal east to Quebec City, brand-new pharmaceutical labs are replacing aging rail yards and foundries, giving Quebec's economy a heart transplant. One of Montreal's big bio-success stories, and a fitting symbol of its resurrection from an old-economy grave, is Phoenix International.

Phoenix does contract research and development in pharmaceutical products. A big multinational without the staff time can hire Phoenix to turn a viable concept into an approved medication. So can a two-person start-up with nothing but good ideas and adequate financing. Phoenix starts with drug discovery and proceeds through full clinical trials. Phoenix Montreal also runs its own 160-bed clinic, which doubles as a research centre. The company has five R&D clinics in North America and Europe. Its ethical and professional reputation has helped Phoenix build a clinical database of volunteers, which at mid-2000 included eighty thousand people. There are old and young; smokers and non-smokers; asthmatics and diabetics; those with high blood pressure and those without; and healthy people, or controls. Phoenix can recruit other specialized populations at need.

The company investigates existing patents and new-drug patentability and also determines the comparative efficacies of new drugs. Montreal has let slip its lead in manufacturing and finance to Toronto, in head offices to Calgary and Vancouver, in port tonnage to Halifax. The Montréalais have watched in helpless rage as stormy provincial politics alienated industry after industry. But Phoenix and its sister firms in biotechnology lived up to their name: they lifted Montreal from the ashes.

Because of this resurrection, Ottawa and Saskatoon are not Canada's only mature technology clusters. A land corridor that starts at Montreal and trends northeastward along the St. Lawrence to Quebec City has the second-largest concentration of biopharmaceutical product development in North America. It is next in size and importance only to the long-established powerhouse of Boston-Cambridge, 400 km south in Massachusetts.

Quebec's technology cluster, like Ottawa's, sprang from close co-operation between industry and government. A key catalyst was the presence of what the NRC's Peter Hackett calls a "research anchor": NRC's Biotechnology Research Institute in suburban Montreal. BRI has already nurtured nearly three dozen biotech start-ups. Next time you take a drug, any drug—prescription or over the counter—check the fine print that shows its place of manufacture. Odds are high that it was made somewhere in Quebec. The knowledge economy is alive and well here, and earning money hand over fist.

———

The kilometres click by. I stop in Quebec City for fuel and lunch but not for interviews: my research time is running short, and I still have much to see. Besides, it's too much of a delight to get back in the car and keep driving. It's perfect early-summer weather, and the air's delicious: it smells like fresh water and new growth. I switch off the air conditioner and put the windows down. (Ah, the difficulty governments have with science. There's a tax on air conditioners in cars, as wasteful of energy. Yet a car that's moving with its windows down experiences so much additional air drag that it wastes more energy than most automotive air conditioners use.)

I cross to the South Shore of the St. Lawrence Estuary, weave through the Monts-Notre-Dame, then head southeast into green New Brunswick.

As my research journey winds down, I think about other endings. Across the country, I've been struck by how people in the knowledge economy regard the end-game, whether it's changing projects, switching jobs or wrapping up a company. Because the old economy loved only winners, its managers and workers hated failure and were reluctant even to discuss it. People in knowledge industries have learned such guilt is needless. They view failure as a source of wisdom, not of shame. It's a value-neutral view: to knowledge workers, failure is just another type of hands-on experience, as valuable as a post-doc practicum or a university co-op term. What the old economy saw as crash and burn, the knowledge economy sees as a golden road to wisdom: what one calls a killer fire, the other calls a cookout.

Here's a practical example. The friend to whom I turned to begin my research for this book is an unfailing source of counsel and ideas in high technology. On summer Saturdays we pour drinks and swap high-tech gossip over the barbecue while our sons raise dust in the backyard.

Mark Heieis is not your typical geek. He brings to the knowledge economy a viewpoint from beyond itself, which vastly increases the worth of his counsel. This is a universal virtue: just as war is too important to be left to the generals, so the knowledge economy is too important to be left to the geeks. Not coincidentally, that was Brian Leeners's lesson too.

Mark's first degree was in physiology. In 2001, he re-entered school to get an M.B.A. from Royal Roads University in Victoria. He is a director of the B.C. Technology Industries Association and is intimately acquainted with the high-tech beast.

In one of his recent jobs, Mr. Heieis earned the nickname "Mark the Knife." Mark's motto, grumbled an employee, was If It Ain't Fixed, Break It. Mark got his reputation as a hit man because he was willing to recognize when a project was a crock. And when he did, he acted quickly and ruthlessly on his perception.

Many managers, perhaps most, labour under a fallacy: any project that's been funded, they think, deserves funding until it's done, if necessary forever. Mark disagrees. To support his contrarian position, he adduces the concept of sunk cost.

"If you don't kill a dog project," Mark says, "you throw good money after bad. Sure it's tempting to hang on a little longer and see if you can rescue things, but there comes a point when you have to pull the plug. Any other action is irresponsible."

Managers covet a "turnaround guy" reputation, Mark says. "But sometimes a project can't be turned around—not by you, not by anybody." And then? "It's the kindest thing you can do to put a bullet in its brain. Ending projects should be as routine as starting them. But people can't seem to do this easily." Can he? "Oh, yes. I was known as Dr. Death at one place, even though no one lost a job and the company became more profitable."

Most knowledge companies, Mark says, lack focus. As they grow, their range of activity gets so spread out that nearly everyone has his own pet project. This can kill a firm if it's unchecked. Here, without knowing it, Mark echoes Jim Crocker of Virtek.

"How often," he says with a head shake, "do I see senior management keep a death grip on an invention simply because it's dear to their hearts. They needlessly toss away millions of dollars." Not just CEOs do this, either. "Nearly every technical professional in every firm has some cherished idea he wants to realize. Give everyone free rein, and you quickly reach a state where your company's trying to tear off in all directions at once. That approach never has made money, and it never will. It's not a strategy. It's an abdication."

Then there's the issue of ending not just a project but your job. People in New York call opting out of the rat race "going fishing." Brian Leeners, the venture capitalist I interviewed in Montreal, left a knowledge firm where he'd been CEO. Would he do it again, I'd asked him—head up a knowledge-company start-up?

Brian had frowned, then shaken his head. "Maybe one day, but not now. It was exciting, sure. But I'd rather be at home with my two little sons than work eighteen-hour days." A lot of people I interviewed felt the same way. No one says on his deathbed, "I should have spent more time at the office."

———————

Bath, Hartland, Fredericton: lush bright landscapes full of leaf crops and green trees. I smell the ocean, though I no longer see it. And on the campus of the University of New Brunswick at Fredericton, I greet Leapin' Lou Visentin.

My God, I love this man: wide as a door, plain as a shoe, vital as a river. He embodies the Mexican proverb. "A good man is ugly, strong, and competent." Lou's competence lies not so much in his original bench discipline of biotechnology as in human interaction. And he's on his way up. As I interview him he's vice-president academic at UNB. By the time I finish my research tour and get home, he's president of the University of Brandon.

"How are you?" Lou's fist is the size of a Swift's Premium dinner ham; I wince as we shake hands.

"Good! Can I buy you dinner?" I ask him. He shakes his head.

"Absolutely not. I can buy *you* dinner, Atkinson."

"What kind of food?"

Lou looks at me as if I've grown a third arm. Italian, of course. Is there any other kind? After all, Lou stands for Luigi.

Lou Visentin grew up in Welland, Ontario, watching the long laker ships glide through the locks of the St. Lawrence Seaway. After earning his doctorate in the States, he worked at a research scientist for eighteen years. He came to Memorial University in St. John's, Newfoundland, in 1985 as dean of science. Then he went to Mount Allison University in Sackville, New Brunswick, and on to UNB. There was a joke going around when he took the second position. You hear about Lou? He's gone to mount Allison . . . Lucky Allison.

"You like it here?" I ask him as we enter a bistro the size of two phone booths.

"What, UNB? I love it. Cool place. '*Scusi!*' he says to a sleepy-eyed waiter lounging in a corner. Lou holds up two fingers. "Grappa!"

"Would the gentlemen like Canadian or European grappa?"

Lou's face clouds. "You would even *suggest* to serve me and my friend, the friend of my heart here, *Canadian grappa*?"

"Yes," the waiter says, deadpan.

"Tell me why," Lou snaps.

The water shrugs. "Because it's better."

Lou roars with laughter as the waiter departs. "Italians," he says. "Always breaking each other's balls." The grappa comes. I take a sip; my eyes mist over. If I had a toupée it would rise in the air.

"See how much better the real stuff is?" Lou asks. I nod, not daring to speak. He smiles impishly; he knows what he's done.

All of us love various friends for various reasons. I like Lou because he was the first to show me you could like science and not have a broomstick up your backside. I still cherish the tale he told me about Sir Francis Crick, co-discoverer of the double-helix DNA model, trying give a formal lecture in the middle of a bun fight waged by two hundred of the world's most senior molecular biologists. I'm not positive Lou started that carnage, but I have my suspicions. When I say that the knowledge economy is a human enterprise with equal parts false starts, brains, energy, blind alleyways, guesswork, and play, I'm repeating a lesson I learned from Dr. L. L. Visentin.

"Got anything for me?" I ask him, when I can speak again.

"You're doing a book on technology. Right?"

"Right. I'll look at anything with an economic impact."

"Try this," Lou says. The University of New Brunswick, he says, has recently spun off a start-up knowledge company called Caris Technologies. Caris applies new computer algorithms devised by two professors from UNB Fredericton. Their software increases the efficiency of air searches for survivors of ship and plane accidents at sea.

But Caris, Lou says, hasn't stopped at a single product. It has extended its expertise to the management of any data that originate in ocean, land, or sky. Caris software has been accepted as a standard by LOTS, the prestigious United Nations Law of the Sea Committee. Countries around the globe now use Caris products to document and support their territorial claims, especially those that reach deep onto the continental shelf. SAMI, Caris's semi-automatic map input, rapidly converts standard data from video screens into a form more easily manipulated by digital computer. This permits fast, easy input of such arcana as map symbols, soundings, spot heights, and text. It also cuts by a factor of ten the time required for a human operator to digitize such data and enter them into computer memory.

I wrap up my notes. "Perfect," I say, and Lou nods.

"It's a sweet little company," he says. "Sometimes I think nobody outside the Maritimes realizes how much new technology is invented here."

"What else have you got for me?"

"Try this!" says Lou proudly, and spreads a brochure before me on the restaurant table. "It's our Renaissance Program. We just finished putting it together. Private donor gave us a couple of million bucks. Local guy."

"Just like that? Walks into your office and peels off twenty thousand $100 notes from a horse-choking bankroll?"

Lou grows a halo. "You wound me, Atkinson. I can't help it if I'm persuasive. Here, have some grappa. You want to hear about this thing or not? Okay, it's an undergrad program with a four-year degree. If you bust your tail and take additional courses, you wind up with two degrees, a B.SC. plus a B.A."

"What courses do you have to take?"

"Some of nearly everything. Math, physics, chemistry, philosophy. Anthropology and languages."

"Why couldn't I stay at home and read books?"

"Because you wouldn't find the right books, schmuck. Plus we have all kinds of visiting experts such as yourself, God help us. Plus you wouldn't get the sheepskins."

"Who's your clientele?"

"Smart kids nineteen to thirty. People who plan to take over the world."

UNB has designed its new program, Lou says, to train leaders for tomorrow, specifically the leaders of Canada's knowledge economy. Lawyers and politicians? I ask. Yes, he tells me, but mostly business people.

"Canada needs a new kind of CEO," he says. "Too many old-style businessmen pursue profit without respecting the environment. Or else they understand technical things but trample on people. Or else they have no clue about what you can and can't do in a functioning democracy. We're out to change all that."

"Why Renaissance?" I ask.

"Good question," Lou says, his eyes lighting. Obviously this is dear to his heart. "It's partly approach, partly the range of stuff we teach. People like Leonardo da Vinci didn't distinguish among the various disciplines, right? Artist, goldsmith, engineer—it didn't matter. The division of learning into disciplines came way later. In a limited way, we're trying to retrieve how it was in Leonardo's time. To knock down the walls." Any other reasons? "Because all this scare talk about the instability of the technology economy is so much horseshit," Lou says. "Christ on a bicycle! It drives me crazy how short-sighted some people are. This isn't 1929, for Pete's sake; it's 1492."

UNB calls it the Renaissance Program, Lou says, because this age is like the Renaissance. In fact, he adds, today is bigger than the sixteenth century; it's the birth of a brand-new age. "Amazing things are about to happen. A world economy based on brains, minimal resource use, maximum recycling. Two-century lifespans, why not? The key to aging, maybe a technology that cheats death.

Pilotless probes to Proxima Centauri within a century. There is no limit."

What about the stock market? I ask him. It's up and down like a drawbridge. People read about the knowledge economy and get excited, then the market glitches and their tech stocks fall. So back they run to bank shares, leaving firms with great technology starved for capital.

"Look," Lou says, "you have to separate the reality from the hype. It was the same deal five hundred years ago: go back and read the documents. *Ye New Founde Lande, where every Yeoman may work off his Schippe-Passage by Seven Yeare Indenture and ye Seas Teeme with Fissche. Vyrgynnia, where Gold and Pearles may be Takene from ye Grounde.* All lies, but so what? They were trying to entice a bunch of poor sods over to populate a royal colony. And what happened? They told the truth without knowing it. The New World *was* rich. People *did* make fortunes. The reality surpassed the hype.

"Look, my parents came from Napoli. Back home the old man was scratching a living out of rocky soil after the war. When he retired in Canada, he owned his own house and two cars. His kids had university degrees and one of his grandkids was a millionaire. The reality caught up with the promises, and that's going to happen here too. The liars have too small an imagination."

Lou jabs the air with his pasta fork. "But this time," he says, "the hype isn't going to take five hundred years to come true. You know what an envelope curve is?" I shake my head. "It's a term from statistics," Lou says. "Markets go up and down. If you plot share values against time, you get something that looks like the edge of a ripsaw—wild gains and losses. Now imagine someone comes along and drapes a cloth over the teeth. What do you see?" A line connecting the tops of the teeth, I answer. "Yah," Lou says. "That's the envelope curve, and it's where the real data are. The market value of knowledge companies falls and rises, falls again; but the *trend* is always up and up. Anyone who runs a business now, even a corner store, needs technical knowledge. Usually in what they make, always in how they make it. Technology is here, it's inescapable, it's not going away. Even diaper factories need digital-numeric process control. No, no, no, the question for the investor is not Should I buy technology? It's Which technologies? And When? And How much?"

I say, "But the losses—"

"Didn't you understand?" Lou says, topping up my glass. "Don't look at the daily variations, *look at the envelope curve!* The knowledge economy's not just going to endure, it's going to prevail and dominate. A public company where advanced technology doesn't play a central part will not *exist* in fifteen years. I don't care if corporations call themselves resource companies, manufacturing firms, service organizations, or something else; they're *all* going to be high tech. The knowledge economy will be the only show in town. It's already happening."

"But the potential for share loss . . ." I start to say.

"Short-term share loss means *dick*," Lou says. "Absolute dick. Do you sell your house the instant its market value dips? Of course not—it's your major life investment. You're in it for the long haul. Why should you treat your stock portfolio any differently? If you're in for real profit, you're in for the long term. That means you don't sweat the day-to-day. You make your killing in years or decades. People who get burned in the markets are looking for the quick flip. I'm not saying invest and forget; you have to keep an eye on what you buy. But some of these ignoramuses want twenty, fifty, a hundred per cent return every year. That's idiocy. If a man approached marriage like that, he'd divorce his wife the first time she got her period. Getting rich quick is for suckers. Get rich *slow*. Find a knowledge company in its early stages and stay with it as long as it's sound. When its stock dives, buy more of it: don't poop your pants and sell. Buy low, sell high, yes? Obvious? So these sophomoric rubes buy high and sell low, then bitch about how technology stocks are dangerously volatile. What morons. Whenever you read about a so-called high-tech meltdown, you're reading the history of a bunch of nerds who got so cute they outsmarted themselves. Stocks fell farther and faster in the Great Depression. And even then, people who held on to what they'd owned in 1929 found they were worth twenty times as much in 1949.

"Today you see some stocks melting down not because the companies are unsound, not because they're even losing money, but *because they're not as profitable as some analysts predicted.* I mean, gimme a break! If I had two free dimes to rub together, I'd be buying into knowledge stocks like there's no tomorrow. Because there *will* be a tomorrow, and knowledge firms will own it lock, stock and barrel.

"Sure, the market is irrational. Fear and greed, that's all it deals with: it's the ultimate crap shoot. But the risk applies only to individual companies. Overall, the only thing the markets are going to evaluate in 2015 is knowledge. Knowledge and nothing else. Your glass is empty again. The evaporation must be terrible in here."

It's late when Lou and I leave the restaurant. The second we step outside the door, the lights go off inside and the Open sign spins to Closed.

"You come here often?" I ask.

"Probably a little too often. When are you going to the Rock?"

"Day after tomorrow."

Lou nods. "I have a contact for you at MUN." Lou means his old digs, Memorial University of Newfoundland. "Guy by the name of Willie Davidson. He was my biochem department head when I was dean of science there. Good man, fine scientist, very principled. Equally important, a mensch." Lou peers closely at me, which is like being inspected by a curious horse. "You okay to reach your hotel?"

"If it's within walking distance. No way I want to drive."

"My son, listen to me. This is grappa we've been drinking. I know you can't drive. I'm asking can you walk?"

———

Canada often considers Newfoundland a poor sister, but old habits mean little to the knowledge economy. I see the truth of this as I meet Dr. William Davidson in his cluttered office at Memorial University in St. John's.

Willie Davidson is a geneticist. I'm lucky to find him here for next month he moves from being a professor of biochemistry at Memorial to become dean of science at Simon Fraser University. He and I swap tales about Lou Visentin, then settle down to discuss a case where medicine meets economics.

In the past five years, scientific fieldwork based on human genetics has quietly turned Newfoundland into a pharmaceutical gold mine. But in doing so, Willie tells me, science has brought into question the right of Newfoundlanders to control a knowledge resource of vast value: their own genes.

Medical genetics, he says, aims to locate the exact genetic errors on human DNA that cause disease. It's a tough task, but with skill, luck and patience, it is possible. Scientists working in Newfoundland are luckier than most: the Rock's human genome is ideal for fostering clinical discoveries.

Contrary to popular belief, the genetic make-up of "Ye New Founde Lande" is fairly diverse. True, whole communities may trace their lineage to one European town. But when settlement occurred, travel was so limited that geographic neighbours were still fairly disparate. In 1800 Devon and Somerset in England were probably as genetically distinct as Beijing and New York are today; yet the two English shires were directly adjacent.

Communication remained poor when immigrants reached Newfoundland, and few new genes have entered the province since settlement tapered off in the 1830s. Both these conditions led to a modern gene mix that's surprisingly like the original. Many outports have come through the centuries with little change in their characteristic genome.

One consequence of this unique history is that many gene-based diseases are far commoner on the Rock than elsewhere. For example, Newfoundlanders have a variety of hereditary cancers; more than twenty eye ailments that lead to blindness; and various kinds of genetically mediated heart disease. A tenth of Newfoundlanders have psoriasis in some form.

Willie Davidson, a "come-from-away" born in Scotland, led a 1995 study of Bardet-Biedl Syndrome in Newfoundland. BBS is a rare genetic disease with fatal consequences. Around the world it affects six people per million; in Newfoundland its incidence is ten times as high. BBS patients may have extra fingers and toes at birth. In childhood, they grow obese; in adolescence, blind. Death by kidney failure may occur in early adulthood.

"The BBS work was a real detective story," Willie tells me. "As well as geneticists, our team needed clinicians, molecular biologists, and pedigree experts." *Pedigree* experts? "We needed them to find tombstone names and dates." With pad and pencil in gloomy graveyards? "Oh no, Newfoundland has extensive genealogical Web sites whose data can be downloaded. Our pedigree team got additional facts from church records and from the Canadian National Institute for the Blind."

The pedigree data told Willie's team where imperfect genes had cropped up in the Rock's population. Here again, the scientists were lucky. Privacy laws in the rest of Canada strictly curtail public access to census information. But since Newfoundland did not join Confederation until 1949, census data recorded on the island before that date are in the public domain.

When the BBS team began research, their working theory was that one settler with flawed genes had caused Newfoundland's high BBS frequency. In most other locales, this hunch would have remained untestable. Newfoundland, with its unique mix of good medical records and accurate genealogies, let Willie's team test its working theory. When the team correlated Newfoundland's pedigrees with their own genetic testing of population blood samples, facts emerged that would have remained buried in other populations. In the end, six BBS families in Newfoundland yielded

more data than fifteen times their population in the rest of North
America.

The BBS work showed Willie that his working hypothesis
was wrong. Newfoundland, it turned out, had at least six BBS
founders. Their bad genes had percolated through the population
to create today's high provincial BBS incidence. So reliable were the
scientists' data that the team ended by locating, identifying and
sequencing the bad genes. After centuries of surreptitious damage, there he was: the enemy, caught in the spotlights and at bay.

When uncertainty becomes fact, those with genetic illnesses
are greatly helped. In the past, for example, Newfoundland patients
at risk of bowel cancer needed a colonoscopy once a year. This was
unpleasant and expensive. Thanks to new research, high-risk individuals now have a blood test that tells if they will get the disease.
Those who test positive can have the colonoscopy excise their
polyps, or have pre-cancerous sections of colon surgically removed.
Those who test negative can stop worrying.

The success of Willie Davidson's work has encouraged other
scientists to investigate Newfoundland's genes. In one group with a
high incidence of bowel cancer, teams identified the gene responsible and deduced the biochemical mutation that leads to the disease.
And when a St. John's dermatologist learned that many of his psoriasis patients were related, he collected pedigree information, correlated it with clinical records, and persuaded a big drug firm to fund
further research. The company now hopes to identify the genes
behind this skin disease. Residuals from any drug or test developed
from this work will be invested in a Newfoundland psoriasis clinic.

"Newfoundland's common ancestry creates a lot of scientific
power," says Willie Davidson. But all the scientific work is mere
prologue to a bigger story—the growing interest of large drug
companies in turning the Rock into a province-sized laboratory
for medical genetics.

It's an appealing idea. Besides keeping excellent records, Newfoundlanders are co-operative, physically and emotionally accessi-

ble, and numerous—560,000 at last census. Best of all for drug companies is the precedent for a province-sized gene lab: Iceland.

Like Newfoundland, Iceland has clinical records that stretch back a hundred years. It has written genealogies ranging back five times as long, and sagas that list founding families from the country's first settlement in about A.D. 700. To exploit these conditions, some native Icelanders formed a company called deCODE in 1996. Their aim was to develop a database with the genealogy of every Icelander who ever lived—600,000 people, including 270,000 alive today.

A national referendum gave deCODE exclusive rights to these historic and genetic data. The result is an enormous family tree–*cum*–medical database on nearly every Icelander. So far everyone on the island but 11,000 people have participated, making the acceptance rate 96 per cent. Hoffmann LaRoche, a Swiss pharmaceutical company, came aboard in 1998 and injected US$200 million into the program. A year later deCODE scientists discovered and sequenced the gene for osteoarthritis, which afflicts forty million people around the world.

Willie thinks that Iceland's experience shows Newfoundland may profitably form an alliance with a cash-rich pharmaceutical giant. Benefits would include a "brain gain," as well-educated Newfoundlanders stream home to high-paying knowledge jobs. There would also be technical spinoffs. In Iceland, deCODE recently donated some barely used but technically obsolete gene sequencers to fish biologists, greatly helping their work. And for the next fifty years, Icelanders have free access to every drug, test, and procedure that emerges from the HR/deCODE liaison.

But this bed of roses also has thorns. Some of the sharpest were the Texas Vampires.

In 1997 some MDs who had emigrated from Newfoundland to Texas returned to their birthplace on a fly-in, fly-out research blitz. They co-opted a small outport hospital, took blood samples from members of a Newfoundland family with a rare genetic heart disease, and went back to Texas, where they identified the ailment's cause. When the family who'd supplied the blood asked about testing, they were told the Texas Vampires had exclusive rights to medical information. The Newfoundlanders were left feeling used: so long, and thanks for all the blood.

Willie Davidson wants Newfoundlanders to avoid any further genetic exploitation of this sordid ilk. "The province has an immensely valuable genetic legacy," he tells me. "The infrastructure to develop and benefit from this legacy—airports, roads, communications, a public medical system, a modern university—is all in place. *Someone* is going to profit from this amazing resource. It would be a shame if the government and people of Newfoundland didn't seize the opportunity to take a leading role. They'd merely be claiming what they already own."

➤ Newfoundland's knowledge economy stands on two types of data: the vanishingly small and the immensely large. One is clinical genetics and its human and economic effects. The other is petroleum exploration and development, including the industries that designed and built the Ocean Ranger and Hibernia oil platforms.

I've become blasé to economists' and geologists' warnings about our imminent exhaustion of Earth's oil and gas reserves. I've seen such hand-wringing lamentations from the day I learned to read. I agree that burning fossil fuels contributes to greenhouse warming and that supplies of such fuels are finite. But world population must level off one day; and alternative means of energy production—from the fuel cell to that matchless source, conservation—are fast becoming reality. By the time the oil runs out, Earth's existing reserves will have proven large enough to buy us the time we need. Just as it's puerile to press for an instant end to old-growth tree cutting, so it's irresponsible to demand an immediate end to our use of oil.

Oil reserves are far more common than we used to think. A hundred years ago, they seemed limited to Pennsylvania and Arabia. Thirty years later oil cropped up in Texas, then Indonesia. Then the North Sea, then Alberta, then the Mackenzie Delta, then the Beaufort Sea, then . . .

Whether petroleum was originally formed by decaying organic matter or arose from inorganic chemistry deep inside the Earth, there seems no end of the stuff. Canada's most recent test sites are on land in the Atlantic provinces. But whether or not these pan out, one thing's for sure: billions of barrels of sweet crude lie beneath the continental shelf southeast of Newfoundland.

It's a tough place to do business. The *Titanic* lay no one knew where for over half a century, and all the time she was in plain view to shipboard sonar—at the bottom of the sea, yes, but *on top* of the bottom of the sea. Newfoundland's offshore oil reserves are thousands of metres beneath that, inside the deep shelf seafloor.

To get at this wealth, new knowledge has come from a variety of sources to help out. DeepDive hard suits let people work in safety, even comfort, six hundred metres down in the bitter blackness. Lessons from the capsize and loss of the Ocean Ranger twenty years ago let marine architects design structures that are safe and reliable even in "the perfect storm." And in the Hibernia exploration, the knowledge economy has once again pushed an obscure academic discipline to centre stage. This time, it's the study of frozen seawater—ice.

Ice gets stranger the more closely you look at it. It's one of the few solids that's less dense than its liquid form. When cold enough, water forms crystalline structures that take up more volume than the free-moving molecules of ordinary water. Second, water and ice flip back and forth into each other at odd times and odd places. In Canada, almost all precipitation starts high in the stratosphere as ice: some of it melts into rain as it falls through the lower atmosphere. We really would be God's frozen people, except that our national game isn't played on ice but on water. The pressures formed when a two-hundred-pound forward slams a few square millimetres of skate edge onto a rink create a layer of liquid water a few molecules thick. The player glides on this as readily as a motor bearing spins on oil. Even Ice Age glaciation, that *beau idéal* of geologists and peerless sculptor of land, may have worked with liquid water. A three-kilometre ice sheet, like a hockey player's skate, might have subjected its lower edge to such astronomical pressures that it liquefied where it met the land. Canada is full of glaciated landforms that cannot be explained entirely by the simple scraping action of solid ice.

Ice has more surprises. When scientists first used sonar—reflected sound wavefronts—to image the bottom of our northern seas, they found the seabed everywhere scored with immense, deep grooves. Some of these were several kilometres long. They pointed in all directions, but tended to align themselves with ambient surface currents. They proved to be the tracks of icebergs huge enough to scrape the floorboards of the sea.

A cube of water one metre to a side weighs one tonne. A cube of glacier ice the same size, less dense, tips the scale at about nine hundred kilos. It is not unusual for *million-tonne* icebergs to ply Hibernian waters. If one of these monsters, driven by wave and wind, hit an offshore oil platform at only thirty centimetres a second, it would transfer half a million foot-pounds of momentum—about seventy thousand Newtons—to the artificial structure. That's the type of design constraint that Hibernia's engineers must allow for—and exactly what the knowledge economy lets them do.

For Newfoundland, the knowledge economy comes with perfect timing. Just as its ancient standbys of fish and timber disappear, new sources of business activity, tax revenue, and employment have sprung up. Although the new disciplines exploit existing human and natural resources, what makes them truly transforming is the most renewable resource of all: knowledge. That alone is turning Newfoundland's potential into real wealth.

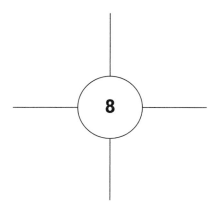

DEMOCRACY

TRIUMPHANT

How dull it is to pause, to make an end;
To rust unburnish'd, not to shine in use!
— TENNYSON, "Ulysses"

Well, it's not always dull; now and then it feels terrific. I've done a thing that startles me: sold my car—West Coast-owned, mild winters, no road salt—to a dealer down the Avalon Peninsula, and I'm flying home. The ancient Greeks believed no state was governable that couldn't be crossed in a single day. Only since the transonic passenger jet came into use has Canada met that criterion. Lord knows how we held the place together for all those decades before aircraft.

It's an unaccustomed luxury for me to log kilometres without driving them myself. I don't regret my slower eastward journey; I learned fascinating things and met intriguing people. All the same, it's nice to do the return trip with my legs stretched out, sipping a drink and looking out the window with a tired, blank mind.

I've finished my initial research. Although the hardest work is still to come—locking myself in my workroom for months to interpret what I've found—that's tomorrow's headache. Just now, rusting unburnish'd feels great.

Yet as sometimes happens when I try to shut my brain down, it runs faster than ever. As I glide across the country in comfort and near silence at a thousand klicks an hour, I find the long view from my window induces a corresponding thing: a mental view exactly like it. Both brain and body occupy the high ground.

That smudge to the northwest, for example: Ottawa again. At the midpoint of my research trip, I had dinner there with a group of friends. We laughed and argued in the crisp spring air, catching up on what all of us had been doing. Suddenly, from a vantage point of nine klicks' vertical distance and two months' intensive research, I realize that our discussions were as vital to my understanding of the knowledge economy as anything my fact-finding uncovered. All that I found in Canada's knowledge economy—IT, nanotech, biotech, new ways to handle resources—rests on a single thing: confidence.

When he hosted the TV series *Civilization*, Kenneth Clark said that two things characterized great ages. One was international-ism. Nations might produce good art when isolated, but they achieved lasting glory only when they opened their borders to the free flow of ideas. Clark's second factor was confidence. Great ages have it; mediocre ones do not. Thomas Mordaunt put it best in 1763, in *The Bee*: "One crowded hour of glorious life / Is worth an age without a name." Nameless ages, Lord Clark said, may believe in something: war, revenge, miscellaneous gods. But they do not believe in themselves, in their absolute fitness for the place and time. Confidence made the Renaissance, said Lord Clark. If Lou Visentin is right, and our age transcends Leonardo's, it's because our confidence as well as our knowledge is greater.

We Canadians aren't flashy about our self-belief; we seldom boast of what we have. But in every pore of our collective skin, we share the robust confidence of our knowledge economy. That's what I learned in Ottawa that cool May night.

―――――――

Maj. Stewart Robertson, Canadian Forces (Ret.) lives in a gabled house on Island Park Drive, one of the prettiest streets in Ottawa. As a career serviceman he was diligent, meticulous, imaginative, and personable. He was also completely frustrated.

The Forces' structure is called a chain of command. The intended image is one of authority and action flowing in straight lines, like forces between adjacent links of chain. The reality is that almost everyone in the structure *is* in chains. After decades of seeing good ideas dead-ended, Major Robertson left the Forces and became plain Mr. Robertson of Ottawa West.

But though Stewart left the Canadian Forces in theory, he stayed with it in fact. As a management consultant who had incorporated his own small company, he found what had eluded him when he was in uniform: direct access to the Forces' top decision makers, and through them the ability to make a difference.

The admirals and generals trust Stewart absolutely, and with good reason. In 1997 he made a proposal to radically change Canada's basic mechanism for providing a military response to domestic disasters—floods, earthquakes, and storms.

God knows it needed changing. When Stewart made his proposal, the plan comprised over three hundred single-spaced pages. Every syllable exhibited an obsession with specifying every conceivable response to every conceivable situation. Those who have not directly experienced the military's obsession with pre-ordering reality can hardly imagine what's involved. In *The Caine Mutiny*, Herman Wouk calls the U.S. Navy "a master plan conceived by geniuses for execution by idiots." A similar thing held true north of the border. The old plan, coded B-GS-055-000/AG-001, contained helpful information such as the following, found in Chapter 3, Paragraph 11, under the heading "Diver Assistance":

> Although provision of diver assistance in humanitarian situations is infrequent, it is included here for clarification purposes. To be considered humanitarian, a dive must be carried out for the purpose of saving life or preventing suffering. In the most frequently encountered cases, those of underwater searches for drowning victims, these criteria are not met since the victims cannot reasonably be expected to survive underwater until the arrival of divers. Under such circumstances, diver assistance would be treated as routine assistance for which costs would normally be recovered.

Say *what?* Such an approach is interminable because it attempts the impossible: pre-thinking all situations and pre-stipulating every outcome. And by compelling people to obey rather than to think, the old plan defeats its own purpose. It both assumes and perpetuates a cadre of zombies with eyes and hands but no minds to make decisions. The *plan* will do the thinking, Corporal: do what it says. This is more old-economy than the old economy—I can't imagine a stronger demotivator.

Stewart himself deftly distinguished the two approaches in a briefing document: "The main difference is the replacement of situation-specific rules with a decision-making framework."

Most people, inside or outside the military, know the old rule-rich tactic doesn't work. Stewart Robertson not only knew it, but knew how to fix it. It did not matter to him that the old plan was enshrined. He persuaded the people in charge to scrap it for something better. How much better, you ask? Stewart's new plan is *one-fifteenth* the old plan's length—twenty pages rather than three hundred. It is short and simple enough that it can and will be read and understood. It assumes, encourages, and rewards the intelligence, perception, and adaptability of the front-line soldier. Here's an example:

> To allow rapid and flexible response to requests for aid, commanding officers . . . have full authority to assign Defence resources throughout their own organizations. A specific list of "right or wrong" situations is not provided, as it . . . would impose a constraint on good judgment.

If cynics among you roll their eyes and predict the new plan's failure, be advised that it formed the basis for the Canadian Forces' successful response to Canada's two greatest natural disasters of recent years: the 1998 ice storm in Eastern Ontario and Western Quebec, and the 1997 spring flooding of the Red River in Manitoba. Both situations showed the military at their finest, winning it national honours and deserved praise. When Stewart's new policy was re-evaluated after these natural disasters, no changes were found necessary. It worked.

Look what's happened here. A single mind, armed only with the courage of its convictions and the confident spirit of its age, gave thousands of soldiers and officers the freedom to use their own judgment and help people more efficiently. It doesn't matter that Stewart's innovation is pure idea, without a complex supporting technology of bells, whistles, lights, and other flashy hardware. Remember Occam's Razor: simplest is best. Some of the most effective solutions in the knowledge economy—PheroTech, UNB's Renaissance Program, the Chapman Creek restorations—hang on one simple idea held by one intelligent person.

Despite Stewart's achievements, I had to pry details of the story out of him: he kept handing away credit to others. Throughout the revision, he said, senior officers such as Rear Adm. Greg Jarvis and Maj. V. R. Howlett championed his new ideas. These people expected excellence from Stewart, and left him alone to achieve it as he saw fit. They dealt with him as the Medici dealt with Michelangelo, and with similar results.

———————

There's a second chapter to this story about confidence.

In 1999 the government of Canada decided to contract out all combat support flying for the Canadian Forces. This activity, which was being performed by Canadian Forces aircrew flying venerable T-33 Silverstar trainer jets and relatively new Challenger aircraft, was abruptly terminated. The Canadian air force had successfully flown such missions for decades, earning praise from allies in the North Atlantic Treaty Organization. In fact, Canada trained NATO pilots as well as its own, and the mighty USAF had often requested the service of Canadian combat support aircraft.

Then, boom! Gone. The Canadian Forces weren't just content to suspend the program by putting planes in storage: all the aircraft in the drone program were auctioned off. It smacks of the Diefenbaker government's immolation of the Avro Arrow. Disband the workers and destroy the plans; don't just kill the program, scorch the earth. You can imagine NATO's reaction when it came time for its next flight-training session. *Uh, guys? Where are the, you know, like the, uh . . .*

You can also imagine Stewart Robertson sniffing the air and thinking, There's an opportunity here. Indeed there was, but it would have lain latent without a lot of imagination, hard work, and above all confidence. In six months, with no full-time staff and two like-minded companions operating from tiny home offices, armed only with phones, computers, NATO military contacts, and colossal nerve, Stewart Robertson and his partners started assembling a consortium to pick up Canada's dropped ball (oops! duh!) in aerial combat training. They located aircraft, operators, and electronic-warfare hardware. They assembled top-notch ex-military pilots ready to fly high-performance aircraft in a combat support role. They established an exclusive teaming arrangement with the largest civilian provider of combat support in the United States.

Over its decade of proposed operation, the project would have been worth roughly $0.5 billion. That impressive figure got their ad hoc company noticed by *Jane's Defence Weekly* several times. All this got under way because of one man.

"At the outset, I estimated our odds of getting the work at a thousand to one against," Stewart says, sitting in his living room with a cat in his lap. "I've recently upgraded my estimate to ten to one. It might never happen. But you know, it just might."

As a postscript, it did not happen. The Challengers have been sold and the T-33s are grounded; the Canadian Forces have yet to issue any request for a proposal. Still, Stewart and his companions don't regret their time and effort. With nothing but chutzpah they came closer than anyone thought possible. Here's a prediction I make with my own confidence: whether on this project or another one, someday Major Robertson and colleagues will scale the mountain and plant their flag. No other outcome is possible.

––––––––––

The plane slips south toward Toronto. Sixty-four kilometres from Pearson International and into our descent, we overfly Newmarket, Ontario, at three thousand metres. That looks like the Spruce Street industrial park. There's the access road and the shop bays. And another memory comes back: a hot day in late spring, past five o'clock but thirty degrees Celsius. Muggy, buggy, close. From inside a small machine shop, the sound of running water. A sign says BAY THIRTEEN—ENGTECH AUTOMATION. The door's open, but no one seems to be around. Then I see a man in jeans, workboots, and an open-necked shirt. He's scrubbing out a sink in a janitor's closet.

"Michael Robertson? President of EngTech Automation?"

"That's me."

"You're cleaning out the sink."

The man keeps working. "You see anyone else around to do it?"

Mike Robertson's factory in Newmarket is hardly bigger than a hole in the wall: shops, offices, janitor's closet, and all, it can't exceed 500 square metres. But in the knowledge economy, inventiveness soars as size dwindles. EngTech, whose factory is smaller than its own parking lot, supplies parts-making machines to automakers around the world. Every door housing for a specific model of Mercury, every dash louvre for a certain Audi may come from one of Mike's machines.

These devices, some of them no bigger than an executive desk, are little miracles of engineering. They are safe, rugged, and dazzlingly inventive. Because of these machines' safety and their relative ease and comfort of use, workers are more relaxed and stress-free on them, and hence more productive. They keep the machines clean, which reduces dirt and foreign objects. That in turn cuts service downtime and boosts productivity further.

And boy, do these machines *work*. Mike's parts-production machines may operate without a pause, 24/7, for years. This is more than a testament to brute efficiency: the machines are elegant as well. They are reprogrammable, so that if an auto manufacturer changes body styling, Mike's machines can adapt to turn out modified parts. From worker safety (high) to maintenance (minimal) to power use (low), each design element is thoroughly thought out and integrated. There's no other word: this engineering has *style*.

Sitting in his office with his feet up on a scarred desk, Mike Robertson (Stewart's younger brother) shrugs off my effusions.

"It's only reasonable," Mike says. "If a machine makes the people who operate it feel good, they'll be willing to stand in front of it loading a part every five seconds for a full eight-hour shift. You have to consider the human element. It's as critical a design parameter as the tensile properties of steel."

In designing his machines, Mike says, he "resists hard spec from a client." That means he won't make machines to someone else's drawings. His machines have to work, perform, and last. They must also *feel* right—another case of engineer's intuition. For Mike Robertson, that means drawing, building, testing, and refining every part of every machine himself. It's a holistic involvement: a work of art. Mike is an *auteur*. He doesn't subcontract his designs; that would be like signing someone else's work. His only regret in the process is that he can't go to the end of the chain as his brother Stewart did and advise the top people among his clients on the engineering consequences of their parts designs.

Yet though his machines are compelled to produce what an automaker wants, they do so in the way Mike says. Both Mike and Stewart remind me of General Patton. "Never tell people how to do things," Patton said. "Tell them *what* to do and they will surprise you with their ingenuity." In the engineering world, telling how is called hard spec; telling what is called performance spec. Mike does the latter.

After earning a degree in mechanical engineering, Mike worked on a drafting board for nine years to design mine hoists. This involved not advanced CAD/CAM, but real old-fashioned Mech Eng: sharpened graphite on sheets of linen paper. If you made a mistake, you erased it and redrew. If you erased too many times, you taped in a patch and started your drawing detail all over again.

When Mike relates this, I start to commiserate, but he's quick to correct me. "I don't regret a day of it," he says. "The discipline proved absolutely central to what I do now. Young engineers who come out of school today knowing nothing but AUTOCAD programs find it harder to develop the same intuitive feeling for what works."

Mike escorts me around his shop. Improved safety, he maintains, comes directly from improvements in machine design. "The machine operators have to work so fast that they don't have time to think," he says. "So I try to make machines that think for them. A good machine is a safe machine, a perfect machine is foolproof."

Mike shows me one new machine, still to be tested and refined before he ships it to his customer. It features a safety device called a light curtain. If the operator crosses this invisible threshold, the machine instantly freezes in mid-action. I see why workers feel safe on these machines; I also begin to see how new knowledge diffuses out from humane innovators like Mike Robertson. It's not just his ideas: it's the self-belief that lies behind them. Whoever uses one of Mike's machines gets an emotional lift, a hit of Mike's own rock-solid confidence.

The excellence of Mike's machines resolves into many small innovations. How, I ask him, does he protect all this intellectual property? Through patents? Mike smiles. "You sound like an IRAP man," he says. "They're always asking me that question." He is referring to the federal government's Industrial Research Assistance Program. "I'll tell you what I tell them," he adds: "You can never afford the time and money to ensure complete legal protection of intellectual property. That's not how this business works." How does it work, then? "It's too fast-paced for lawyers," Mike explains. "Too much legal activity would only slow things down. Besides, I don't need patents to protect my technical knowledge. It would take someone so long to reverse-engineer one of my units that I'd build a better one before they'd finished."

Shades of Tundra, I think. I ask him what keeps everyone in this business honest, if it's not the law.

"Reputation," Mike says instantly. "This community [auto-parts machine design] is incredibly close-knit. If I tried something shifty, if I reneged on a deal or didn't do what I said I would, in two hours it would be all across town. By lunch next day it's all across North America and by 5:00 p.m. around the world. Whereupon I'm gone, done, dead. This business works the way Hong Kong works. I do deals on a phone call: I don't even need a handshake.

Sometimes I get a fax as hard-copy backup." You're kidding! Nothing more? Mike shrugs. "You find out right away who can be trusted. They also find that out about you. If they can't trust you, they shut you down. Simple as that."

Simple to the confident, maybe.

The Prototype: Greatest Commandment

ACT FROM TOTAL CONFIDENCE.

Calgary at sunset: from eleven thousand metres, the city looks like a piece of lapidary work. Orange lights outline the freeways, and the collector roads glow topaz yellow. I'm still in my long-view trance, going to the general from the particular. Right below me, I recall, something is happening that's changing the face of the entire knowledge economy.

Like most Canadian cities of any size, Calgary has a vigorous university with a faculty of computer science. Its graduate students and professors may use mass-produced software like Microsoft Windows, Word, or Power Point to write letters and make slides, but their original research requires far more elegant and powerful tools. One of the most important of these is a computer program called LINUX.

LINUX is a core or 'kernel' computer operating system invented by Linus Torvalds, a brilliant young Finn, when he was barely out of his teens. His new OS began life as a good design, but that's not the story. The real saga is how LINUX went from good to terrific.

Linus Torvalds was not just brilliant, he was lazy too. In most of us, laziness is despicable. In an IT geek, laziness works like Occam's Razor, paving the way to the most powerful and elegant solutions.

Torvalds couldn't be bothered to spend years sweating out the millions of possible glitches in a new operating system. Besides, he didn't want riches from software sales: he wanted a bulletproof OS. And in his inspired sloth, he conceived a new way to obtain it. The method he developed to test and improve his new code proved to be a developmental engine more important even than the software it created. It is an engine powered by the entire geek fellowship.

Before LINUX there were earlier, cruder, and less effective operating systems. They include the one for the Apple Macintosh, the first personal computer with a graphic user interface; MS-DOS, which made billions for wunderkind Bill Gates; and IBM's OS-1 and OS-2.

While Windows is the world's best known and most widely used operating system, for more than a decade Apple OS remained the best. It was a model of clarity that Windows could only hope to imitate. In fact it's debatable whether early marques of Windows can be called op-systems at all. Right up to Win ME, the real OS behind Windows was (and is) ol' granddaddy DOS. Atop DOS, Windows balances like a crazy back-bayou shack, a Rube Goldberg structure that let PC users delude themselves that their machines are really Macs. An NRC computer scientist once described this to me as hanging silks on a cow and entering it in the Kentucky Derby. Other IT professionals routinely refer to Windows as 'MS Bloatware.'

All these operating systems, good, bad and ugly, share a common trait. Their guts—called source code—are owned outright by their corporate originators, who guard their software like crown jewels. State secrets have nothing on the fervour with which a computer firm shields its OS source code.

LINUX was different from the first. Linus Torvalds posted his source code on the Net, making it universally accessible at no charge. Yes, you read right. He listed LINUX in every detail, down to the uttermost code character, in the public domain, permitting and even encouraging universal review. And he asked, Do you like it? Does it work? Can you make it better? The term for Torvalds's approach was *open source*.

The geeks took up his challenge. Today, after years of fiddling, tugging, gutting, reassembling, and refining, LINUX has emerged as so simple, strong, and bulletproof—there's that word again, the Holy Grail of IT—that it makes most proprietary operating systems seem what they are: clumsy and half-baked.

This work of noble note was done for fun, for nothing. Further, it was *not* done by people "contributing their time." That's a term reserved for philanthropy, along with "giving till it hurts." The geeks who developed LINUX created their shared masterpiece, their work of collective genius, by giving because it was enjoyable. Though their work was most definitely for the good of the public, they did not donate it to help the unfortunate. They did it as an act of enlightened self-interest, to help themselves. They no more thought of making source code secret than soccer players think of hiding the ball.

I find the LINUX story fascinating because it's a great example of the Big and Little debate. A small guy, a young unknown, came up with a dynamite initial concept—a self-powered, self-renewing process for software development that tapped effortlessly into the best brains in existence. This happened at a time when, according to conventional wisdom, individuals were powerless against megacorporations like Microsoft or IBM. The LINUX process mobilized the immense force of the worldwide geek collective. It catalyzed that community into an unpaid, democratic, spontaneously cooperating team—close to the original Marxian idea of true communism, where central control and even socialism wither away. The young Finn showed the big boys where the real power lies. Even Consolidated MegaCorp seems puny when set beside its entire economic sector.

Torvalds's concept of productive anarchy flies in the face of old-economy wisdom. What, *give away* something useful? And when LINUX began to sweep the IT world, in defiance of the mega-corps' sneers, their response was: *There's a chance here for us big firms—*

smart, devious, in love with secrecy—to swipe LINUX and resell it! It's a gold mine!

"The big firms thought they could grab LINUX and make it theirs," one CEO told me. "But they just don't get it. In the IT community, things don't work that way. The geeks see through these oh-so-clever firms and treat them with contempt. The geeks know the big firms are trying to sell back less than they've taken."

Will the big firms succeed? "Not a chance," the CEO said. "Their old-line monopolistic strategies won't do 'em a bit of good. By the time a big firm issues a proprietary version of LINUX, the geek fellowship on the Net will have vastly improved it. No way will the old economy win this battle. It can't."

Nearing Vancouver now, past the big peaks of the Coast Range, moving steadily up the Fraser Valley. This river was a gateway to the Northwest, and down it moved a steady stream of white man's goods—muskets, blankets, beads, and also preconceptions. The trade items were tangible; the ideas behind them had a more lasting impact.

One of the assumptions that the whites brought with them was the whole notion of property. Concepts of ownership varied among aboriginal cultures, but nearly all were puzzled by the white man's belief that something he couldn't carry could be possessed like a hat. Land, for instance. Grade it, mine it, cut its trees: dispose of it, *control* it. Crazy.

Except for personal artifacts such as weapons, this idea of fee-simple ownership was largely foreign to the Amerind mind. Earth was Earth. We walked on her, we lived with her, and we hunted and were hunted by her creatures, of whom we were one. All living things had souls. The very rocks had souls. Human slavery was accepted but not the perpetual enslavement of things. Even human slavery had a time limit.

If all this seems impossibly noble to a modern society whose concepts of ownership are so abstract that it that rents air and sells things that don't yet exist, think again. Even our property-obsessed culture retains a vestige of the laws that hold important things in common. By the United Nations Law of the Sea, for example, the territorial rights of nations are restricted to the continental shelf. Both the moon and Antarctica are prescribed from corporate or national ownership. So are the deep ocean, the deep seafloor, and space. In Canada, open water larger than a pond belongs to the Crown—not the modernity-challenged crew in Buckingham Palace but a convenient legal fiction for all Canadians acting in concert. We're not as private-enterprise as we like to think.

A similar thing has happened in the development of open-source code by an anarchistic rabble of IT geeks. This ad hoc collective, based on ingrained notions of fairness and commonality oddly like those of aboriginal North America, has voted against a property-based approach to source code. Something as basic as an OS, say the geeks, is like air and water: it is from all and for all, and may not be packaged or sold. This judgment of the geek collective is so final that geeks in many companies will not accept advertising from any big firm intent on sealing LINUX OS into a proprietary wrap.

And yet a host of small, sharp, successful companies has recently sprung up based on LINUX. The geek collective finds these newer firms acceptable. What's the difference? It turns out that LINUX is just a recent member of a long, honourable open-source tradition. Long for IT at any rate: two decades.

"You'll never hear this from Microsoft," says Dana Epp, a software engineer and CEO of IT consultants Merilus of Chilliwack B.C. "But the Internet is run today, and always has been run, on free, open-source, universally accessible software. One of the biggest closed-source programs in use today is Microsoft Internet Explorer. Yet even that appropriated its original code from Mosaic, which was an open-source program.

"I teach software at the University College of the Fraser Valley," Dana adds. "My students all think that Windows owns the Net. I disabuse them of that quaint notion."

Barry Carlson, CEO of Parasun down below me in New Westminster, tells me: "Open source code is like money: it works best on low-end applications that everyone has to have. It's like money. Currency is a shared-use application: a dollar must be the same and do the same things no matter who uses it. Mass applications demand uniformity." It's only when you get into highly specialized applications, Barry says, that you have to start amending the original shared code, and that's where the new companies can make a geek-approved buck.

"The Bank of Montreal, say, needs to do different things with its ATMs than the Bank of Nova Scotia," Barry says. "And they want to keep these variations confidential. If open source is like money, tailored apps are like involved financial transactions—stock warrants and the like—that require highly paid experts to assemble and use. So the instant you diverge from a mass app, the instant you have to modify a commonly held open-source code for specialized ends, that's the point where you diverge from shared code, even if your stuff began as open-source development. And that's the point where you can legitimately charge for your new development work."

All very well in theory. But in practical terms, how can small firms that adapt open-source code make their way? How can they charge for something that they themselves believe with all their heart should be free?

I put this question to Dana Epp; he is amused. You're writing a book, he says. Will you give it away? Of course not! I reply, outraged. I have copyright on whatever I create. And do you also copyright the English language? he answers. Long pause. Riiiight, I say.

Dana's point is stronger than mere analogy: it's indisputably true. English belongs to everyone who speaks it. Yet when I as a writer apply this freely accessible, communally held resource to an individual application, I reconfigure it in a special way. I stamp ideas on it: I sculpt something unique, for which I can then ask and expect a fee. Companies such as Dana Epp's Merilus do this. They snip and sew LINUX and other open-source codes, tailoring a solution to each client.

"We like to say we offer our customers LINUX without the learning curve," Dana says. I've shied away from predictions in this book, but here's one: watch out for small, young, LINUX-based companies such as Merilus. They have everything they need: advanced knowledge, business smarts, happy clients, and—what the big firms have so far ignored—the soul of the geek. In five years these new firms may dominate Web-based IT, and through it a large part of the knowledge economy.

Merilus, Dana tells me, specializes in B2B applications. One of the paths they are taking toward that goal is through the individual consumer. Consider the main specialty of Merilus, which is digital security. Gateway Guardian, the firm's B2B software package, is a firewall system that costs several hundred dollars. Home Guardian, a simpler version suitable for home PCs, is available for download from the Merilus Web site without charge. Geeks find such Netware, or free Net software, irresistible. Dana is banking that many geeks who download Home Guardian, install it, and find it useful will afterwards order the B2B version for their commercial workstations. So far it's proven a sound bet.

A human resources manager would say Dana came to his firm by "push-pull." The pull was the opportunity to start and run a business according to his strict beliefs about the ethics of new IT knowledge. What pushed Dana from his previous position was the inadequate technology with which he was forced to work.

Dana began his career writing computer code for security and auditing functions. One day when he was creating a mail server using a Windows NT platform, he "decided LINUX was the key to faster, more elegant software. I wanted my solutions to be limited only by my own creativity, not by the operating system I happened to be using. I found that a Windows platform was too slow and clumsy."

Today, Merilus's B2B solutions embody an engineering philosophy that Dana calls Crystal Box. The metaphor is in sharp contrast to the big firms' Black Box approach. Black Box software is deliberately made permanently mysterious to its users: they cannot improve, modify, or even understand it. It works, is all . . . at least until it doesn't. Users of Black Box are thus forced to rely on their software suppliers.

The contrast with a Crystal Box philosophy could not be greater. When clients use a Crystal Box product, they can inspect every line of code before they order it, at no charge.

"In 1999 a brand new ship in the U.S. Navy developed a buffer overload in its onboard IT systems," Dana explains. "It had Black Box software, which no one on board knew how to modify. The ship had to be towed thousands of kilometres back to the U.S. because nobody on hand knew how to fix a fairly simple problem."

A more sinister aspect of Black Box software, he tells me, is that its engineers may build in what the industry calls a back door. This is a hidden port that lets anyone with a secret access code hack in from anywhere on the planet. The intruder can then change or disable code functions or even shut down the program altogether. Big firms don't talk a great deal about back doors, but I have heard reports from several sources that various security agencies routinely request back-door data from big North American software developers. Further, they usually get it.

By contrast, Crystal Box software is perfectly transparent. Its user knows precisely what's in it, to its ultimate function and its last line of code. It's democracy triumphant: the bane of the sneaks.

Not all firms sees things this way, Dana admits. But to him and Merilus, the advantages of Crystal Box are too great to ignore.

"Crystal Box is less vulnerable," he says. "When we find a glitch or a virus in any of our codes, we simply post a notice on our Bug-Master Web site. We include a patch that lets our clients neutralize the bug within minutes. From that point on, our client's software is invulnerable to that particular threat. This compares to weeks or months to get a Windows fix from Microsoft."

To date, Dana's most enjoyable projects have involved clients that had been Windows-based and whose systems consequently locked up or crashed several times a day.

"We gut their operating-system code," Dana says. "And then we substitute LINUX for Windows. But we keep the graphic user interface, so that for these clients nothing visible changes. Their systems become much, much faster and more reliable—that's all that happens. 'What did you do?' they ask us. 'Everything's working the way it should have worked all along.'"

Pause a minute, and savour the irony. Windows began as a shell program, a user interface that aped Apple. Now its own guts are being scooped out, leaving nothing behind but its good GUI looks. Inside there's something far better: LINUX, the uncrowned king of open source.

————————

New Westminster falls behind me: the plane has nearly reached Vancouver. The Fraser splits into deep channels that wind among sandy islands. There's UBC, Delta, Vancouver Island. And far to the south, a blur on the horizon, Redmond, Washington: the home of Microsoft. As my journey ends, I find myself thinking about how central that big firm has made itself in the whole knowledge economy.

Linus Torvalds is the prototypical underdog, and we have reasons to like such creatures. Some reasons are social: most of us identify with an unknown challenger who breaks the champion's nose. But there's another reason why we like underdogs, and that is evolutionary biology. Its lesson is simple: don't put all your eggs in one basket. We have learned this so often over countless millennia that it's embedded in our genome.

Simplify! Thoreau said. *Diversify!* replies biology, and gives better advice. Absolute reliance on one person, crop, or technology sooner or later leads to grief. The greater your diversity, whether of foodstuffs or of clients, the better off you'll be.

This explains the enormous harm done by recent computer viruses. The term *virus* is almost literally accurate. Both protein and software are agents of sabotage. Both infiltrate and destabilize a complex system by scrambling its administrative data. Sir Peter Medawar, a Nobel laureate in medicine, defined an organic virus as "a bit of bad news wrapped up in protein." That's the computer virus to a T.

A virus of either type, byte or protein, uses its host's own machinery and energy to replicate itself and spread infection; the host dies, but not before the virus has subverted and used it. Here is where diversity protects. Not everyone is equally susceptible to a given pathogen. Thousands of children ingest live polio virus and get only a sniffle, and there are Kenyan prostitutes who shrug off HIV. If every human were genetically the same—same appearance, same enzymes, same metabolism—we'd all be vulnerable to the same threats. The key to our survival lies in our varied genes.

Unfortunately, we haven't designed our IT systems as well as nature designed us. In mid-2000 the Love Bug, a virus assembled by a hacker in the Philippines, raced around the world and shut down large parts of the global business community. Its perpetrator designed his virus to preferentially attack one type of computer, the IBM-developed PC and its clones; one operating system, Microsoft Windows 95/98; and one E-mail program, Microsoft Outlook Express. He didn't bother to target Macintosh, LINUX, Apple OS, Eudora, or Quark; there was no need. IBM rules hardware, and Microsoft rules IBM. To kill, you go for the heart.

Decades ago, Microsoft began to use its vast size and marketing smarts not only against competitors such as Apple but also against firms like WordPerfect who as Microsoft allies had thought themselves immune (WordPerfect ran on DOS and Windows). Microsoft's success established a dominant IT monoculture that grew to span the world. As the roots and fibrils of this identical software ensnared us, we enjoyed the benefits (software intercompatibility) and endured the drawbacks (poor reliability, weird glitches, restricted choice, high cost to acquire and learn). The Love Bug woke us up to the greatest risk of all: having the world's eggs in a single basket, especially a basket so loosely made. Perhaps it's no accident that at the exact time the Love Bug appeared, the courts ruled in favour of a U.S. government antitrust suit alleging Microsoft's ruthless extermination of any possible competitor.

In mathematical terms, an Internet net made up of many different firms and systems is described as "robust." Its stability, adaptability, and resilience let it encounter many different threats and stresses, yet soldier on. That was the idea behind the Net in the first place: that nothing and no one should kill all of it part of the time, or part of it all of the time. If Bill Gates wilfully set out to dominate the Net—as certainly seems the case—he had a reciprocal obligation to maintain Net security by making his software bulletproof to hackers and their viruses. Whether he did this I leave to you to decide; but as for me and my house, we will use Eudora.

The Love Bug had an aftermath exactly like that of a biological plague. Some of its victims recovered; some were left crippled; some died. And humanity, the afflicted species, underwent natural selection. We the survivors finally learned to appreciate the danger of monocultures. Just in time, we developed an interest in diversity. Alternative IT systems got shots in the arm: especially LINUX, the Robin Hood os. Apple products benefited as well. Mac users laughed as heartily at the Love Bug as they did at the now-infamous y2k glitch—another pest restricted to the Microsoft/ibm hegemony.

How did Gates and company come to dominate in the first place? Again biology explains things, in a concept called the founder principle. This holds that the first species to dominate an ecosystem may continue to dominate even when later, better-adapted forms appear. Note that the founder principle refers neither to the first organism to appear nor to the form that is the fittest, but merely to the first species to proliferate and dig itself in.

The founder principle is as universal in the knowledge economy as it is in biology. The big money goes to those who come along after a penurious genius, snap up his ip for chicken feed, and market it. Charles Goodyear invented and named the vulcanization process that uses sulphur to make natural rubber tough, flexible, and temperature resistant. He died a pauper, without seeing the company that filched his name and his ideas. Nor did Edison invent the electric light. It already existed in various forms, illuminating the stages of urban theatres. Edison merely put it in a form that could be mass-produced. Like Edison and Goodyear, like the great god Zeus, for that matter, Bill Gates wasn't first on the scene; he merely walked in on an existing operation and took it over. And like Zeus he remembers his enemies and is ill at ease. Zeus recalls his imprisoned father, Kronos. Bill knows that even now, linux is at the Gates.

No one need worry about actively toppling Microsoft. It will happen spontaneously: Microsoft will subvert itself. It may already be happening. In statistics, the effect is called regression to the mean: it's what gives a chance to baseball teams besides the New York Yankees. As surely as the telcos or the great nineteenth-century industrial trusts, the People's Republic of Redmond will one day overreach itself and trigger its own demise. The trick is to topple Microsoft without crushing too many innocent companies who rely on its software. *Topple* is in fact too violent a verb: *ease out* or *transform* would be better. As we develop multiple systems to ensure a diverse and robust Internet, as we ensure that these disparate systems share protocols through which they interact, the Net (and the World Wide Web based on it) will grow less vulnerable and more dependable. As it sheds its current Microsoft monoculture, the transformed Net will attract and retain the universal use that has so far eluded it. It will work so well, and so reliably, that we no longer see it; in IT terms, it will be perfectly transparent. The Diverse Net will power the commerce, the leisure, and the creativity of the world. Best of all, it will free us from the terror that some lone hacker may collapse the world's knowledge economy with a few malicious lines of code.

––––––––––

Everywhere in my field research across the country, I was struck by the reach and vigour of Canada's knowledge economy. I was also deeply moved by the boldness of Canadians involved in it. Their confidence in the knowledge economy, their self-assured place in it, went beyond that of the owner-operator who projects a cool image even when he's quaking in his boots. The confidence I sensed was far deeper and more serene. It shone from directors, researchers, technologists; it came from loading-dock workers and from those who answered phones. I was staggered by the people I saw— their knowledge, their ingenuity, and above all their cast-iron gall. Something is happening here. Far from having peaked, far from having been defeated by stock-market glitches, the change is accelerating. Just what is going on?

I think that Laurier's prediction has at last come true. *The twentieth century belongs to Canada*, said Sir Wilfrid when he was prime minister. Since then, Laurier has been widely ridiculed for his words. Economic nationalists and free traders alike tell us that the United States eclipses Canada in degree of innovation, quality of life, and every other index of success. Furthermore, they say, it will continue to do so.

Balls. Laurier was perfectly accurate: he just made his prediction a hundred years early. The twenty-*first* century belongs to Canada—and along with it, the Age of Knowledge it contains.

Right, Sir Wilfrid: glad you believed in us. Now fasten your seat belts, everybody. You're in for the ride of your lives.

Glossary of Terms and Abbreviations

2 I/C   Second-in-command

AC   Alternating current (electricity)

APP   Application (software)

ASP   Application service provider (Internet software)

ATP   Adenosine triphosphate (energy molecule)

B2B   Business-to-business (application software)

B&W   Black and white

BNR   Bell-Northern Research

BRI   Biotechnology Research Institute (NRC)

CAD   Computer-aided design

CBDN   Canadian Bacterial Diseases Network (NCE)

CCA   Cost of consumer acquisition

CEO   Chief executive officer

CFO   Chief financial officer

CIO   Chief information officer

COD   Cash on delivery

CPU   Central processing unit (computing hardware)

CRT   Cathode-ray tube—see also VDT

CTO   Chief technology officer

DC   Direct current (electricity)

DNA   Deoxyribonucleic acid (genetic molecule)

DOS   Disk operating system (Microsoft)

EDI   Electronic data input

E-M   Electromagnetic

EPA   Environmental Protection Agency (USA)

FSF	Fabrication-less semiconductor firm
GM, GMC	General Motors Corporation
GMF	Genetically modified food
GMO	Genetically modified organism
GPS	Global positioning system
GUI	Graphic user interface—see also WIMP
GT	Games Traders
	Gene therapy
HDTV	High-definition television
HGH	Human growth hormone
HO	Head office
HQ	Headquarters
HR	Human resources
HSV	*Herpes simplex* virus
HZ	Hertz (Frequency unit: 1 HZ = 1 cycle/second)
IBM	International Business Machines
iff	If and only if (logical biconditional)
IP	Intellectual property
IPO	Initial public offering
IRAP	Industrial Research Assistance Program
ISP	Internet service provider
IT	Information technology
ITA	Industry Technology Adviser
LAN	Local area network
LOTS	Law of the Sea (United Nations)
LSD	Lysozomal storage disease
M&A	Merger and acquisition
MBA	Master's degree in business administration
MBO	Management buyout
MEG	Magnetoencephalograph (brain science)
MIID	Micro-immuno-isolation device (medicine)
MODR	Missions operation and control room (NASA)
MS	Microsoft
NCE	Network of Centres of Excellence (Canada)

NDA	Non-disclosure agreement
NEP	National energy program
NPV	Net present value
NRC(C)	National Research Council of Canada
OEM	Original equipment manufacture(r)
OS	Open source (computer software)
	Operating system (computer software)
P&L	Profit-and-loss statement
PBI	Plant Biotechnology Institute (NRC)
PC	Personal computer
PCR	Polymerase chain reaction (Biotechnology)
PENCE	Protein Engineering NCE—see also NCE
PRL	Prairie Regional Laboratory (NRC)
QUAGO	Quasi-governmental organization
R&D	Research and development
RAM	Random-access memory (information technology)
RF	Radio frequency
ROI	Return on investment
ROM	Read-only memory (IT)
RTO	Reverse takeover (Stock exchange)
SAMI	Semi-automatic map input (Caris Technologies)
SATAC	Satellite Artificial Chromosome
S&T	Science and technology
SFU	Simon Fraser University
SYLVER	Silvicultural impact on yield, lumber value, and economic return
TASS	Tree and stand simulator (SYLVER subroutine)
TCRL	Thalamocortical resonance loop (neuroscience)
TIIS	Technology-intensive industrial sector (NRC)
TNF	Tumour necrosis factor (medicine)
UBC	University of British Columbia
ULF	Ultra-low frequency (audio)
UNB	University of New Brunswick
UNBC	University of Northern British Columbia

UNLOTS   United Nations Law of the Sea
UWaterloo   University of Waterloo (Ontario)
VDT   Video display terminal—see also CRT
VICLAS   Violent crime linkage analysis system (RCMP)
VRL   Variable-retention logging
WIMP   Windows/icons/mouse/pull-downs (IT protocol—
see also GUI)

The Prototype

Attributes for the Ideal Knowledge Organization

1. Scientific, technical, and strategic knowledge should be as simple as possible.
2. An organization must be humane.
3. If it isn't fun, don't do it.
4. Exploit a niche market with unique technology.
5. Think big, act small, avoid debt, stay lean, control growth, grow via partnerships, treat your people well.
6. Skunk Works work.
7. ACT FROM TOTAL CONFIDENCE (The Great Commandment).

Appendix

E-mail: Toward an Etiquette of Use

E-rule #1: *Think*

An energy barrier in a communication medium is not all bad. The time cost of writing longhand or on a typewriter, like the phone's instant two-way voice contact, discourages hasty outbursts. Slag the older media if you wish, but credit them with fostering sober second thought. E-mail can be the moron's darling, the fast, sure way to shoot yourself in the knee. Is there a user of E-mail who has never groaned in anguish as an ill-considered message winged away?

E-rule #2: *Write*

While E-mail is fast and efficient, it can also make you seem illiterate. People forgive bad grammar and misspellings on a Post-it Note, for it's scrawled in haste. But an E-mail appears in type as clear and readable as a hard-cover book. Messages such as 12 PM MGRS OFFC or HOPE YOUR BETER are like jabs in the eye.

E-rule #3: *Condense*

Restrictions acceptable in other media create eyesores in E-mail. The worst of these is length. One executive I know restricts her E-mails to one screen: anything longer must go by snail mail. Shovelling megawords into E-mails is an imposition.

Here's Dr. Prabhakar Ragde, a professor of computing science at the University of Waterloo.

"People can justly expect you to remember a long letter better than a long E-mail," Prabhakar writes to me (via E-mail, of course). "You invest less time in composing and processing E-mail, and you get more information by E-mail than you do by personal letter. Both these things give written mail more intrinsic heft. A physical letter cues us to pay attention." In letters as in forests, it seems, volume and value are two different things.

Issues growing up around E-mail are both legal and social, Prabhakar tells me. "Legally, you could E-mail someone the *Encyclopedia Britannica* and then testify you briefed them on the habits of the Algerian fennec. Socially, that's a mistake."

Discussions of length lead naturally to the topic of word overload. "The sheer quantity of my E-mail messages is a problem," writes another correspondent, Dr. Robin Cohen. Like Prabhakar, Robin is a computer-science professor at UWaterloo. She offers a solution: E-mail could "introduce a standard subhead that indicates the nature of the message. Currently, a sender's name doesn't telegraph an E-mail's importance. Is this message from my friend Jane Doe with a dinner invitation, or Jane Doe my committee chair with the minutes of a meeting? When I see a number of unopened messages, I need to know at once which ones are vital and which are optional."

E-rule #4: *Don't Spam*

A big part of overload involves junk E-mail. Computer geeks nickname this *spam*, after the only thing on the menu in a Monty Python skit. Spam may comprise advertisements or the electronic equivalent of mass mailing. Greed tempts to the former, sloth to the latter. Why send selectively when you can scatter your note to the winds and reach anyone who's remotely involved? But temptation must be resisted: you must think about your addressees as well as your message. "I find spam very irritating," Robin grumbles. "I'd like to see it hit with a blanket ban."

E-rule #5: *Be Circumspect*

Is E-mail a private communication like a letter, or a publication like a newspaper? If it's a publication, how many people must receive a message before it becomes a magazine?

"I don't know what the law thinks," says Prabhakar Ragde, "and I suspect the law doesn't know what it thinks either. Such questions will be decided not by legislatures, but case by case."

Prabhakar believes that creating a Web page, or posting an E-mail to a news-group list, is clearly publication. Still, questions remain. "Should E-mail carry the same weight as paper publication in cases of libel? This is not a legal issue—it's a social problem. We will resolve it as a culture."

E-rule #6: *Assume It's Public*

Another hot E-mail issue is privacy. Here are the considered comments of a legal expert in the subject, who is also president of the University of Waterloo, Dr. David Johnston.

"It's a good analogy to consider E-mail a postcard, rather than a letter," David writes. "There's no way to guarantee the content of an E-mail will be concealed. But while someone sending a post-card knows that anyone may read it, few people realize that E-mail has a similarly public nature. Because they compose, send, and read E-mail in solitude, they assume it is as private as their thoughts. E-mail horror stories usually involve people who discover they've been thinking out loud in the wrong company."

Such stories often involve E-mails that are modern variants of that ancient cliché, the indiscreet letter. A hundred twenty years after he said it, Mark Twain's wry axiom "Do right, and fear no man; don't write, and fear no woman" rings true for users of E-mail.

Some people believe that as technology created E-mail, tech-nology can safeguard it. Knowledge companies are springing up, promising to encrypt messages and give an E-mail the same secu-rity as snail mail. But this approach is not a blanket solution, Prab-hakar Ragde writes.

"Encryption may answer some questions," he explains. "It can transmit a message when both sender and receiver want to exclude everyone in between. But who encrypts everything they do, every time? Unless people can configure every one of their mailers to encrypt all text automatically, encryption technology will not be used." Besides, Prabhakar says, the weakest links in any crypto-graphic system come at its ends. "All it takes to violate security is for someone to leave unencrypted text on a hard drive, or to print out a copy and leave it unattended."

As for E-mail etiquette in general, here are David Johnston's wise words: "There are things that you'll say to your dog that you would, and should, never utter to another human being. It is not hypocrisy to understand this, merely prudence. Effective use of any medium demands a constant knowledge of occasion."